Benedict Cumberbatch, In Transition:

An Unauthorised Performance Biography

Lynnette Porter

Paperback ISBN 9781780924366
ePub ISBN 9781780924373
PDF ISBN 9781780924380

Published in the UK by MX Publishing
335 Princess Park Manor, Royal Drive,
London, N11 3GX
www.mxpublishing.com

Cover design by Jules Coomber.

Contents

Foreword

For us, of course, it all started with Sherlock.

Or rather, with the reaction to that first trailer that aired on the BBC in the mid-summer of 2010, which took the form of *"Why have they got the creepy guy from* Atonement *to play Sherlock Holmes?"*

As is often the case, knee jerk first impressions and, indeed, preconceptions are *very* bad things. He may have a name that delights certain sections of the media, an unmistakable appearance, and a voice that can weaken knees, but the ultimate reason for the continued rise of Benedict Cumberbatch is his supreme focus on performance as an actor and artist. Be it a biographical drama of scientist, painter, or counter-culturist; an often frantic airline captain; creature/creator; repressed spy; 'intergalactic terrorist'; or the greatest detective the world has ever known, Cumberbatch is not a man to sit still or allow himself to fit into any particular mould.

It's fitting then, that this book may not be what you are expecting. Lynnette Porter has written not a typical celebrity biography, obsessed with every little nugget of personal information that feeds many a tabloid column inch, but instead a serious, analytical study of an actor's craft, intensively researched from almost every source imaginable. In this age where gossip reigns supreme and social media can twist words contextually, it's refreshing to see the professional rather than the personal handled in this manner. What the book also does though, and rather astutely, is quietly disseminate the culture of celebrity in both traditional media and the burgeoning online world, effectively using Benedict as a case study of how those column inches treat actors throughout their careers.

It is foolhardy to assume you can ever know someone you see on the stage or screen on anything other than their own terms, and your preconceptions of them based upon those performances are always likely to be wrong. As we personally realised with that jump from *Atonement* to Sherlock, an actor is someone who, by choice, *pretends,* and is not a person to pigeon hole into your own imagined thoughts of him. The work actors give us for our entertainment may often be all they are willing to share of their life, and ultimately that work is always the most important thing.

But for us, of course, it all started with Sherlock, a fixed point that his career seems to have thus far rotated around, leading us to his superb earlier work while eagerly awaiting what is to come. Writing this mere weeks ahead of the opening of *Star Trek: Into Darkness,* where servers in the UK buckled under the strain of demand for pre-booking cinema tickets online, and seeing Cumberbatch forming the film's marketing push in bus stops across much of the world, it's easy to see that fixed point on the verge of shifting, with this book as a fitting retrospective of a possible first stage in a career that is about to slingshot away into superstardom.

SHERLOCKOLOGY
www.sherlockology.com

Introduction: Head and Heart

"I've never really made a
head-over-heart decision like that before." [1]
Benedict Cumberbatch, 2011

Benedict Cumberbatch is having a remarkable career, especially since 2010. *Tinker Tailor Soldier Spy, War Horse, The Hobbit, Star Trek: Into Darkness, Parade's End*—not a bad list to add to a resume, especially within a single year. BAFTA-winning *Tinker Tailor Soldier Spy* (best British film of the year) and Academy Award-nominated *War Horse* started 2012 on the red carpet. Next came roles in two of the biggest franchises ever—Peter Jackson's *The Hobbit* films, building on the cinematic legacy of *The Lord of the Rings,* and J. J. Abrams' rebooted *Star Trek.*

After filming these potential blockbusters in early 2012, the publicity machine kicked in later that year in preparation for cinematic releases in 2013, when Cumberbatch would be revealed to the world as the next great *Star Trek* villain and, a few months later, would be heard as Smaug in the *Hobbit*'s middle film, *The Desolation of Smaug.* The HBO-BBC period piece *Parade's End,* broadcast in the U.K. in August/ September 2012 and in the U.S. in February 2013, was compared to critically acclaimed *Downton Abbey* and received the most Broadcasting Press Guild nominations by a single project and won four awards, including best drama. (Cumberbatch received two best actor nominations—pitting himself as *Parade's End*'s

1

Christopher Tietjens and as Sherlock Holmes in *Sherlock*—and was named "best actor" for both.[2])

Then there are the stage roles. The National Theatre's *Frankenstein,* directed by Danny Boyle in 2011, sold out performances so quickly that patrons lined up at 4 a.m. in hopes of getting one of the coveted day tickets held back from regular sales. National Theatre Live's global broadcasts of *Frankenstein* proved to be so popular in spring 2011 that they were rebroadcast in theatres around the world in summer 2012. Although alternating the roles of Victor Frankenstein and the Creature surely provided Cumberbatch satisfaction in meeting a rather daunting acting challenge, receiving an Olivier Award as best actor—the highest accolade in the British theatre—is a fine reward for a job well done.

2013 began in a similar high-profile way, with roles lined up or being discussed in several feature films, including biographies of Julian Assange, Alan Turing, and Brian Epstein; a new series of BBC radio's *Cabin Pressure;* and, on the awards front, Golden Globe and National Television Award nominations. In January 2013, *Forbes* named Cumberbatch one of the new stars to watch.[3] In March 2013, as previously mentioned, he was honoured as best actor by the Broadcasting Press Guild. As the *LA Times* wrote in their 9 May 2012 feature, Benedict Cumberbatch "lights it up"—with roles on radio, television, film, and stage—but the spark igniting Cumberbatch's recent career and international fame is one role, one series: *Sherlock.*

In the U.K., the BBC series won the BAFTA as best drama in 2011. *Sherlock* has also been named best drama at the BAFTA Cymru awards; best terrestrial show by the Edinburgh International Television Festival; and, in Canada, best continuing series at the Banff Rockie Awards. It continues to receive, for example, National Television, Emmy, and Satellite award nominations, and among its many trophies, won as best series or best drama at the RTS (Royal Television Society), Television and Radio Industries Club, Television Critics Association, TV Quick, and Peabody Awards. In 2012, the Crime Thriller Awards, the first to present *Sherlock* with an award in recognition of its excellent initial series, again rewarded the programme's outstanding second series. Additionally, the Crime Thriller Awards named the leads— Cumberbatch and Martin Freeman (John Watson) as, respectively, best actor and best supporting actor. 2013 began on a similar note for the series: *Sherlock* received Royal Television Society awards for best drama series and best drama writer (Steven Moffat).[4]

Through the years, "Sherlock" Cumberbatch has won or been nominated as best actor by BAFTA, the Broadcasting Press Guild, TV Quick, Satellite, National Television Awards, Golden Globe, and Emmy Awards— and those are only for his television work. Perhaps he can't win them all, but he at least is nominated, year after year, for the most prestigious awards.

In 2013, around the time that Cumberbatch received a Golden Globe nomination as best actor in a television movie or miniseries and, a few weeks earlier, won a Satellite award, also for *Sherlock,* the media again questioned whether series' leads Cumberbatch and Freeman had outgrown their now-famous television roles. After all, filming of the third series was delayed from January to March (and the shooting schedule compressed)

3

in deference to the actors' extremely busy professional calendars. Nevertheless, both actors seemed committed to the show that, although it had not launched their careers internationally, at least had given them a substantial boost. A frequently quoted comment by Cumberbatch is that "Making [*Sherlock*] is all about availability. Martin Freeman has the same kind of pressures on him now. [The show is] a thing of quality not quantity."[5] In a separate interview, Freeman noted that "*Sherlock* is one of the best written things I'll ever do. If I live to 100, I won't do many things that are better written than *Sherlock*,"[6] which seems a positive indicator that he would be willing to continue as John Watson. Certainly the actors' fan bases, spanning the world, revere them in the series and hope it continues.

Cumberbatch has flirted with international fame before, with an award-winning television performance as Stephen Hawking in *Hawking* (2004), as well as a memorable if creepy role in *Atonement* (2007). In 2011, he starred in two independent films: *Third Star* and *Wreckers,* which received good reviews for both actor and the films at festivals in Europe and North America. His talent has never been in dispute—he has been called one of Britain's finest young actors for at least a decade. However, he does not fit the typical Hollywood model of a television or film star or comfortably deal with the level of celebrity to which many people aspire.

In many ways, Benedict Cumberbatch challenges the popular definitions of *celebrity* or *star*. He lacks the idealised physical perfection of a young Brad Pitt or Tom Cruise. He looks and sounds "posh" (as illustrated in a 2012 Jaguar commercial in which he starred as an elite young man about London), and he has been both glorified for his magnificent voice and criticised for his unique, what some have called "alien," appearance. According to his sister, Cumberbatch laughingly compares his striking long face to that of racehorse Shergar "in self-defence, to get in the criticism about himself first."[7] A series of well-publicised Internet photos comparing Cumberbatch-as-Sherlock's expressions with those of an indignant otter made the international entertainment news. The combination of exquisite talent/unique looks and name that makes Cumberbatch appealing to his fans is also making him a rising international star whose time finally has come.

Fans trying to get tickets to the British Film Institute's *Sherlock* preview in December 2011 caused mayhem online, on the phone, and in person the moment the box office opened. The lucky 450 who saw Cumberbatch in the Q&A following the screening clearly adore the actor and the show—several fans had flown overseas just to attend the event. (I was one of them.) When the second series of *Sherlock* arrived in the U.S. in May 2012, PBS held an online lottery to randomly select 100 fans (who each would receive two tickets) to attend a similar screening and Q&A with Cumberbatch in New York City. In response, PBS received more than 10,000 emails.[8] Beginning at 7 a.m., the line of fans hoping for a last-minute ticket stretched several rainy blocks, although the screening was scheduled for 6:30 p.m. Another 3,000 fans watched the live-stream from NYC that evening.[9]

A *New York Times* feature about Cumberbatch reported that an average of 10 million viewers watch *Sherlock* in the U.K. After the 6 May second-series premiere, PBS issued a press release touting *Sherlock*'s "remarkable ratings"[10] in the U.S.; the *New York Times* listed 4.6 million as its average PBS viewership for the first series' episodes.[11] BBC Worldwide has sold the show to more than 180 countries and territories so far, and the market keeps growing; *Sherlock* was BBC Worldwide's second most lucrative export in 2011.[12]

Sherlock has become a cult favourite around the world and a mainstream hit in the U.K., and its writing, production values, and chemistry between leads Cumberbatch and Freeman have won it a devoted following. Much of the acclaim is the result of the perfect blend between actor and role: Cumberbatch and Sherlock. In some ways the two seem similar: highly intelligent, inquisitive, intense, research oriented, and dedicated to "the work." Cumberbatch is the kind of actor who has read Sir Arthur Conan Doyle's canon[13] but also taken violin lessons, "practices" the art of detection in his observations of people, and changes his diet and fitness regime to better encapsulate Sherlock's physique as well as his peerless mind.

The critical acclaim for and popular fascination with *Sherlock* indicate a major shift in Cumberbatch's professional profile and in his new role as international celebrity. In 2011-12, the actor began to decide which roles to take and through which media to display his talent based on slightly different criteria. After a successful National Theatre run of *After the Dance,* Cumberbatch was tapped to take the show to Broadway. However, he turned down the opportunity in favour of more film work (in addition to his commitment to *Sherlock*); this was one of his first "head-over-heart" decisions that disappointed fans, especially in the U.S., who hoped to see him in person more often on stage. He further worried *Sherlock* fans in August 2012 when *The Big Issue* reported his remarks that "for film you have to play a long game . . . . I am just starting to do that, where you wait, you campaign for roles. There will be time out of work, but to be frank, I could do with a bit of a break, anyway."[14] Yet Cumberbatch made it clear that he is not finished with theatre; in 2011 he shared the lead roles of Victor Frankenstein and the Creature in the multiple-award-winning National Theatre production of *Frankenstein* and in summer 2012 mused that he would like to play Hamlet in the near future. The heart-head debates over role choices have led to a highly varied career to date, and the actor once said he has "no regrets" about his career up to 2010 "because I've loved the journey I've gone on. I was doing exactly what I wanted to do, landing lovely roles and getting the respect of my peers."[15]

In addition to his highly visible work on film, television, or stage, his distinctive baritone garners him plenty of voiceover work, whether in commercials or on radio. He voiced two roles (a Hugh Grant-style Prime Minister and Alan Rickman-as-Severus Snape) on pop culture's most durable barometer of television cool, *The Simpsons*. His radio work includes roles in one of radio's most popular series, *Cabin Pressure,* and one-off dramas, such as *Tom and Viv* (playing T.S. Eliot) or *Copenhagen* (playing physicist Werner Heisenberg), with his role as the angel Islington in Neil Gaiman's *Neverwhere* gaining plenty of media attention in 2013. He is in demand for public or recorded readings of everything from short stories to war letters. When *Sherlock* was dubbed into German, Michael Schlimgen, author of the German version, commented that few German viewers will "know Cumberbatch's original voice," so choosing a German actor whose voice matches the role, not the actor's sound, became most important. (Schlimgen may need to revise that assumption about audience familiarity with Cumberbatch's voice.) However, insights into the quality of voice needed for the role reflect Cumberbatch's unique sound, which Schlimgen described as having "conflicting aspects . . . . He is young, and he has a rather deep voice."[16] No matter what Cumberbatch's future holds in the way of leading-man roles, he could rely on his voice alone to have a very lucrative, long-lived career.

Some of the actor's choices may seem strange—such as a voiceover for a dog food commercial[17]—but his dossier for 2011-13 includes such high-profile performances (in addition to *Sherlock, Star Trek: Into Darkness,* and *The Hobbit* trilogy) as a plantation owner in the Brad Pitt-starring/produced *Twelve Years a Slave,* scheduled for U.S. release in late December 2013, just in time for Oscar nominations[18]; a browbeaten son in the George Clooney-produced *August: Osage Count;* and the lead in Dreamworks' Wikileaks biopic *The Fifth Estate,* a role that some critics expect to bring acting-award nominations. Cumberbatch also participated in readers' theatre *Look Back in Anger* and poetry reading at the Cheltenham Music Festival, Q&A sessions about *Sherlock* both at home and overseas, the opening narration to the BBC's coverage of the London Olympics, and narration of *The Snowman* sequel. His most literally commercial roles helped sell Jaguars as well as introduce the world to a new Google format. His presence on the runway helped launch a men's collection during London's fashion week. Although he throws his heart into his work in these artistic or purely commercial ventures, his head clearly thought through the impact these choices would have on his bankability as an actor of incredible range but also specific strengths (such as his voice).

His heart may be displayed in roles he fell in love with, including Christopher Tietjens in *Parade's End*, a joint venture among the BBC, HBO, and Dutch television, but he is clear headed in realising that this is his moment—not the promise of fame whispered after roles in *Hawking* or *Atonement*. He may joke that he has been the "next big thing" for more than a decade, but a more mature Cumberbatch is poised to achieve what few actors ever do—to balance heart (roles he loves to play, however much or little they will pay monetarily or with critical acclaim) with head (roles designed to keep him in the public eye as well as to stretch and enhance his talent as well as bankbook).

As if this professional balancing act were not enough to handle, Cumberbatch also faces an even more interesting dichotomy, that between *actor* and *celebrity*. In 2012 he was named to several "top" lists ranging from sex appeal to global influence. In the former he beat David Beckham[19]; in the latter, U.S. President Barack Obama.[20] He received professional recognition with the Olivier award for *Frankenstein* and many television awards, based on critics', actors', or fans' votes, for *Sherlock*, but he also was photographed on the red carpet for film premieres in London, Brussels, Cannes, New

York, and Los Angeles, not always for his own films. He has become a photographable celebrity invited to high-profile entertainment and society events.

When he is absent from the London spotlight because of filming commitments, newspapers rehash old interviews or speculate on what he has or has not said or done. When he grants interviews in relation to a project or an event, his words are scrutinised for weeks in all media, sometimes taken out of context to provoke even greater public commentary [such as reported quotes about the perils of being a posh actor in the U.K., his need to leave theatre or television behind in order to become a (Hollywood) movie star, or the superior quality of his BBC miniseries over any rival period piece]. Whereas he once was able to shop like a "normal" person—and sometimes had to get a bit cross in order to get his deli order[21]—he now seems baffled at the way other shoppers react when they see him in the frozen pea section.[22] He has taken to wearing a quasi-disguise of baseball caps or hoodies, and his dark shades are seldom far from those famous eyes, but he also marvels at the public's incorrect assumption that the famous "just walk from chauffeur driven cars to red carpets and basically have people wiping our arses for us."[23] Trying to balance the everyday aspects of life with those uniquely the province of actors and celebrities seems to be increasingly difficult as Cumberbatch becomes more of a media commodity. Head and heart both may tell him that celebrity is another part of his job, but whether it enhances or manages to subtly undermine his ability to do "the work" is a chapter of this book, one just being written in Cumberbatch's life.

Benedict Cumberbatch's career is the perfect case study to understand modern acting, the actor's profession, and the perks and perils of celebrity. As a professional actor for more than a decade, Cumberbatch is interesting not only for his performances but his preparation for roles. He analyses characters, modifies his appearance in order to inhabit the character's physical space (not an easy task when he shifts, for example, from the ethereally slender Sherlock to the plumper Christopher Tietjens within a matter of days, or when he tackles the sly slinkiness of Smaug within the confines of a motion-capture suit and the muscle-defined bulk of a *Star Trek* villain at roughly the same time). He learns new skills, including equestrianship and musicianship, as well as new dialects. He seems to be always working in a variety of roles and media—more than might be expected for an actor who has already achieved a high level of recognition and fame. Within a decade he has accumulated a significant body of work to study, as well as to enjoy.

Additionally, he talks a lot about his roles and provides a wealth of information for students of acting as well as fans who simply want to know more about him. Perhaps because he has spent a great deal of time in the theatre (and grew up around actors, many, including his parents, who frequently work there), even when he discusses a television or film role, he elaborates on the role and his preparation for it. His interviews are often difficult to break into simple sound bites, because he adds so much detail to his answers and is effusive, intelligent, and informative, not merely verbose. Even if the interviewer asks superficial questions, Cumberbatch provides thoughtful answers that allow those who want to learn about acting something to think about. As the role model of a modern actor, Cumberbatch is not only knowledgeable, but he shares his off-stage/camera perspective in print, on radio, and before a camera.

However, Cumberbatch is also at a pivotal point in his career, and that trajectory—especially as documented in tabloids, magazines, newspapers, and entertainment media—permits a closer examination of just what it means to be a celebrity or star in Britain or the U.S. and how an actor may be perceived very differently in London or Hollywood. As an actor and as a burgeoning film star, Benedict Cumberbatch is far more than Hunk of the Year, eligible single, or sometimes controversial interviewee.

Whatever the role—and Cumberbatch has played monsters as well as heroes—the actor makes each character *human,* complexly flawed, vulnerable or doubting, as well as cunning or confident. He can make historic figures doomed to villainy by generations of interpretations seem understandable and even likeable. He gives voice to the misunderstood in history (e.g., Vincent Van Gogh, Werner Heisenberg, Guy Burgess) or literature (Frankenstein's Creature) and makes audiences re-evaluate the human experience. He tackles iconic roles such as Sherlock Holmes and attracts new fans to the canon as well as a most modern adaptation because he imbues the character's genius with love and vulnerability. Such is the talent of Benedict Cumberbatch, an actor who embraces a well-written role and brings new dimensions to interpretation of character. That this artistic genius also now illustrates the predominance of celebrity culture in the arts, as well as the tension between the professions of celebrity and actor, further makes Benedict Cumberbatch important to current popular culture and entertainment history.

In a 2012 interview, Cumberbatch cautioned the way his career should be "read": "'[Fans] know you from the trail you leave with your work,'. . ., the slightest edge of frustration in his voice. 'They assume things about you because of who you play and how you play them, and the other scraps floating around in the ether. People try to sew together a narrative out of scant fact.'" [24] In this performance biography, I do not attempt to draw con-clusions about the actor himself from any similarities or differences with each of his roles; a performance biography is a critical evaluation of the actor's effectiveness, including his preparation and performance. In the following chapters, I analyse Benedict Cumberbatch's road to stardom, beginning with his first youthful forays into drama; to early stage, film, radio, and television roles; to the transition front and centre before international audiences. Because not all readers may work in the theatre, some sections explore in greater detail the demands placed on an actor and the typical activities that take place backstage. Although some biographical information is included, especially in the first chapter, this performance biography is centred around two emphases: Cumberbatch's roles through 2013 and the way his career has been developed.

Because this actor has blessed his fans with so many roles in a relatively short career, I cannot attempt to adequately analyse each role and have instead emphasised a variety of performances, some less well known to more recent fans or critics, that illustrate specific aspects of Cumberbatch's preparation or performance quality. I also, as much as possible, have selected performances or events that are available to hear or view as downloads, CDs or audiobooks, DVD or Blu-ray discs, media footage, or photographs. Readers new to Cumberbatch's work may want to review his back catalogue in light of the commentary about or reviews of his performances.

I thank directors Nick White (*Inseparable*), D R Hood (*Wreckers*), and Hattie Dalton (*Third Star*) for previous PopMatters interviews and/or new interviews or information specifically for this book. I also am indebted to staff members at the National Theatre and archives, Victoria and Albert Museum performance archives at Blythe House, British Library, Westminster Reference Library, British Film Institute, and BFI Reuben Library.

Chapter 1 What's in a Name?

"What's in a name? That which we call a rose
by any other name would smell as sweet.
So Romeo would, if he were not Romeo call'd, retain that
dear perfection which he owes without that title."[25]
Juliet, *Romeo and Juliet*

Benedict Cumberbatch. Seldom has a name piqued so much curiosity or media comment. When a *Washington Post* journalist "accidentally on purpose" misspelled his name, #BandersnatchCummerbund trended on Twitter,[26] and online newspapers around the world immediately carried the story. Within days of the *64th Annual Emmy Awards* broadcast, host Jimmy Kimmel explained that the actor "has a very silly name" and took a camera crew to Hollywood Boulevard to ask "What is a Cumberbatch?"[27] Although a *Montreal Gazette* blogger quickly noted one of many tweets criticising Americans for being "late to the party" to celebrate the actor's talent and increasing celebrity,[28] U.S. media mavens have not been the only ones known to tease Cumberbatch about his name. *Chatty Man* Alan Carr prefaced his questions about the actor's name by noting that "it's the kind of thing the police ask you to say when they think you're drunk." The actor agreed that it sounded a bit "like a fart in the bath" and confided a more sexual interpretation bestowed by one of his university friends (then apologised to his mum for saying it on television).[29]

The Londoner born Benedict Timothy Carlton Cumberbatch on 19 July 1976 has varied his professional name throughout the years. He was originally known professionally as Ben Carlton, following his father Timothy Carlton not only into acting but using a more common stage name.[30] Certainly that variation was easier to say and spell, but it also failed to be as memorable as the young actor's performances. "When I started, I just assumed I couldn't be called Benedict Cumberbatch," he told *The Guardian* in 2008.[31] When he changed agents, he agreed to change his professional name. His agent thought that the name Benedict Cumberbatch is formal and unique, but the actor himself originally considered it "a bit bumbly and messy."[32] The name change was part of a "rebranding process," he explained on radio program *French and Saunders* in early 2011 but joked that "I don't change my name as often as I change my pants" when the hosts prodded him to talk about the name change. The discussion led to a bit of history about his surname, which supposedly means "a person who dwells in a valley with a stream." Cumberbatch told the story of how, one day on the *Creation* set, a cast mate happily told him that the name has Welsh origins; however, the name also was reputed to come from the very English town of Cumberbatch, in Cheshire, which the actor's mother, Wanda Ventham, confirmed was the true origin.[33]

Going back farther than any link to Cheshire is the name's German origins. Long before acting became a family profession and generated new wealth, a branch became plantation owners in the Caribbean (Barbados) and, as was common with that profession, also were involved with the slave trade. One article claimed that "generations ago the family had made a mint as owners of a sugar plantation in Barbados." Playing roles like

Edmund Talbot in *To the Ends of the Earth* and later, in 2012, a U.S. plantation owner in *Twelve Years a Slave* helped him, he once said, "draw on this part of his DNA," although other roles, such as abolitionist William Pitt in *Amazing Grace*, were "a sort of apology."[34] Despite that connection to family wealth, Cumberbatch's half-sister Tracy told *The Sun* in 2011 that the actor's father "had to scrimp and save to pay for Benedict to go to private school" and "set up a trust fund even before he had the idea of having Benedict."[35]

Cumberbatch once described his upbringing as a sort of hybrid. On the one hand, he went off to boarding school at age 8; he attended public schools Brambletye Preparatory School in West Sussex and later Harrow, "whose former pupils include eight [Prime Ministers]."[36] On the other, unlike his classmates who went on skiing holidays between terms, for example, he visited his grandmother in Brighton. Indeed, she helped pay for his education.[37] When criticised for making comments about posh actors, the actor differentiated himself from his landed or titled class peers. Despite having the benefit of a public school education and the social connections it includes, Cumberbatch has tried diligently in public to straddle a middle (or perhaps a middle-class) line between being affluent and just a regular guy.

Celebrity from an Early Age

Cumberbatch might have been expected to have a show biz life, given his parents' circle of friends and colleagues in the British entertainment industry and the amount of press given to them during his childhood. Baby Ben was only five days old when the *Daily Mirror* published photographer Freddie Reed's first picture of him. "Little Big Ben takes a bow" the paper wrote under the headline proclaiming him "Wanda's Little Wonder." Indeed, his parents look very happy in the photo: his mother beams at the camera, his father pecks her on the temple. Front and centre is nine-pound Benedict, looking more alert than most new babies, gazing calmly back at the camera. The paper noted that the new father had "helped to bring Ben . . . into the world at Queen Charlotte's Hospital."[38]

The *Daily Mirror* often chronicled the youngster's life in its reports of Ventham's television and theatrical career. For six months after her son's birth, Ventham was largely out of the limelight, but she decided to return to acting when she received a contract for *Crown Court.* Carlton, then working in the television version of *Dick Barton,* worked during the day but looked after their son when Ventham performed in the theatre during the evening. Ventham's return to television in a *Doctor Who* episode generated press about the role, but she also mentioned her little boy: "[My] one regret about *Dr. Who* is that Ben is still too young to watch."[39]

Ben seemed much more precocious at three. His mother, then starring in television drama *Fallen Hero,* described her son's confusion about Father Christmas. According to the *Daily Express,* Ventham explained that "this is the first year he has really understood about Father Christmas, and he is very excited. But he is a bit puzzled because he has been taken by friends to see two separate Father Christmases and he can't understand why there were two faces! He's worried, too, that Father Christmas will come down our chimney and land on the electric fire." Even as a three-year-old, Cumberbatch was thinking ahead and making some interesting observations. Ventham's solution was to remind Ben that the family would be spending the holiday at his grandmother's, where the fire would be extinguished in plenty of time for Father Christmas' visit; a side note added that the parents "will have an old rugger sock on Benedict's bed" to hold the presents Father Christmas would surely bring.[40]

Descriptions of Cumberbatch as a child vary widely, depending upon whom is asked. His mother recalled her son as a sweet boy considerate of her, but Cumberbatch referred to himself as a hyperactive nightmare.[41] Sometimes, however, even his mother was less than pleased with her little boy's conduct. When Ventham was interviewed at home in 1979, she apologised for her three-year-old's "vile" behaviour that day; Carlton, who his wife said was good with their son, entertained the child the interviewer dubbed "boisterous Benedict" in another room. First impressions are memorable, however, and the article initially describes the boy as "an energetic handful who was treating the living room like a sports stadium." The youngster's tonsils had recently been removed, and, according to his mother, "his temperament has gone slightly loopy in the last day or so."[42]

Ben must have matured a bit by the next year (or he was on best behaviour around his mother's friends.) Una Stubbs, who worked on movies with Ventham and decades later would be cast as *Sherlock*'s Mrs. Hudson, remembers going out in her Kensington neighbourhood "with my pram, and Wanda and I would be talking," while "poor little Benedict, who I suppose was about four, [was] standing there while we were gossiping in the high street for hours!"[43]

Such "quiet" memories have been seldom recorded in the press, whether through his own interviews or as referenced in his parents'. Often his life away from acting seems thrilling or daring—at least, far from sedentary or quiet—and the best anecdotes indicate Cumberbatch's fearlessness. The actor once said that star Elaine Stritch early on determined that he would be successful as an actor: she "predicted my future career when I was a little boy . . . . She saw me walking across a field in my red dungarees despite the presence of a bull. 'That boy,' she drawled, 'is going to be a star.'"[44] His ability to charm anything in his path was a worthy trait to turn toward acting.

Although a 1980 article claimed that Ventham found full-time domesticity difficult and thoroughly enjoyed her acting career, she did not want to miss out on her son's childhood. She explained that "Ben starts school next year and because I'd worked for some long spells away from home making *Fallen Hero* last year, I decided to spend as much time as possible with him [this year]. I turned down any job which involved leaving London for more than a few days."[45] The bond between Cumberbatch and his parents seems strong; they often visit, even when he is working overseas, and, in an appropriate turnabout, he often mentions them during interviews.

Being at least peripherally in the public eye for much of his life did not seem to hamper his inner child as he became a working actor, and he seems not to have outgrown some behaviours noted in descriptions of young

Benedict. An early *Sherlock* article described how the actor kept cast members in stitches with his impressions of other people or how he sat nervously on his hands or bounced his leg up and down during the interview, unable to contain his energy.[46] A scriptwriter's blog comments that Cumberbatch still giggles.[47] These descriptions echo an early school report that "Ben is slightly more controlled, but he must try to be less noisy. A good start, but we hope Ben will calm down a little next term."[48]

Talkative and energetic seem to be keys to the actor's personality at any age. During a 2010 radio show, when asked about her son as a very young child (Cumberbatch muttering in the background "oh, great"), Ventham remembered that he "always talked a lot. He had a very loud voice. . . . He was active, but he always slept. I think he knew he had an older mummy, and he was very kind to me." In the background, Cumberbatch added, "I'm very grumpy without eight hours sleep, which is a luxury in adult life." As an older child who accompanied his parents on a six-week tour during a half-term break from school, young Ben received permission to sit just off stage while his mother worked and "got terribly overexcited because of the laughter. And he was standing there, actually shivering, saying 'I wish I could come on with you.'"[49]

Cumberbatch developed observation skills early and studied the people around him. He remembers that he and his parents "lived sort of in the shadow of the Royal Garden Hotel in Kensington," where "there were floors and floors of all these silhouettes and I was fascinated with people doing things. I was far too young to know what was going on, if anything was going on. But I always listened through the [door] jamb to this adult world, to see what was going on."[50] (As he became famous and easily recognizable on the street, he mourned the loss of such opportunities to observe others unaware: "One of the fears of having too much work is not having time to observe. And once you get recognised, there is nowhere for you to look any more. You can't sit on a night bus and watch it all happen."[51])

Soon enough Cumberbatch was acting in school plays. Recalling an early role as Joseph in his prep school's nativity play, the young actor gained notoriety by shoving Mary off the stage because he was "furious about how self-indulgent she was being."[52] Unwittingly, he earned a laugh from the audience, but playing to the crowd to get that laugh was not his intention. He simply wanted the performance to go as it should and, even as a youngster, was more focused on the work than courting audiences'—or his parents'—approval. "Mum and dad were mortified" [53] but even then might have realised their son's dedication to his future profession.

What Cumberbatch once called his "first, big, silly role at school was as Arthur Crocker-Harris in [Terence] Rattigan's *The Browning Version*, where my job was to make schoolmasters' wives weep with recognition."[54] Other roles during his school years included Titania, Queen of the Fairies, and Rosalind. He was encouraged to act on stage as a way to direct his energy other than fighting, or, as he once put it, "to repress the tearaway in me."[55] Harrow typically produces about twenty plays per academic year, which certainly provided plenty of opportunities for the young actor to participate in theatre and study with the department's director, Martin Tyrell, who has described Cumberbatch as "the best schoolboy actor [I] have ever worked with."[56]

Cumberbatch's preference for sports, especially rugby and cricket, also helped to acclimate him to a life on stage, not only by honing his natural physical prowess but by introducing him early on to teamwork. During the BBC documentary *The Rattigan Enigma,* Cumberbatch points himself out in two group photos taken during his years at Harrow in the early 1990s. A blond lad "with wicketkeeper's hands" represents the sporty side of Cumberbatch's Harrow education, but a later photo of the teenaged thespian shows him wearing his "rats" tie in honour of playwright Terence Rattigan, who not only attended Harrow but once lived in The Park, the house where Cumberbatch lived as a student.[57]

In November 2012, as master of ceremonies celebrating Harrow's Jubilee Churchill Songs in Royal Albert Hall, Cumberbatch jokingly recalled the "mixture of nostalgia and terror" that summarises his memory of the school but praised the way Harrow prepared him for his career:

> I was thirteen and a Shell the last time I sang Harrow songs here. It was an extraordinary occasion and one I found a little terrifying up on this stage in case anyone was looking at me . . . [I]t cannot be denied those years were formative—though at the time it is a rare thing to be able to deduce where those experiences will lead you. For example, little did I think my time at school would lead to the BBC asking me to play Sherlock Holmes.[58]

After Harrow, Cumberbatch travelled to Asia for his gap year "to make use of the opportunities I had at school." He wanted to teach English to Buddhist monks at a Tibetan monastery but realised "I had to do something about it really quickly; otherwise it was going to get allocated. I was very decisive. I worked for six months to drum up the finance as it was voluntary--there was no income. I worked in Penhaligon's the perfumery for almost five months and I did waiting jobs." His work ethic paid off, and he secured the gap-year position in Tibet.

In addition to the satisfaction of his teaching duties, the trip was valuable in showing the young man how to live with a great deal less. However, the trip was not always austere. During a two-week visit to Nepal, he went white water rafting and camping "out under the stars."[59] This early trip abroad began what would become the first of such adventures, often to filming locations (such as South Africa, where he enjoyed scuba diving and horseback safaris in 2005) or simply getaways for a thrill (such as tandem skydiving in New Zealand early in 2012) that made Cumberbatch a man of the world in the best sense.

Perhaps a surprising choice for university was Manchester, but it provided Cumberbatch with a wider range of associates ("a thoroughly healthy—and unhealthy—mix of friends"[60]) and a long-term partner, actor Olivia Poulet. After graduation, he attended the London Academy of Music and Dramatic Art (LAMDA), which in 2012 proudly touted Cumberbatch as one of its alumni: "Scarcely a year goes by without our graduates being honoured at a major film, television or theatre award ceremony. Already in 2012, Benedict Cumberbatch has been named best actor for his performance in *Frankenstein* (National Theatre) by the London Evening Standard Theatre Awards, the Critics Circle Theatre Awards and the Laurence Olivier Awards."[61] The requirements for his one-year MA degree in Classical Acting for the Professional Theatre included study of Shakespeare's plays; works from the Jacobean, Spanish Golden Age, Restoration, and French Classical Theatre periods; and classes in acting, voice, movement, textual analysis, stage combat, and dance[62]—truly a rigorous course. In addition to preparing students for the rehearsal process, LAMDA also showcased their pupils' talents through performances open to the public and, more important to a career, agents.

Cumberbatch's passion is recalled even by those who knew him only briefly in school. A former university acquaintance who blogged about seeing *Frankenstein* noted that the aspiring actor was always standing in the kitchen during parties to discuss acting with his friends.[63] Although at one time Cumberbatch considered a career in law, he never truly doubted his ability as or desire to become an actor. He confessed to *The Telegraph* in 2012 that he is not "someone who's naturally confident, [but] I just knew no matter what [acting] held for me, I was going to pursue it."[64] There is the much-repeated story of, after being moved by a performance, Carlton telling his son that he is the better actor; Cumberbatch's parents seem proud of their son but also professionally appreciative of his talent. Instead of questioning whether he should become an actor, the key issue would initially become how to distinguish himself from other equally committed actors. Finished with formal education at 24, Cumberbatch gained his first agent and began the series of performances, many discussed in this book, that illustrate his talent as an actor but also his increasing "presence" in the profession.

What Makes Cumberbatch Distinctive—
Other Than His Name?

Although Cumberbatch may seem to be a "late bloomer" when it comes to the fame game, his talent has never been disputed, and the majority of his projects in any medium have been highly successful. He has consistently worked as a professional since his graduation, and since 2010 his name has seldom been out of the press, whether in announcements of new or rumoured roles or publicity for anticipated or just-released films or television productions. In addition to his memorable name, what makes this actor attractive (in ways other than the physical) to his fan base? The following list summarises what his supporters like best about the talented Mr. Cumberbatch:

• His inquisitive approach to acting underscores his intelligence and immersion into roles. A *Guardian* reporter once wrote "More studenty than Stanislavski in his approach to roles, he likes to read or interview his way into a part."[65] Cumberbatch does his homework, and his professional "education" into history, art, politics, science, or music is impressive. He reads texts from the periods during which his characters live, as well as original works from which scripts have been adapted. He asks questions of scientists, for example, when he needs to understand the terminology and theories that form the basis of his characters' dialogue. He tackles new skills (e.g., horseback riding, playing an instrument, speaking in a specific dialect) with gusto. Cumberbatch is a student of life and throws himself into preparation for his roles.

- Because of his talent and success as an actor, his profession affords him remarkable opportunities to meet and talk with people otherwise outside what might be expected as his "normal" circle of acquaintances or friends. He talks with royalty at film premieres. Beginning with preparation to play Stephen Hawking in *Hawking* and continuing over the years as Cumberbatch narrated Hawking's science documentaries, the physicist and the actor have conversed about a great number of topics—including, according to one observer, *Star Trek.*[66] Such opportunities to interact with the famous in other professions or the unique from different walks in life not only enrich his acting life but indicate to fans his diverse interests and intelligence; he can converse knowledgeably about a wide range of subjects with just about anyone.

- His increased fame, level of professional recognition and respect, and willingness to give back to the community have led him to participate in cultural or philanthropic events. He works with the Prince's Trust (e.g., attending several Celebrate Success events through the years and, most impressively, raising more than £23,000 during the Palace to Palace bike ride in 2012[67]). He has been featured at Cheltenham literary or music festivals. He is invited onto professional panels or juries, such as that to select finalists for the EE British Academy Film Awards' 2013 Rising Star award.[68] He served as the guest director of the 2013 Cambridge Science Festival.[69]

• Family and friends are important to him, and fame is a family affair. His niece is his personal assistant. His parents, famous in their own right, often join him on location or at events, such as they did in New York following the PBS *Sherlock* series two premiere. He noted in one interview that he hoped to travel with his parents in New Zealand after completing filming on *The Hobbit* trilogy. An often-repeated story is how friends, late at night during the Christmas holidays, helped the actor with what turned out to be an impressive *Star Trek* audition—filmed in their kitchen on an iPhone.[70] Although Cumberbatch benefits from the support of family and friends, he also works to keep these relationships vibrant, even while he travels far from home to make movies.

• He chooses roles according to his long-range view of his career and the parts that interest him most—he directs his career and seeks or accepts roles that offer new challenges. For example, he initially turned down *After the Dance* because he failed to see Rattigan's relevance to modern audiences and thought that he had played similar roles. Only when he understood how the playwright could speak to modern audiences did he agree to taking on a role that brought him excellent reviews and greater exposure.[71]

- He is eloquent, erudite, and expressive in discussing roles and projects, which allows his audiences to understand the historic or cultural context of a play, film, or television series, as well as better appreciate Cumberbatch's character's background and motivations. He speaks his mind, even if, to his horror, he ends up being misquoted or misinterpreted by the media.

- He does not seem attention seeking, even at events when he is expected to promote himself and his projects. He is smart about publicity and knows how to give good sound bite, and he is most often gracious around the press or fans but, even in 2013, seems overwhelmed by the increasing number of paparazzi who turn up unexpectedly on his doorstep or dog his steps when they see him in public.

- He still becomes nervous before live performances, such as television's *The Turning Point*. Although his audition recordings for *The Hobbit* and *Star Trek* wowed the director and fellow actors (such as *The Hobbit*'s Ian McKellen), Cumberbatch still seems surprised to hear the praise. He admitted to being nervous in flying to Los Angeles and going directly to the studio to begin *Star Trek*. Even after filming was completed and the press invited to a large-screen preview, the actor said, "I always get incredibly nervous, especially on an empty stomach having only had a macchiato. It makes your heart beat a lot faster and I don't like it. I look away when it's me. I don't like being my own audience. It's very weird. . . . You probably saw my nostril hairs, counted how many pores I've got on my nose and which one of my teeth is wonky."[72] Because these responses seem real and spontaneous during interviews when the actor is surprised by a question or relieved in the immediate aftermath of a performance, they signal to fans that the actor is still humble and human and not all about self-promotion or ego.

- He admits to some flaws and resists being placed on a pedestal. At times, even the usually publically even-tempered Cumberbatch does not suffer fools well or becomes impatient when he is hampered in doing something he needs to do straight away. "I can be a bit irate or impatient at times," he told NPR, "and my mum worries sometimes I might be turning into [Sherlock]. [Sometimes] I can sort of see the picture of what's in front of me and expect everyone else to get it as fast as I do."[73] When trying to submit that long-distance *Star Trek* audition, for example, he was fortunate that friends and an iPhone finally recorded it. He had been called during a Gloucestershire vacation to submit an audition but grew frustrated when no one could film it during the holiday season. Then, after going to such an extreme to send the iPhone recording right away, he faced delays in receiving feedback—the director was on vacation.[74] Cumberbatch takes his work very seriously, and he can become very focused when he needs to accomplish something, whether it is as mundane as getting someone to take his deli order[75] or more professionally significant like working on a role. Although in public with fans as well as in the media he has been praised as

30

a most gracious, solicitous man, Cumberbatch occasionally reveals that he is, indeed, humanly capable of having a temper.

Another less endearing quality is tardiness. He apologised for being late to the *French and Saunders* radio interview with his mother, claiming that traffic delayed his taxi. He was one of the last to be seated, after Steven Moffat, Mark Gatiss, and other cast members at the BFI screening of "A Scandal in Belgravia" (although that could also have been a result of keeping him safely tucked away in a green room). Even viewing the very first episode of *Sherlock* with his colleagues turned into a broadcast delay for those closest to the production—Cumberbatch arrived late at Gatiss' house, and so the cast was aware of Twitter exploding with excitement about the episode about fifteen minutes before they actually watched the pilot's conclusion.[76] In a 2008 interview, Cumberbatch claimed the phrase he uses far too often is "Sorry I'm late!" and admitted "I'm a terrible time-keeper." However, he also told the *Independent* interviewer that he is not being wilful with such lateness, but he simply is disorganised.[77] For his fans, if not his colleagues and potential employers, Cumberbatch's tardiness may be thought of as an endearing quirk that proves their idol is, after all, only human.

Certainly Benedict Cumberbatch is not the world's only actor with these attributes, but when they are blended with a reported determined work ethic, well-documented number of roles in a short period of time, media saturation, and ability to mediate press storms—in addition to his acting talent—he becomes more highly prized as a "watchable" and "bankable" actor. Such financial and commercial realities may attract the attention of more filmmakers and producers who seek him for their projects, but the actor's long-time fans can only wonder why it has taken the rest of the world so long to catch on to the fact that Cumberbatch is more than an entertaining, successful actor. He is intriguing because his public persona often seems at odds to the excess, bad behaviour, or entitlement of a star or celebrity, and, although media interest in his family since before he was born would seem to indicate that he would never be surprised by public attention, Cumberbatch still does not seem to grasp the fact that his fans would do just about anything in order to meet him.

Chapter 2 The Pre-*Sherlock* Theatrical Career

"You need to be a very good mime artist for radio, to be
able to avoid walking into furniture and able to learn lines
for the stage, and as far as TV is concerned, just don't
look into the lens! I'm being facetious, but I could give
you a half-hour lecture on each one. It's important to
remember that integrity in all is paramount.
And, no matter what the medium, the challenge is
thinking rather than showing and doing–
that's the best way to tackle it."[78]
Benedict Cumberbatch, 2005

Two photos taken by photographer Simon Annand
reveal Cumberbatch the actor in moments not usually
captured on film—backstage at the theatre. On the
photographer's website, he explained the significance and
rarity of these photographs: "The dressing room is a
physical space that allows for concentration and privacy
so the psychological negotiation between the actor and
this fictional character can take place. When 'The Half' is
called over the loudspeaker backstage, it is the start of a
35-minute countdown to facing the audience and there is
no escape."[79]

In his book and a photo exhibition entitled *The
Half: Photographs of Actors Preparing for the Stage,*
Annand captured Cumberbatch at work, and the results,
especially amid the dozens of portraits of actors "at rest,"
such as smoking a cigarette or gazing into a mirror or the
camera lens, explain a lot about the actor-as-subject-of-
art. The first photo (part of a set of three making a photo
spread of individual shots of Martin Sheen, Martin

Henderson, and Benedict Cumberbatch "checking props," according to the caption) presents Cumberbatch as a "thinker" in the moments before going on stage. His photograph is less intense in expression and action than the other two in this set; with one hand Cumberbatch holds his suit jacket in place while the other hand checks his coat pocket for the prop. He is looking down, and his attitude is relaxed—this is a man simply doing his job, ensuring that he is ready to go on stage, in this case for the Almeida's 2005 production of *Hedda Gabler*. He does not seem rushed or concerned, merely attentive. In the background of the small dressing room are the usual real-life props: photographs on the wall (in this case, a flower, costume designs, and a ship), a mirror surrounded by bright bulbs, and a mostly empty water bottle capped on the table next to the actor, as if he just finished it before standing to check props one more time.[80] A second photo of Cumberbatch, displayed during a London photo exhibition, reveals the actor during the long make-up process required to transform him into Frankenstein's Creature. In this photograph, Cumberbatch-the-actor is still visible as a hand tugs into place the Creature's cap of scarred and sutured flesh.[81] The actor's complete concentration seems turned inward as psychologically he inhabits this difficult role while his body is being hidden beneath a pattern of warped prosthetics, such as the lines of stitches and raised, twisted flesh crossing his chest. A hint of Victor Frankenstein is evident in this photograph, too, where one of Cumberbatch's long sideburns is still visible. Annand beautifully captured Cumberbatch in transition to play the breakthrough, star-making role of his theatrical career, with both Creature and Frankenstein are conveyed in this single shot. What is most impressive is Cumberbatch's seriousness; his eyes are the focal point of the shot, but his gaze is clearly turned inward. In these photographs, Annand well illustrates the theatrical presence of Benedict Cumberbatch.

Perfecting Theatrical Performance: From Regent's Park to the National Theatre

Theatrical roles have the power to make or break a young career, especially in markets like London or New York. In 2005, Cumberbatch discussed his first big theatrical break as the King of Navarre in the Regent Park's Open Air Theatre 2001 production of *Love's Labour's Lost.* Then the actor teasingly reconsidered. "Or perhaps playing Anne in *Half a Sixpence* at the age of nine with a very bad wig—it was the first time I realised I looked good in girls' clothes."[82]

At the other end of the emotional spectrum, the 2002 Regent's Park production of *As You Like It,* in which he played Orlando, brought what Cumberbatch later described as his most embarrassing moment on stage: "Losing my voice . . . and with a microphone, hardly being heard saying the lines after the wrestling match when he's lovestruck with Rosalind: 'I cannot speak to her'—and hearing a mixture of derision and sympathy from the audience; and hearing Tam [Mutu], my brilliant understudy, say the first few lines of the next scene as I cycled home in tears all the way to Shepherds Bush."[83]

That the actor lost his voice is not surprising. The play's first performance was rained out halfway through, and the weather did not improve for the second—

although, perhaps because the press might not return a third time, the show went on and stayed on, despite the rain. Critic John Gross even wrote about the rain in his *Sunday Telegraph* review: "Drizzle alternated with downpour, until downpour took over completely . . . . [T]he cast must have been soaked to the skin."[84] The *Independent* noted that "Playing the hero, the excellent Benedict Cumberbatch brings out the eager, emotional neediness in this ill-treated son . . . . Though [Rosalind and Orlando] had to throw themselves down and lie in various attitudes of love-languor on a sodden stage, nothing dampened the youthful ardour of this couple."[85]

During his very early professional theatrical career, Cumberbatch played such requisite Shakespearean roles in theatre in the park and took roles in small venues, such as the Drayton Court in Ealing. The earliest reviews of the King of Navarre from the Regent's Park Open Air theatre (15 June-22 August 2001) indicate that he had already caught the critics' eye. The *Daily Mail*'s Michael Coveney, who would continue to praise Cumberbatch's performances in subsequent plays, first wrote that Cumberbatch is "going places" and his King of Navarre "finds humour and silliness where none previously existed."[86] By 2003, when Coveney reviewed *The Lady from the Sea*, he commented on the fine performance "from rising star Benedict Cumberbatch as a consumptive sculptor."[87]

Initially, critics described Cumberbatch's work with the New Shakespeare Company as "fresh" as well as "excellent," but some reviewers criticised aspects of his performances. Cumberbatch's Orlando was faulted because he "once or twice falls to ranting," although he "more than makes up for it with his ardour and openness."[88] This production of *As You Like It* was faulted by another critic; the modernisation "seems undecided which personality to adopt. . . . As brawny wrestler Charles (a perfect ad for steroids) takes on scrawny, pasty Orlando [Cumberbatch], it all starts to look less like a costume drama and more like a comic book."[89] Similarly, that summer's other production, *Oh! What a Lovely War,* received a few less-than-enthusiastic reviews for the 17-person ensemble of which Cumberbatch was a member. *Time Out* concluded that "it's as if this ensemble piece has been given the Regent's Park treatment (two Shakespeares are always followed by a jolly musical), and the result is satire with a slightly dulled edge."[90] The *Mail on Sunday* was harsher: "Acted with the cartoon zest of a student revue, this is an amiable show that honours the dead with fondly nostalgic frivolity."[91] Cumberbatch, however, was neither singled out for praise nor criticism.

Within a brief few years, these roles led to larger ones on London stages and eventually to award-winning performances known to critics and fans around the world. One standout theatrical role, which earned Cumberbatch an Olivier nomination as best supporting actor, was as George Tesman in the Almeida Theatre's *Hedda Gabler.* The actor enjoyed working there, as he stated in an Almeida Brand Video promoting the theatre. "It's a very intimate place," Cumberbatch said on camera, joking that he had the most fun in that auditorium, then correcting himself with a smile. "Well, that's a lie. I've had more fun on stage, but that's because I'm an actor," adding later in the video that "the privilege of getting that first job here was . . . fantastic. . . . I do love this theatre."[92]

This production of *Hedda Gabler* drew even more attention because it was the first after the Almeida's refurbishment, and critics came to see the remodelled theatre as well as the play. Eve Best, playing the title character, garnered most of the attention in the press, although Cumberbatch also shared the spotlight. (For example, he is featured on the cover of *Theatre Record*, a publication that announces and collects reviews of newly opened plays, but he is there primarily because of an article featuring Best, the focal point of the cover shot.) For some critics, Cumberbatch had to overcome perceived miscasting: "Initial misgivings that Benedict Cumberbatch as her youthful, enthusiastic husband—far from the usual smug pedant—had been miscast give way to the realisation that this is Tesman as he really is rather than how Hedda sees him."[93] The *Financial Times'* Alistair Macauley acknowledged that "the most arresting interpretative decision comes from the excellent Benedict Cumberbatch as [Hedda's] husband, who suggests at the end that she is now useless to him and that he means her for Judge Brack."[94] This interpretation is vastly different from the common portrayal of Hedda becoming bored with George and becoming ensnared in the Judge's web as she looks for ways to escape the constraints of her marriage. Not everyone understood Cumberbatch's interpretation of George Tesman, but it earned him an award nomination and greater awareness from the theatre-going public. The play was popular enough that after its run at the Almeida (16 March to 30 April 2005) it

38

was transferred on 23 May to the West End's Duke of York.

By 2006, reviews of the Almeida's *Period of Adjustment* praised the "widely feted Benedict Cumberbatch."[95] Even if many critics did not like the Tennessee Williams play or this particular production, they enjoyed the actor's "strong supporting performance."[96] The role of newlywed George Haverstick, who marries and abandons his bride at a friend's house after a botched attempt at lovemaking, is difficult to make sympathetic, but the actor won over at least a few critics. "Benedict Cumberbatch, another of London's fast-rising actors, finely catches [Isabel's] husband George's [fierce] façade and the shakes that keep returning to him (a legacy of warfare). He brings him a virile warmth that makes us hope for the marriage."[97] The *Spectator*'s Lloyd Evans was "hugely impressed by Benedict Cumberbatch . . ., who extends his range here as a damaged, sexual inadequate."[98]

Although films and television offer him a wider audience and greater international fame, Cumberbatch and theatre seem especially well suited to each other. His voice resonates in a theatre, and audiences can better appreciate the very physical nature of acting when they watch Cumberbatch on stage. When he is cast in a revival or new adaptation, his work attracts a great deal of attention and many good reviews, even if not everyone agrees that a production or a performance is spot on. His most recent theatrical roles illustrate his progression from respected supporting actor to lead to star.

In 2007, Cumberbatch performed in a series of plays at the Royal Court Theatre and, during post-show talks, discussed with the audience his roles and the political nature of *The Arsonists, The City,* and *Rhinoceros.* In 2010, his leading role as David Scott-Fowler in the National Theatre production of *After the Dance* gained him even more acclaim in London theatre circles and, after the runaway success of *Sherlock* a few months later, brought more attention to this recently-completed theatrical performance because of the public's immense interest in Cumberbatch. In early 2011, between the global distribution of *Sherlock* and the start of the second series' filming in May, Cumberbatch had become a television star, and fan and critical interest in his breakthrough performance helped propel him into true theatrical stardom in *Frankenstein.*

Cumberbatch's theatrical performances bring something new to well-established characters. Reviewers following his progress from Regent's Park to South-bank's National Theatre frequently commented on his increasing status in the theatre community, but until *After the Dance* he was mainly considered a supporting actor. The roles at the National—especially in *Frankenstein*—assured him lead status and elevation to the hierarchy of Britain's best stage actors.

The following sections further analyse Cumberbatch's stage performances—including dis-cussions of his work through podcasts or post-show Q&As. The actor's work from 2007 through 2012 is discussed in this chapter, although *Frankenstein* is thoroughly analysed in Chapter 5 as a turning point performance.

Rhinoceros

In 2007 Cumberbatch was a member of the same cast performed *Rhinoceros* and *The Arsonists* in repertoire at the Royal Court. Following a lengthy post-*Rhinoceros* Q&A, the audience was told of the cast's difficult schedule; the next day they would be rehearsing *The Arsonists* but would again perform *Rhinoceros* in the evening. Both plays received mixed reviews and were deemed somewhat controversial, and Cumberbatch's reviews were similar to the play's. No matter what critics thought of the plays or the actor's overall performance, he shines in at least one difficult scene in each and, in *Rhinoceros,* takes the complacent Berenger to emotional heights that also reveal Cumberbatch's physical dexterity as well as his ability to play comedy.

When casting this play, director Dominic Cooke, who had seen Cumberbatch "in lots of things where he was brilliant," knew that he needed an actor to play Berenger who could help the audience connect with the character. After all, Berenger is "in every scene, I mean there's five minutes when he's off the stage, and it's really unusual . . . . [E]ven Hamlet has a quarter of the play off at least. . . . I thought Benedict would be the right person . . . and I also wanted someone around Benedict's age for that part, because it's often cast as older . . . . [T]here was something about the 20-something, 30s generation that will connect with this play."[99]

Not everyone was won over by Cumberbatch's performance. *The Guardian*'s critic wrote that the actor "doesn't succeed in making Berenger anything more than a nay-saying cipher,"[100] but the British Theatre Guide thought otherwise. "Leading the cast, screen regular

Benedict Cumberbatch, who has made his name on stage in much grimmer roles, particularly when playing opposite Eve Best in *Hedda Gabler*, shows that he also has a talent for comedy."[101] *The Independent*'s critic also mentioned Cumberbatch's previous work in a review of *Rhinoceros*, calling Cumberbatch "marvellous in the lead. Cooke is a great actors' director and he releases something in Cumberbatch we have not seen before. On Sunday, Cumberbatch was spot-on on the TV in *Stuart— A Life Backwards* with Tom Hardy, who is surely the Marlon Brando of our era. Here, in Martin Crimp's excellent translation, he surpasses himself."[102] Nevertheless, this critic found the play itself rather boring, a comment found in more than one review.

Certainly Eugene Ionesco's play is not to everyone's taste. The playbook cover's summary of Martin Crimp's new translation underscores the play's absurdist premise. "When a rhinoceros charges across the town square on Sunday afternoon, Berenger thinks nothing of it. Soon, however, rhinoceroses are popping up everywhere and Berenger's whole world is under threat. What will it take for him to stand up to the increasing menace of rhinocerisation?"[103] For Ionesco, this "rhinocerisation" was the rise of Nazism, but the director and cast broadened the interpretation to suit a modern audience.

The production, as seen in a recording made for the Royal Court, is imperfect, and Cumberbatch has little to do as Berenger until late in the first half, when his friend Jean begins to transform into a rhinoceros. In fact, this transformation is so mesmerizing for the audience that much of Cumberbatch's frenzy as first he tries to help his friend and then becomes terrified of him is undoubtedly underappreciated. However, after the interval, Cumberbatch-as-Berenger often has the stage to himself. As at least one critic mentioned, the actor mines the humour from lines, but his greatest dramatic moment is far from funny. Near the end of the play, isolated and questioning whether he should hold out against conforming to the new social norm, Berenger even tries to become a rhinoceros and despises his body because he cannot be transformed. Cumberbatch illustrates this crisis by tearing at his clothes, screaming, biting his lips, and even spitting as he forces out lines. It is a powerful moment on stage, even more so than his final defiant line, "I'm not giving in!"

Throughout the second half of the play, which takes place in Berenger's flat, where he has barricaded himself to avoid interaction with the growing number of rhinoceroses, Cumberbatch displays his physical flexibility and grace. As required to express Berenger's changing emotions, from paranoia to anger to fear to vulnerability to love, he portrays emotion physically. He perches on chairs, becomes so tense that tendons stand out in his neck, slides across the floor, or balances on the balls of his feet as he crouches. In some ways, this physicality heralds the fluid grace and command of his body he would display a few years later in *Frankenstein;* in most of Cumberbatch's theatrical roles, he has not been required to accomplish as much physically, but *Rhinoceros* requires Berenger to act out his changing emotions, especially while he is physically confined in a small space. Although Berenger does not become transformed into a rhinoceros, Cumberbatch must use his body to indicate the tortures of a man who deplores such transformation but physically responds to the growing horror of being surrounded by that which he fears he may become.[104]

To become Berenger, Cumberbatch had to believe in the reality presented in the play. *"[B]eing is the essence of believable performance. Being means that [an actor] totally accept[s] the given circumstances and [is] aware of the moment-to-moment reality. It means actually living in the reality of the scene—not pretending, not waiting for [the] next cue, not thinking of how [one is] going to 'act,' not thinking of choices, and not speculating on how a good a job [one is] doing."*[105] Cumberbatch's believable performance is a testament to his ability to *be* in the moment. In a post-show discussion of the play, when the cast was asked how they could take seriously the embodiment of a rhinoceros on stage (one hovers, for example, in a doorway near the end of the play while Berenger debates to himself whether he could even become one), Cumberbatch again provided one of his patented long explanations that explained the politics of the play, as well as his preparation for playing Berenger:

> [T]o take it seriously for me is a fear of what's happening around me, and to try to make the situation as real as possible. I—well, we all— looked at a lot of footage and writing to do with Nazism, which was obviously what the play was written in reaction to. . . . [I]t's about any level of conformity and being isolated from that conformity, any totalitarian forces

and [he took a breath] it helps, because we've rooted the play very much in the time it was written, for me, at least. When I say the [the character of the] logician [has] turned into a rhinoceros, I'm seeing him with a Nazi armband When I'm saying, "not Monsieur Papillion" [Berenger's employer, who also turns into a rhinoceros], I'm seeing him with a tiny little badge, a little lapel pin.[106]

One of the most important cast resources was a Holocaust survivor who shared her recollections of the gradual transition into Nazi Germany. Her insights obviously became integral to Cumberbatch's interpretation of Berenger, who remains human, even when everyone around him—his friends, his employer and co-workers—become, over the course of the play and for various reasons, rhinoceroses. Cumberbatch recalled hearing of the woman's experience as a nursery school pupil whose teacher arrived one day to make an important announcement: "'Children, now I want you all to listen to this. Come closer; gather round.' And they all thought he was a bit strange anyway, but they gathered round. He then said, 'Look at this.' And there was a tiny swastika on his lapel. And he said, 'From now on, things are going to be different.'"[107]

During this important section of his reply to an audience member's question, Cumberbatch enacted the scene in the classroom, telling of the children's perceptions of their teacher as an aside, but then voicing the teacher authoritatively. Even in this type of interaction with the audience, the actor shines through and mesmerised his listeners with the woman's story. No sound other than the actor's voice could be heard in the theatre; all gave him their rapt attention. Cumberbatch then summarised his reaction to the story and underscored its importance to his performance: "And [this situation is] horrifying. You can't imagine. This was a play written in response to people, human beings being herded onto cattle trains, which is interesting, because I myself [as Berenger; the actor "becomes" the character here] say that the rhinoceroses should be herded into pens and put under some kind of house arrest, which is [like] the pogroms" [only for Nazis, not Jews].[108]

To conclude and summarise the point of this answer, Cumberbatch added, "So there's a lot of history and reality to draw on that makes the absurdism or any level of what that may be for an audience to enjoy on a humorous or objective level actually very chilling." The audience sat in silence for a moment. Finally, the moderator asked if other cast members wanted to comment further. Most said no, but one ventured, "I think Ben's done very well," and the cast laughed. Cumberbatch joined in the laughter, mocking himself "blah blah blah blah blah."[109]

The actor's familiarity with the text was not limited to this interaction with outside resources. He recalled reading about a story Ionesco told of one of his friends immediately becoming a Nazi during a conversation—the conversion was that fast.[110] Such a scene occurs in *Rhinoceros,* and Cumberbatch mentioned that connection between real experience and the play to the audience. Cumberbatch is not an actor who talks just to hear himself or to impress others; he participates in conversations, with cast and audience, in this case, and references materials he has read as well as his interpretation of texts.

The Arsonists

The role of Eisenring, in playwright Max Frisch's *The Arsonists* (1 November-15 December 2007), was perceived as more controversial than his usual roles. The playbook describes Cumberbatch's character as "[p]robably the son of a well-to-do family/Never known envy/Probably very well read/And horribly pale . . . ready to do just about anything/The ends justifying the means/(So he hopes)."[111] Dressed as a formal waiter in dark trousers, waistcoat, crisp white shirt, and black bow tie, Cumberbatch's character slyly works his way into the Biederman home and gleefully sets up incendiary devices with which to burn down the house, but he also gets to drink wine, smoke cigars, and enjoy a fine meal with the Biedermans while his plans are slowly revealed. Although Eisenring only appears in scenes three through six, he is a key player as one of the titular arsonists.

The strength of this play is its ability to be interpreted in a number of ways. Just who are these arsonists burning down the city? Are they evildoers in general, political anarchists wanting to bring down society, or a specific socio-political group making their own headlines in London papers? During a post-show talk after the 13 November performance, director Ramin Gray explained that the original "arsonists" in Frisch's Germany were Nazis. Alistair Beaton, who translated the play from German into English, said that he preferred an open-ended interpretation of the modern adaptation so that the audience could define evil for themselves. Gray, however, opposed such an ambiguous point of view for the play and suggested that multiple interpretations of the play may water down the material. Thus ensued a lively discussion among members of the company, who joined Gray and Beaton on stage to discuss their individual interpretations of evil. Such analyses also had taken place during rehearsals and helped the cast prepare for their roles. Gray emphasised that he does not want to be racist but sees a threat to Western Europe's liberalism from Islamic fundamentalism; he further explained that he does not have a problem with Muslims but with some interpretations of Islam. With that preface, the audience asked questions of the actors, and Cumberbatch was asked a very long question about the meaning of the play and the way his character "disassociates himself."

"From what?" Cumberbatch immediately responded. The man who asked the question clarified that Eisenring is an intellectual who disassociates himself from what he started. "Yeah," the actor agreed, and the audience member repeated that the character is an intellectual ("Yeah" again agreed Cumberbatch) who understands the political situation and can warn others. Here the actor jumped into the discussion. "But as an intellectual, isn't the fundamental aspect of that—forgive me the use of the word 'fundamental'—but isn't it to do with reason? *He has the reason why he initially said what he had to say* [actor's emphasis], so if it isn't Islamism, what would you suggest it should be?" Although the actor's voice softens toward the end of his answer, he slowly, clearly, and rather forcefully paused between words to emphasise his answer. In reply, the man

48

mentioned that it could be then-President Bush's fundamentalism. Considering this answer, Cumberbatch thoughtfully hmmmmed "yeah, yeah, OK," but never agreed with this statement. The discussion monitor then closed off this line of discussion to proceed in another, lighter direction.[112] As would become more common as the actor gained fame, Cumberbatch seems to attract "serious questions" during Q&A sessions, and he easily expresses his opinion. Because Cumberbatch engages with those who interview him, he often is sought to answer more difficult questions in Q&As, not just the puffy or funny questions frequently posed by tabloids or fans.

Although the audience may have revelled in the socio-political interpretations evidenced in this post-show talk, critics were not so easily impressed with the play. *The Telegraph* simply noted that Cumberbatch and co-star Paul Chahidi "mingle ingratiation with silky menace as the arsonists,"[113] theatrical magazine *Curtain Up* wrote that "the double act of dodgy houseguests are a delight of nihilistic manipulation and easy conquest,"[114] but Music OMH's reviewer more harshly evaluated both play and Cumberbatch's performance, calling the actor "far too dapper" in the role and "lacking menace."[115] (With his later radio role as the "demonic" angel Islington in *Neverwhere* or as a much-publicised *Star Trek* villain, however, Cumberbatch proved he could do menace very well.) *Variety* contradicted this review and effusively praised the play as "a smart choice for the Royal Court. Complacency in the face of creeping political threat is everywhere. You don't have to be a conspiracy theorist to spot contemporary parallels of terrorists living and working within a community that ignores the issue." Cumberbatch also received kudos for his sly villain: "As he proved on screen in Joe Wright's *Atonement*, Cumberbatch has a strong talent for smiling while portraying a villain. Here, too, his shamelessly bright-eyed behaviour neatly contradicts his malign intent."[116]

The Arsonists and Rhinoceros in particular were part of a "controversial" series of plays designed to make audiences think, living up to the Royal Court's promise of delivering innovative and influential plays "built by generations of gifted and imaginative individuals."[117] Benedict Cumberbatch is now part of that esteemed history.

The City

When Martin Crimp wrote *The City*, performed at the Royal Court Theatre from 24 April 2008 until 7 June 2009, he indulged his "love/hate relationship with theatrical realism." Crimp "wanted to write a play that escaped my control sometimes"; not only do the actors (and thus the audience) take a psychological journey, but objects also have their own journeys throughout the play. Items like a knife, piano, and pink jeans become recurring "characters" who help create the mood of uncertainty and precariousness of society, which, Crimp explained, was once felt only "at the very bottom of society but now it is filtering all the way through."[118] A focal character trying to adapt to this growing sense of uncertainty in the middle class is Christopher (Cumberbatch), a married father of two who loses his job and must adapt to his changing perceptions of who he is in light of his redundancy, along with the perceived critical viewpoints of his wife Clair (Hattie Morahan) and society. The play also analyses Chris and Clair's changing relationship as a couple. Director Katie Mitchell wanted the play to seem like a very intense dream, as if the characters imagine themselves in their own surreality; yet the play is presented realistically, with a "lurch" of surrealism in certain scenes. When neighbour Jenny-the-nurse visits Clair at home and presents her with a knife (which will be "useful with small children . . . . To cut up their food"), Clair comments on their "sitting in front of the fire like this, unwrapping our gifts," although that is not what is taking place, a fact underscored in one of the few liner notes in the playbook ("There is no fire. They are not sitting." [119]). Not only the odd comments about out-of-sight children and the knife, but the obvious contradiction about what is happening on stage and the characters' perception of reality enhance the surreal nature of the play's final scene.

Cumberbatch explained that that "there are moments when that ['lurch' into surrealism] is very obvious. There are sort of spikes, either in the action or in the interaction, that are just strange and, I think on the whole, by the end of the play . . . there's a crescendo . . . and it gets to the point where you feel, playing it, that you are in your own dream and everything is skewed out of your control and there is a way that your subconscious can take over."[120]

On the surface, Chris seems like a nice guy who does not know what to do when he suddenly lacks a job to occupy his time. Most strange interactions with his children are only described through dialogue, not shown on stage: Did the children lock themselves in the playroom, or did he lock them in? Are they screaming because they simply are playing loudly in the back garden with him, or are they screaming in terror? In the lone on-stage scene with his daughter, Chris encourages her to recite an inappropriate limerick. He notices blood in her coat pocket but does nothing about it. Is Christopher doting or secretly abusive? Is he emotionally stable, even in the face of working wife's potential infidelity and his continued demotion in the workforce, or do his periodic outbursts signal something darker? When Chris tries to tell Clair a story leading to good news about his job prospects, for example, she has news of her own: she has been invited by a writer (an acquaintance who may be having an affair with her) to speak at a Lisbon conference. Chris nonetheless gets caught up in his increasingly fragmented story until he shouts "What is it exactly that you're trying to say to me?"[121] These outbursts add a stark reality to some scenes, whereas the dreamlike quality of others allows audiences far greater leeway to interpret what is going on.

When asked about his greatest challenges in tackling this role, Cumberbatch thoughtfully responded in the longest answer (2 minutes, 45 seconds) given by a cast member during a podcast with Crimp, Mitchell, and Morahan. Similarly, although he was only directly asked one question in a recorded discussion session following a performance, the actor eloquently spoke about the role for nearly 3 minutes, long enough near the end of the session that the moderator called for a final question once Cumberbatch finished his response. He laughed apologetically and sounded a bit embarrassed as he quietly commented, "That's more than we needed now.

I'm sorry."[122] However, Cumberbatch's fans enjoy these discussions and broadcasts in large part because the actor intelligently and precisely explains the nature of acting, from research to character observations to approach to a role. He is truly in his element when he permits non-theatrical audiences to understand why they are moved by a performance or how his understanding of the role becomes realised in line delivery or gesture. Through these interactions with audiences on a professional level (as opposed to impromptu encounters with paparazzi), Cumberbatch's enthusiasm for acting and his intelligent (some would categorise it as intellectual) approach to his work are most evident.

Take, for example, the lengthy answers to the rather "easy" questions posed in the *City* podcast and after-show talk. In the former, the actor was asked about his challenges in playing the role of Chris. Cumberbatch noted that he would not have been interested in this part if it had not provided challenges. He detailed these:

> I'd say one of the main ones is parenting . . . .
> [In the play] I am a father of two, and while I
> can occasionally be very broody [in real life],
> the actual reality of that is . . . I've only spent
> no more than a couple of hours fair-weathering
> it with friends' children. [Parenting is] an
> incredible [sigh] mind-set or focus to have, and
> I think also the idea of being the breadwinner
> and being someone who financially is
> responsible for three other lives . . . is
> something that I have to sort of focus on.[123]

Chris has just been made redundant, an economic challenge that becomes more personal and debilitating as he interacts with his still-employed, successful wife and his children. Cumberbatch noted that redundancy is the greatest challenge:

> [W]e live in that factual state of uncertainty as actors, but when you have a job you have a very set, defined time in which you're working, but this man has a mind-set . . . which is very much to do with having a job for life, and these thoughts that are probably a generation old now but that . . . this young man has installed in him, hardwired into him, [and] is something he has to adapt to losing, so that's a very big challenge as well.[124]

In comments like these, Cumberbatch's ability to itemise and discuss the character's problems and motivations only hint at the amount of preparation that goes into a role. He easily compared himself with the character (at the beginning of this answer even referring to Chris as "I") and indicated ways that he has to compensate for his lack of (in this case, parenting) experience in order to understand the character's mind-set.

Bearing the weight of a relationship that is no longer working is another aspect of *The City* that Cumberbatch analysed in response to the simple audience question "Is this the sort of play you need a hug after?" "F---, yeah," he replied, to audience laughter, before immediately apologising for his language. Whereas many actors would have stopped with this flippant if spontaneously heartfelt remark—especially when it generated a laugh—Cumberbatch was only warming up. He takes audience questions seriously and honestly tries to give a complete response, and his answer to this question was typical:

> [F]rom the point of view of playing [the gradual estrangement of a couple] is a very painful realisation that you can have the most intimate and physical relationship with someone and yet never really scratch the surface of what's going on in their head and what their experience of their life was like that day . . . . [Y]ou've got this surface level where people are consistently colliding or missing each other, and underneath there's a huge wealth and need for each person to understand who they really are. So we did a lot of work . . . based on who those people are. . . . [The play's] about a frustrated process of communication.[125]

In this recorded response, as in many such Q&A sessions before a live audience, Cumberbatch often begins quietly and sometimes repeats or "stutters" on a word as he gathers his thoughts. But then he gains speed and volume as he elaborates on his ideas and captures the audience's full attention. At times his voice descends into the gravelly depths when he is at his most serious, but when he is in full "performance" mode, he enacts lines of dialogue in a character's voice (or many characters' voices), his pitch higher and his voice louder as he glibly explains his perspective on the play. When audiences get to see Cumberbatch the actor behind a role, they benefit from glimpses of his thought processes and his concentration on getting across his point—even if sometimes that leads to a bit of profanity (for which he apologises) or inadvertently saying something that makes the audience laugh. These moments, as well as during official performances as a character, have enchanted and enlightened fans.

During public conversations about *The City*, such as a podcast and after-show Q&A, Cumberbatch's immersion into the role, and the director's appreciation of his (and fellow cast members') work, becomes emphasised. In the *City* podcast, Mitchell exclaimed that she had "three racehorse actors, who are so precise and brilliant" that, by the time the play opened, the actors could take their own notes and were "self-directing."[126] In reply, Cumberbatch praised the director's approach in rehearsal: "It is very empowering because you are given a very clear, very practical toolkit. And from that you can concentrate on every given moment. It just gives such focus . . . and intention and purpose to all of your doings as an actor."[127] The actors and director took a journey of discovery together throughout the rehearsal and performance process. During a post-show discussion after a May performance, the cast explained to the audience that they were given few stage directions but were more often directed to consider pauses; the director allowed the actors to discover the motions or locations on stage that worked best for a scene.[128]

When given the chance to talk about his approach to a role—without the time constraints of sound bites on a red carpet or the clamour of dozens of journalists vying to ask questions during a media conference, Cumberbatch's eloquence is obvious, and his words offer insights into his research methods and character development. These reflections on his theatre work also indicate an actor who may have difficulty with the rush-rush of celebrity, when his thoughts must be reduced to a few words or possibly synthesised into a controversial statement devoid of an entire conversation's context.

Another interesting sidelight to these theatrical performances is the actor's highlighted credits in theatre, on television, and in film. To fans today, these "highlights" may seem minor stops on a much longer and far more lucrative career journey. At the time, however, they chronicled an already-impressive number of roles. The *Arsonists, Rhinoceros,* and *City* cast credits list Cumberbatch's television roles, ranging from then-most recent *The Last Enemy* and *Stuart: A Life Backwards* to earlier guest shots on *Spooks* and *Cambridge Spies.* His television awards from the Monte Carlo Television Festival (in 2004 for *Hawking* and 2006 for *To the Ends of the Earth*) are mentioned, along with a Third Prize Ian Charleson Award for his performance on stage in *Hedda Gabler*,[129] an important step in his theatrical trajectory but not quite the breakthrough role needed to make him a star of the London stage.

Hedda Gabler

This performance (in 2005) took place before Cumberbatch's work at the Royal Court, but it, more than the previously discussed later roles, indicates his success in more commercial theatrical roles and highlights the first performance that truly marked him as a theatrical star about to make that big breakthrough. The actor looks boyish and, in early scenes, beams with the enthusiasm of a young man on the verge of a wonderful career and happy home life. (The performance video was recorded less than a week shy of the actor's 29th birthday.)

Cumberbatch once described his interpretation of George Tesman, Hedda Gabler's husband, as more "sympathetic" and "three-dimensional," "to give him the integrity that is often overlooked." However, "being an emotional punching bag eight performances a week takes its toll," and the actor reported that playing Tesman did his ego no good—he took pains to make sure the play's leading lady, Eve Best, still liked him.[130] As some critics noted, Cumberbatch played Tesman sincerely, as an academic so bound up with his work that he fails to notice his wife is bored; he tries so hard to please his new bride that he pushes aside his own feelings until they can be submerged no longer. When this Tesman comes to a pivotal scene—realising that his wife has done something terrible in order to protect him and ensure no one is above him in his profession—the rapid shift in emotion seems honest and is thus believable.

In this emotional rollercoaster of a scene, Hedda reveals to her husband that she has destroyed the work of a man whose brilliance could outshine her husband's. Because Tesman desperately wants an academic appointment, the demoralisation of his rival is helpful, to say the least, to his career. When Hedda exclaims "I did it for you!" as she watches her husband's horrified expression, Cumberbatch hesitates a second, then delivers perhaps the most honest line of the play: "Is that true?"

The recorded performance shows how giddy Tesman becomes when Hedda breaks the news about his rival's work; he smiles and scarcely dares to hope that his wife loves him as deeply as he does her. He confesses that he doubted her love and immediately wants to share this good news with his favourite aunt. Only then do the consequences of Hedda's action begin to soak in, and Cumberbatch gradually sobers. Tesman, however, knows that ruining another for his own benefit—even if it "proves" his wife's love—can only haunt him for the rest of his life. He gradually becomes more distraught as he determines the course of action the couple must take. Cumberbatch expands and contracts Tesman's emotions throughout this scene, but the range is believable because of the honest interaction between Tesman and Hedda.

Only much later, after Hedda's actions lead to tragedies of varying degrees for everyone around her, does Tesman become fed up with his wife's behaviour and, realising that she only cares for herself, decides to abandon her to the destiny she has determined with her actions. Tesman gives up his own career in order to salvage the reputation and re-create what his rival had done—he understands that he will never have the golden life he envisioned at the start of the play. Through Cumberbatch's variation in pace—from dancing delight and quick dialogue to underscore Tesman's joy, then a slower, more deliberate delivery and "heavier" step and dedication to his work to illustrate Tesman's growing awareness of what his future will be. When he agrees to work every evening away from home, so that Hedda may entertain the Judge, his back is turned to her, and the actor delivers lines ironically, turning his head to talk over his shoulder. Tesman obviously is finished with his wife.[131]

After the Dance

Just as *Hedda Gabler* brought Cumberbatch to greater public and critical attention, so *After the Dance* marks another watershed in Cumberbatch's career, not only in the theatre but as a whole. Up to this point he earned good to excellent notices for his performances at the Royal Court and, in particular for *Hedda Gabler*, garnered a great deal more attention for his work. By this time his resume also included a number of high-profile U.K. television programmes, such as *Hawking*, for which he was nominated for or won acting awards. His film career branched into internationally acclaimed films; his role in *Atonement*, although creepy, gained him attention and eventually led to his casting in *Sherlock*. Despite this progression in multiple media, Cumberbatch still was not a household name and could be best defined as a successful actor, not yet a star and still free of the notoriety (and lack of privacy) associated with becoming a celebrity. In many ways, *After the Dance* was the calm before the *Sherlock* storm, and his performance as David Scott-Fowler would lead to an important "head or heart" choice to determine his career's direction.

As a PopMatters feature explained in early 2011, "on the morning after Cumberbatch took home a best actor award, an Internet-fuelled rumour claimed that he would be heading to Broadway next spring. Discussions reportedly under way with Actors Equity to allow the British cast to come to Broadway developed an interesting twist. Cumberbatch, according to the online articles, wanted his co-stars from the National Theatre production of *After the Dance* to accompany him to New York. This implies that the actor's name recognition has improved to the point where his requests become part of the negotiations."[132] Of course, Cumberbatch often is suggested to be cast in a play or film, but either negotiations have not worked out or the casting was merely a rumour (such as one about becoming a Bond villain, of which Cumberbatch assured fans at the Cheltenham Literary Festival that he had not even heard).

However, the possibility of taking *After the Dance* with the original London National Theatre cast to Broadway (much as later hints that *Frankenstein* might someday come to New York with the original leads) thrilled in particular American audiences who could not travel to London to see the play. The actor's interest— and his clout in negotiating terms of taking the play to Broadway—signalled a very different career environment for Cumberbatch at the conclusion of *After the Dance*'s London run from his and the play's status at the beginning, in 2010, shortly after the actor completed filming duties on *Sherlock* but months before its U.K. premiere. As the PopMatters piece suggested, "Cumberbatch's future celebrity may depend upon the way the actor is marketed in the U.S. *After the Dance* may bring him physically to the U.S., but roles in blockbusters make more audiences aware of his work. Like Colin Firth, this year's best actor Oscar winner, Cumberbatch may become more famous as an actor but not infamous as a celebrity."[133] *After the Dance*, like *Sherlock*, helped create a perfect storm of opportunities that would soon flood the entertainment market with roles for Cumberbatch; he emerged, a little more than a year after his star turn as David Scott-Fowler, as a star of television and stage, with more of an eye turned toward film.

After the Dance's programme, like those published by the Royal Court, illustrates this turning point quite well; Cumberbatch's biography continues to list what would later seem minor roles but, at this time, still held more weight and attested to his range of skills as well as the genre and medium of performance. The programme notes the actor's resume highlights: in theatre, "*The City, The Arsonists* and *Rhinoceros* at the Royal Court; *Period of Adjustment, Hedda Gabler* and *The Lady From the Sea* at the Almeida; *Oh What a Lovely War, Romeo and Juliet, As You Like It, A Midsummer Night's Dream* and *Love's Labour's Lost* for the New Shakespeare Company; and *The Visit* at Drayton Court. TV includes *Imagine: Vincent van Gogh* [the title changed to *Painted with Words*], *Turning Point, Sherlock, Small Island, Miss Marple: Murder is Easy, The Last Enemy, Stuart: A Life Backwards, Broken News, To the Ends of the Earth* (best actor at the Monte Carlo TV Festival and Golden Nymph Award), *Nathan Barley, Hawking* (best actor at the Monte Carlo Television Festival and BAFTA nomination for best actor), *Dunkirk, Fortysomething, Spooks, Cambridge Spies, Tipping the Velvet, Silent Witness, Fields of Gold,* and *Heartbeat.* Film includes *The Whistleblower, Wreckers, Four Lions, Creation, The Other Boleyn Girl, Atonement, Amazing Grace, Starter for Ten, To Kill a King* and *Hills Like White Elephants.* Radio includes *Far Side, Mr Norris Changes Trains, The Odyssey, Kepler, The Sergeant's Mate, D-Day, The Cocktail Party* and

Mansfield Park."[134] Whereas the number of roles is impressive, it is interesting that *Sherlock* receives no special mention and is embedded in a list that includes guest roles on continuing series *Miss Marple* or *Spooks*, for example. Within a few months of this programme's publication, many of these earlier performances and awards would be largely forgotten by all but hardcore fans in light of the many later awards for theatrical blockbuster *Frankenstein* and the television phenomenon that is *Sherlock*.

Even an early first note about wigs needed for *After the Dance* inadvertently comments on Cumberbatch's long series one "Sherlock" hair: "Benedict Cumberbatch (David Scott-Fowler) will need a haircut by the end of next week once his filming commitments are over. There will need to be a discussion about colour at a later date."[135] The physical transformation from Sherlock to David made the actor seem to age from a young man to an emotionally jaded older character, not only when his hair was cut, darkened, slicked back, and severely parted, but with the shift from Sherlock's manic deductions and quick movements while on a case to David's deliberate motions and careful poses. In both roles, Cumberbatch was commended for paying attention to details, and the aspects of his performance that define Scott-Fowler reveal an actor who carefully develops a character and, perhaps especially on stage, conveys through body movement and pace the "inner life" for which television directors also would come to praise him.

"Detailed" and "deliberate" are the keywords to this National Theatre performance. Cumberbatch pays attention to detail, even when audiences are unlikely to notice the results of his concerns. A note to crew handling props requests "personal cigarette lighters for David (Benedict Cumberbatch) and John (Adrian Scarborough). Mr. Cumberbatch has requested his to be a 'Dunhill' style lighter."[136] He also would need a cigarette case.[137] During Act Two, Scott-Fowler smoothly pulls the lighter from his pocket, lights a cigarette, and takes a long draw from it. His perfunctory exhale only further establishes his boredom with his life.[138] The lighter is an important prop, but the audience cannot easily see its design, and it is only useful to allow Scott-Fowler to smoke on stage and establish his character's mood—it is not in itself a prop worthy of special attention in order to understand the story. Nevertheless, Cumberbatch's smooth handling of the prop and its elegant design—even if noticeable only to him—help him introduce the character to the audience. The actor, not the plot or the audience, required a certain type of lighter to establish Scott-Fowler in this scene.

Because the majority of characters smoke their way through the play, the actors had to light up on stage, performance after performance. The cast sampled several brands before choosing what they would smoke for the next several weeks. Prop masters were again asked to provide "herbal cigarettes (NTB brand) for actors to practice with out of space please."[139] Cumberbatch, however, "requested that he test both Marlborough lights and ultra lights to decide his preference."[140] (Comments about his off- and on-again smoking habit have been made as footnotes to sightings or interviews,[141] as well as on the *Sherlock* second-series DVD commentary.[142]) After several days of the cast trying various brands, the rehearsal notes jubilantly proclaim "Cigarette preferences are in! Total smoked currently stands at 30. The company would like a mixture of Herbal NTB (brown packet) 17 per show and Marlborough (light/ultra lights TBC) 13 per show."[143]

Other notes seem directed to Cumberbatch in particular. Most other characters are already on stage (and talking about David) before Cumberbatch makes his entrance about twenty minutes into the first act. Because the actor in real life often has been teased for his tardiness, one production note seems humorous, simply because no similar instruction was written about another actor. (To be fair, most entrances take place before David's, and Cumberbatch did not have to be in place as early as most cast mates.) "Make sure that you have Benedict," is written in the show bible, and "if you haven't by the time the doorbell rings, get [a crew member] to call him again, or if he arrives let [that crew member] know he is there."[144] Whatever the reason for this note, Cumberbatch faithfully made his entrances on schedule.

David is indeed a posh character in a period piece—the type of role that the actor is often accused of repeating. However, David is not just a wealthy thirty-something living in the past glory of his misspent youth or a cynical partier drinking himself to death. He seems above emotion to the point his wife fears to be a "bore" if she ever admits her love for him, and he similarly fails to reciprocate, repressing any real emotion he feels for her. However, David also can be vulnerable regarding his writing talent, obtuse in understanding his wife, fearful to hope for change, and ultimately self-sacrificing. He discerns the difference between the man he wishes he were and the one he has become, and for a moment he dares to believe that he can change and live up to his former promise. Physically, as shown in a National Theatre recording, Cumberbatch easily embodies playwright Terence Rattigan's character with casual elegance as he "poses": drink in hand, all long lines in his fashionable suit, his dark hair slicked back and severely parted on the left. David's actions and speech are carefully fashioned to create an effect—the character plays a role as much as the actor does. When David is bored or sarcastic, Cumberbatch draws out his phrasing, lowers his voice, and heavily emphasises words to indicate his sarcasm. Every gesture is casual, high class, deliberate; David's only "tell" when he is reflective or uncomfortable with conversation is to smooth his hand back over his hair, suggesting a comforting motion. David's persona on stage highlights the big contrast between pleasant, boyish Cumberbatch being photographed during costume fittings and the much older looking, jaded David.

As with other roles for stage or screen that involve learning or brushing up on a skill, *After the Dance* required Cumberbatch to play piano. He sang and played a few bars of "Dinah"; David entertains his family and friends with the pop song but then softly switches to Chopin when no one is in the room. (Rehearsal notes from late April 2010 request sheet music for "Chopin, Avalon, and Dinah for Benedict Cumberbatch to practice with as soon as possible."[145])

The dichotomy between David's inner persona (the man he would like to acknowledge openly or would hope to become) and outwardly outgoing personality becomes obvious in such a scene. Privately, David prefers classical music and quiet pursuits, such as his desire to be a historian, but even to his wife and closest friends he maintains the lifestyle of a cynical man above common concerns; he lives to excess. Thus, when the crowd re-enters the room, David again loudly plays upbeat popular tunes and is forcibly jolly.

One of the few times that Cumberbatch-as-David jumps on a line and acts impatient in speech by quickening the pace of his part of the conversation takes place when author David wants to hear new paramour Helen's evaluation of his book. Even a simple "Well?" indicates what David truly cares about. When Helen says the book is all bad, David again slides his hand over his hair. As she provides more details about what is wrong with the book and advises him to start over, David becomes progressively more defensive. His arm gestures become larger before he abruptly shuts down by thanking Helen for her trouble and then changing his body language. He crosses his arms and almost hugs himself as he closes himself off and becomes a smaller target for her criticism. In a very quickly delivered, angry speech, David reveals that he wanted Helen to lie to him because he cares about writing and wants her good opinion—even if it is all a lie. He wants to be perceived as the writer she believes he can be, even as he realises that his work is subpar.

Physically and metaphorically protecting his heart, which David perceives as his weakness, is evident in yet another emotional scene. After David's wife Joan "falls" from a balcony to her death during a party after she learns that David is going to leave her, David reveals that he is emotionally broken by Joan's death. When Helen first mentions Joan's demise, Cumberbatch-as-David sits down, bent over with hands clasped between his knees. He keeps his head down, and his voice breaks. Similarly, in a later scene, when a guest crassly discusses how Joan died at the party, David again doubles over and begins to cry. Cumberbatch emphasises David's physical pain as one result of refusing to show emotional pain until he is at the breaking point. The action of physically and symbolically protecting the character's vulnerable heart is poignant and helps the audience understand the vast contrast between Scott-Fowler's public and private selves.

At the end of the play, David stands alone on stage. He decides to "give up" his life—actually a noble gesture to "save" Helen from being dragged down, as he now understands he inadvertently did to Joan, by pursuing his former lifestyle instead of the reformation Helen seeks for him. He takes from his desk the book Helen wants him to read as "homework" for his writing, flips through pages, stops, drops the book on the sofa, and reluctantly walks toward the balcony doors as if he is being pulled there. Unlike his entrance in Act One, when he stomps onto stage, the actor's footsteps are almost silent. David braces himself physically and emotionally as he looks down from the balcony. He stumbles back into the house and decisively pulls the doors closed. Although direct suicide horrifies him, he nonetheless chooses his own form of self-destruction and pours himself a drink. The conclusion saddens audiences because, although David is far from an ideal or romantic figure, Cumberbatch again reveals a character's vulnerability and makes him worth empathy, but not necessarily sympathy.

The curtain call in the National Theatre's recorded performance underscores the difference between actor and character by catching Cumberbatch out of character immediately after the play. Following "Joan" (Nancy Carroll), he jogged to the stage and bowed, hands braced on thighs—the customary, expected company bow. He left with his arm around Carroll, who whispered in his ear; they both did a little dance move and seemed lost in conversation as they headed off stage.

Critics praised the entire production as "the National Theatre at its best: an obscure yet excellent English play, directed with tact and vision, and stunningly performed" and noted that, although "Cumberbatch's physical pose is remarkable, it's his voice that is the real marvel: dense as treacle, but unerringly precise."[146] Another critic wrote that "Benedict Cumberbatch conveys not just the surface smoothness of the self-destructive David but also the intelligence of a man who realises he is a wastrel."[147] Although Cumberbatch was not nominated, as Carroll was, for an Olivier award for this performance, the media duly praised his well-received star turn. As with *Hedda Gabler,* for which he received an Olivier nomination as best supporting actor, *After the Dance* emphasised Cumberbatch's presence in the theatre and was another milestone on his way to the performance phenomenon of *Frankenstein* at the National Theatre in 2011. (See Chapter 5 for a discussion of *Frankenstein.*)

Unlike *Frankenstein,* which attracted plenty of fans to the stage door night after night, *After the Dance* was not bombarded by Cumberbatch fans. At times, however, the intensity of media interest in *After the Dance* and the role of the former bright young thing prompted Cumberbatch to take a breather. One interviewer described the actor's transition from David Scott-Fowler back to Ben: "After the show the actor had showered, danced around to 'Skeleton Boy' by Friendly Fires to 'shake off' the interwar years, and dived into the National's Green Room to have a drink with his friends, but then escaped to the fresh air of a balcony, alone. 'I just felt, "This is too much." I was hot. So I walked away from everyone.'"[148] That feat would soon become much more difficult to accomplish.

The Rattigan Enigma

Within a year of the well-regarded, popular National Theatre's production of Terence Rattigan's *After the Dance*, the first London revival of the 1939 play in seven decades, BBC Four presented a one-hour television special, *The Rattigan Enigma*, in July 2011. Cumberbatch narrates the biography and appears on camera throughout, while his background and career—as an actor starring in one of Rattigan's plays—is compared with the playwright's. Cumberbatch reportedly wrote the script, and reviewers commented that the hour is as much about the actor as about Rattigan. For Cumberbatch fans, that is not a criticism but a bonus. During the programme, Cumberbatch takes viewers to his and Rattigan's former school, Harrow, where the actor points out photos of Rattigan as well as a few of young Ben.

The special is interesting not only because it provides a glimpse into Cumberbatch's life but because it suggests how he writes and reveals himself to others. *Rattigan* is yet another display of Cumberbatch's "public persona" that seems to disclose interesting, sometimes inconsequential background information and offer viewers insights into the actor's real life but limits its "insider information" into publicly accessible records and far-from-intimate topics. However, this self-written documentary, like another self-written travel article about a vacation to the Seychelles,[149] seems more of a promotional piece. The Seychelles travelogue promotes the resort and activities the actor enjoyed during his visit; *Rattigan* goes beyond providing biographical information about the playwright to further introduce BBC television star Cumberbatch and, secondarily, the National Theatre's *After the Dance,* to a wider audience.

Although Cumberbabes likely enjoyed yet another hour of Cumberbatch on the BBC, television critics were less kind. One of the harshest wrote that "Like Rattigan, Cumberbatch had been to Harrow, and some far-from-advisable attempts to yoke their two stories together followed. Throughout the programme, Rattigan stubbornly refused to come to life, mainly because Cumberbatch had nothing of interest to say about him."[150] However, another arts critic disagreed with this assessment, calling the programme a "quietly absorbing survey of Rattigan's life and work" and Cumberbatch "a sympathetic and thoughtful guide, [who] evidently feels a rapport with the playwright, not least because they both attended Harrow School."[151]

Live Theatre Broadcasts and One-off Performances

The most popular, to date, of Cumberbatch's theatrical performances undoubtedly has to be *Frankenstein*, but it is not the only play to have been broadcast live[152] to a wider audience. In summer 2009, he co-starred in *The Turning Point,* a play designed as a one-time live performance upon the stage within a small studio before a live audience, but the play simultaneously was broadcast in the U.K. as part of the *SkyArts Theatre Live!* series.

In this two-character production, Cumberbatch plays Guy Burgess to Matthew Marsh's Winston Churchill. In some ways, Cumberbatch's performance echoes his role in *After the Dance*, which was set only a few years before, in the late 1920s. Both plays are period pieces that encourage their characters to smoke and drink on stage, and both characters' inner persona and agenda are very different from the way the world perceives them. There the similarities end. In Burgess' case, the man encouraging Churchill to re-enter politics instead of living in retirement in the country later becomes well known as a socialist spy working for the Russians; he is a man with a mission and a clear agenda who plans to make a difference in the world. Audience members unaware of Burgess' historic importance or real-life role in history should be surprised that such an interesting, persuasive, apparently upstanding British citizen could, in fact, be working as a Russian agent; those who already know about Burgess may become caught up in Cumberbatch's ability to make this national traitor such an appealing character.

Within a short span of time (little more than an hour on stage), Cumberbatch brings great nuance to the part. Although his character is less well known than Churchill (and possibly allowed him greater leeway in interpretation because Burgess is not as familiar a name and his life has not been dramatised so often as Churchill's), Cumberbatch makes Burgess likeable and reasonable. When discussing the role, the actor noted that "when you're playing someone who actually existed in history, there's always a danger getting the impersonation wrong, or the interpretation rather, which I tried to lean more towards. . . . In the case of Burgess, there's not a lot of first-hand footage." Cumberbatch's research methods in preparation for a role have become well known, but his fear as well as exhilaration of live performance might be more surprising because he "grew up" in the theatre. "That was one of the reasons I really wanted to do it. [Live television is] a challenge that, certainly my generation hasn't had at all . . . . It will help raise awareness and concentration of the game. And also the joy of the audience knowing" that the performance is live.[153] Doing live performance is *de rigueur* for actors in the theatre, but having a single live dramatic performance broadcast on television to a much larger audience is another matter.

Other one-off performances, including readers' theatre (e.g., *Far Away/Churchill,* a rehearsed reading of stories in celebration of Caryl Churchill's seventieth birthday, directed by Martin Crimp at the Royal Court Jerwood/Upstairs in 2008; *Look Back in Anger* at the Duke of York in 2012) or a philanthropic event such as *The Children's Monologues,* have taken place in front of a smaller audience without being filmed for immediate or future broadcast.

Cumberbatch earns respect from fans and peers because of the way that he becomes involved with philanthropic projects such as the latter performance. Instead of discussing his upcoming performance at the Old Vic, for example, Cumberbatch focused on the point of *The Children's Monologues* event: raising funds for a children's community and arts centre in South Africa. He talked with *The Guardian* about the project a few days before the mid-November 2010 benefit: "These children are not only vulnerable to the worst of Africa's deprivations but they're also often the most vulnerable because they're the quietest sufferers; they don't have a way of expressing what they have suffered . . . .You can't believe how much they've carried with them in such short lives, on such small shoulders."[154] The dramatic monologues based on these children's experiences provided the thematic backdrop for a host of performances by, in addition to Cumberbatch, such popular actors as Tom Hiddleston, Gemma Arterton, and Ben Kingsley. However, at least for one long-time fan, Cumberbatch was one of the standouts because he truly acted his role—superbly—instead of reading from a script, which, the fan added, was understandable given the actors' short preparation time for the event.[155] Cumberbatch wins kudos from the press and fans for the quality of his theatrical performances, certainly, but also for using his talent to help others and being down-to-earth instead of expecting star treatment.

Although many of these earlier performances and awards may be largely forgotten by all but hardcore fans in light of the actor's many later awards for *Frankenstein* or *Sherlock*, each has been a significant achievement in Cumberbatch's theatrical career; they also signal that his ever-broadening acting career encompasses far more than the London stage. In mid-2012, Cumberbatch sent mixed messages to his fans about his theatrical ambitions and worried theatregoers that he may focus on other media in the near future. In summer 2012, however, the actor thrilled fans with a few one-time live performances.

His sold-out poetry- and dramatic reading at the Cheltenham Music Festival drew a fervent fan crowd. Cumberbatch pleasantly signed whatever fans brought, and even his mother chatted with a few fans while she waited for her highly in-demand son. Also in July, he, along with *Parade's End* co-star Rebecca Hall, performed a stage reading of *Look Back in Anger*. The cast worked without a set and with a script, but Cumberbatch's acting involved more than exquisite line interpretation. His body language and emotional range—including his well-known ability to cry on cue—went far beyond audience expectations of a "dramatic reading." Fan site Sherlock-ology commented that Cumberbatch, playing the lead role of Jimmy, turned the reading into a far more explosive performance: "While it would be very simple for an actor to simply remain seated and read the lines by rote off the page, Benedict was an animated presence through[out] . . . .[Cumberbatch acted] out the stage direction of the script, plus his own embellishments.. . . As well as being furiously funny and angrily impassioned, some moments of the play allowed Benedict to demonstrate his famous ability to cry on cue, as well as his gifted vocal and impression skills, changing his accent through numerous permutations and countries as Jimmy's comedically bitter rage continued to spiral out of control."[156]

Cumberbatch seems to enjoy such performances, even if he is increasingly mobbed after them. He even suggested that his next theatrical venture might be *Hamlet*, a "must" in a serious actor's career, as well as a role that would generate a great deal of critical and fan interest. "I hope to return to the theatre soon, hopefully as Hamlet, as it's a role I've been interested in for a long time . . . . I don't know if there is such a thing as a right age to play the part, but 36 or 37 seems appropriate to me, so I need to do it before long."[157] In August, a *Reader's Digest* interview[158] included a quotation sure to worry fans who hoped to see their favourite on stage; the actor planned to concentrate on films instead of television series or theatre, because those take much longer than making a movie. However, Cumberbatch reiterated late in 2012 that he would return for a third series of *Sherlock* and saw no reason why he and Freeman, schedules permitting, could not continue the roles for years to come.

Such mixed messages provided through published interviews illustrate that Cumberbatch has transitioned from working actor to a star who can choose or suggest roles and whose schedule often is in flux, depending on which projects become viable or catch his interest at a specific time. His fluctuating emphases among interviews hint that he may concentrate on films for a while, but he has not ruled out future theatrical roles. Perhaps as consolation to fans who worry that the actor's time in the theatre is ending, at least for the near future, is the reminder that Cumberbatch manages to do those projects that interest him most; his roots are firmly in a theatrical

76

background; and he likes to undertake a variety of roles in a wide range of media. Whether he achieves his goal of playing the Dane within his ideal time frame perhaps is a moot point; it is highly unlikely that Cumberbatch will leave the theatre for good, but he may put the theatre on hold while he attempts to gain true stardom in film.

Chapter 3 Pre-*Sherlock* Television and Film Performances

"I spent every day . . . running for my life, getting beaten up, . . . dodging bullets from an assassin, . . . running down corridors or having politicians ruin my life."[159]
Benedict Cumberbatch (about *The Last Enemy*), 2008

As is typical of hungry young actors, Cumberbatch early in his career earned guest roles on popular television series and starred in short films. In some, he simply looks cute and seems affable; in others, he plays rich bad boys. Bit parts in television or film are a mixed bag as a means of assessing Cumberbatch's talent; he does his job well but often does not stand out as *the* actor to watch when he only has a few lines or his greatest acting challenge is to stagger drunkenly or be a convincing dead body (*Silent Witness,* 2002[160]). However, even brief performances sometimes glimmer with *presence* that suggest Cumberbatch would do well playing a much larger role in that production.

Such is the case with a brief scene in the second of four parts of BBC miniseries *Cambridge Spies,* in which Cumberbatch has six lines as a British reporter covering the war in Spain.[161] Sitting in a Seville bar, his character, Edward Hand, mostly provides exposition about one of the Cambridge spies' future lovers. Cumberbatch's sly, knowing delivery of "Welcome to Spain" as he raises his glass in a mock toast proves that he can make dialogue interesting, and his deepened voice makes the line memorable.

Of course, through the series of small television and film roles discussed in this chapter, in conjunction with his early work in the theatre and on radio, Cumberbatch paid his dues as a working actor and moved up the professional hierarchy to larger parts in ensembles or lead roles. This chapter summarises what is memorable about Cumberbatch's early television or film roles and emphasises his first leading roles in BBC miniseries or movies and independent films.

Bit Parts in Television and Film

Although he often played to a "type"—usually wealthy, entitled, and arrogant—even brief television guest roles hint at the talent just waiting for more to do. In two episodes of the television drama *Heartbeat,* for example, the young actor played two characters linked only by their class status. Charles accidentally kills a young woman while driving his rich uncle's "borrowed" car and then tries to blame someone else ("The Good Doctor," 2000),[162] and Toby Fisher, an obnoxious young man who "borrows" petrol to fill his car because the rural station is closed, seems to have a lot of trouble not being the best at everything ("No Hard Feelings," 2004).[163] Both characters feel that societal rules should be bent for them and that the circumstances surrounding their legal transgressions can be suitably explained away. Cumberbatch makes Charles and Toby distinctive despite similarities in social class. Charles is much more obsequious and tries to blackmail his uncle's employees into silence, but he is also very wide eyed and naive in his belief that he can avoid being caught for his crime. Toby is arrogance personified and is so confident in always being right—or bullying others into accepting his opinion—that he seems the more dangerous of these two posh bad boys.

In contrast, Cumberbatch offset this type of character with friendly, beau-next-door types, such as Freddy in BBC movie *Tipping the Velvet* (2002[164]). Sweet Freddy is lead character Nan Astley's first gentleman caller during her teenaged years as an oyster girl in her father's restaurant. Cumberbatch acts endearingly boyish, whether clapping enthusiastically during a scene in which he watches stage entertainment or trying to get to third base with Nan during their sexual fumblings. When Nan falls in love with male impersonator and music hall sensation Kitty Butler, Freddy falls out of favour (and out of the movie) after its first half hour.

Cumberbatch similarly played a "good boy" in his first recurring role in a television series. Rory Slippery of ITV's *Fortysomething* (2003) hardly stretched the actor, but the role granted him more national television exposure. "You're just too nice for this world, Rory,"[165] his mother says fondly as she bids him goodbye on his first day at work at homeless shelter Sidestreet (a foreshadowing of Cumberbatch's much more prominent role working with the homeless in *Stuart: A Life Backward* in 2007). In the pilot episode, Rory seems almost the cliché of the good son, who is put upon as the eldest of three boys. When his brother seduces his girlfriend, who then decides she prefers the Slippery's middle son, Rory enacts almost a caricature of anger as he confronts the lothario. By the second episode, however, Cumberbatch and Rory had settled down and were much better at being one of the family's calm, problem-solving central characters. Rory becomes exasperated with his father's midlife crisis and his brothers' schemes and squabbling, but he can be relied upon to suggest solutions to the episode's problems and to show wry humour at the family's foibles. When, by the sixth and final episode, Rory leaves home to share a flat with his troublesome brother, he seems more mature—stable, reliable, witty, and even a bit sexier.

Although Cumberbatch frequently acted in television dramas, his work in sitcom *Fortysomething* and subsequent repeat roles as harried accountant Robin in *Nathan Barley* (2005) or as *Broken News'* (2005) on-the-scene reporter Will Parker showed he could handle comedy. He played nervous anxiety especially well but could also mimic the self-important seriousness of television broadcasters who really have nothing new to say. These comedic roles were interspersed among modern dramas or period pieces as Cumberbatch moved into more significant roles in television [e.g., *Hawking* (2004) and *To the Ends of the Earth* (2005) on television and *Starter for 10* and *Amazing Grace,* both films released in 2006]. By 2008, when he played a small yet important role in enduring favourite Miss Marple's *Murder is Easy* television movie, Cumberbatch's career was mostly "above" such guest roles. By then he had played leading roles in television movie *Stuart: A Life Backwards* (2007) and miniseries *The Last Enemy* (2008) and been more frequently seen in bigger budgeted films marketed internationally, such as *Atonement* (2007).

Even when Cumberbatch's profile in the U.K. was rapidly becoming more prominent through BBC productions like *Small Island* (2009) or *Van Gogh:*

81

Painted with Words (2010), he still was not known far beyond British shores. Very small roles in films better known to festivalgoers and indie fans than to mainstream audiences nonetheless offered him additional exposure, in particular to North American audiences. Brief roles in *Four Lions* and *The Whistleblower,* both released in 2010, gave the actor something different to play—as, respectively, an absurd hostage negotiator and an American-accented peacekeeper in Bosnia. Keep in mind that these roles took place during Cumberbatch's parallel ascension in the London theatre, and this range of increasingly visible roles in television or film becomes all the more impressive.

Avoiding Typecasting

Despite what seem to be a variety of roles and well-received performances, Cumberbatch faced two criticisms of his pre-*Sherlock* work on British television and films. Some critics scanning his resume have written that he has played (too) many posh characters and that these characters often are set in period pieces. The *Times* benevolently praised Cumberbatch, in the days before the "Great 'Posh' Controversy of 2012" (discussed in Chapter 7), for brilliantly conveying "male comradeship, of the old-fashioned, posh sort."[166] Whether praised or criticised for such roles, the actor is presumably well suited to them because he has the voice, diction, and physical appearance easily lent to historic characters or stories featuring aristocrats or intellectuals who have time to pursue knowledge at their leisure. But how true are these assessments that the actor's roles may not have exemplified the variety he likes to tout when he discusses choosing the parts he wants to play?

The following two tables categorise Cumberbatch's roles in films, television miniseries/movies, or television series in which he had the same role in at least two episodes. (Roles in which he had only a few lines, such as in the miniseries *Cambridge Spies* or film *Tipping the Velvet*, are not listed in these tables.) The first table lists roles set in a now-historic time. In the following tables, "period" is loosely defined as a production set in a time prior to 1950, although traditionally a "period piece" takes place much earlier. (For many of Cumberbatch's young fans, the mid-20th century is indeed a far distant time.) The second table lists roles in productions set after 1950.

Table 1. Cumberbatch's Key Roles in "Period Pieces"

Setting	Character	Role	Title	Release
Late 1700s	William Pitt the Younger	Britain's youngest Prime Minister	*Amazing Grace*	2006
Early 1800s	Edmund Talbot	Aristocrat, adventurer	*To the Ends of the Earth*	2005
Mid-1800s	Joseph Hooker	Intellectual, scientist, staunch supporter of Darwin	*Creation*	2009
Mid-1800s	William Ford	Plantation owner	*Twelve Years a Slave*	2013

83

Setting	Character	Role	Title	Release
Late 1800s	Vincent Van Gogh	Artist	*Van Gogh: Painted with Words*	2010
Early 1900s, World War I	Major Jamie Stewart	Cavalry officer	*War Horse*	2011
Early 1900s, World War I	Christopher Tietjens	Conservative intellectual	*Parade's End*	2012
1930s-1940s	Paul Marshall	Paedophile who marries his victim	*Atonement*	2007
1930s-1940s	Bernard	Businessman, soldier	*Small Island*	2009

Table 2. Cumberbatch's Key "Modern" Roles

Character	Role	Title	Release
Rory Slippery	Sensitive son in family sitcom	*Forty-something*	2003
Stephen Hawking	Student physicist	*Hawking*	2004
Robin	Anxious account manager of an overbudget arts-funding program	*Nathan Barley* (2 episodes)	2005
Will Parker	Parody of an on-the-scene television reporter	*Broken News* (3 episodes)	2005

Character	Role	Title	Release
Patrick Watts	High-strung intellectual leader of a university quiz team	*Starter for 10*	2006
Joe/Charlie	Dual roles as identical twins with very different lifestyles	*Inseparable*	2007
Alexander Masters	Community worker helping the homeless, writer of a book about one homeless man, Stuart	*Stuart: A Life Backwards*	2007
Stephen Ezard	Brilliant scientist entrapped in a government conspiracy	*The Last Enemy*	2008
James	Terminally ill man taking one last buddy road trip	*Third Star*	2010
David	Young husband and teacher with a dark past	*Wreckers*	2011
Peter Guillam	Spy	*Tinker Tailor Soldier Spy*	2011
Sherlock Holmes	Consulting detective in modern London	*Sherlock*	2010-
"Little" Charles Aiken	Sensitive, belittled son in a beleaguered family	*August: Osage County*	2013
Julian Assange	Wikileaks founder	*The Fifth Estate*	Filmed in 2013

As these tables show, the majority of Cumberbatch's roles (with the exclusion of some performances with no or few lines, e.g., Nick Kaufman in *The Whistleblower,* that would fill out either table) fall fairly evenly between the "period" and "modern" categories. Two crucial films fit neither category: Peter Jackson's *The Hobbit* trilogy (which features Cumberbatch as both the dragon Smaug and the Necromancer primarily in the second and third films) and J. J. Abrams' *Star Trek: Into Darkness*, the second film in the relaunched science fiction franchise. Fantasy, especially the history-rich setting of J.R.R. Tolkien's Middle-earth, cannot truly be classified as a "period" piece, although its unique world requires a particular acting quality to make a rustic historic setting seem real and perhaps even "modern" in its universal themes of good versus evil or its extolled virtues of friendship, loyalty, and bravery. *Star Trek*'s futuristic time period requires a similar suspension of disbelief—or rather the belief in a world unlike ours that still manages to convey the same universal themes espoused in a fantasy film series like *The Hobbit.*

If any "typecasting" is going on in these more recent and highly acclaimed roles, it is that Cumberbatch, like many British actors before him, has begun playing "bad guys" in films geared for wide distribution internationally. *Spears* editor Josh Spero cautioned the actor about his fear of being typecast as "posh" and retreating to America's less class-obsessive entertainment industry. Spero noted on radio's *Good Morning Wales* that many British actors who make it big in Hollywood do so because they are frequently cast as villains.[167] If Cumberbatch feels compelled to leave the U.K. because of being typecast as posh, he might consider how Hollywood might choose to typecast him because of his uniquely attractive appearance and seductively dark voice.

The posh category perhaps holds more weight than the claim that Cumberbatch is best suited to period pieces. In addition to such early roles in *Heartbeat*, all roles listed in the first table fit the description of elite characters: William Pitt the Younger (*Amazing Grace*), Edmund Talbot (*To the Ends of the Earth*), Joseph Hooker (as a scholar/scientist more than an aristocrat in *Creation*), William Ford (*Twelve Years a Slave*), Paul Marshall *(Atonement)*, Christopher Tietjens (*Parade's End*), Jamie Stewart (an officer, not an enlisted man, in *War Horse*), and *Sherlock,* with his reluctance to receive a knighthood, his plummy tones and expensive wardrobe, and his close association with that "minor" official in the British government. Even a plantation owner like William Ford, who typically would work long hours to ensure the success of his property, is nonetheless a land (and slave) owner who thus maintained a higher distinction even in "classless" America. Paul Marshall, by virtue of being a business entrepreneur with social connections to much older money, is a member of an upper social class, even if his recent money (and highly questionable sense of morality) make him less socially refined. A man like Joseph Hooker *(Creation)* must have time for his intellectual pursuits, even if a man of science did not have to be wealthy in order to achieve an "elite" distinction as an intellectual. Similarly, although Christopher Tietjens has a job and eventually becomes a soldier, his upbringing and intellectual conceits, as well as his amount of leisure time and ability to pay the bills for friends, mark him as more socially elite than many of his peers.

What distinguishes Cumberbatch's characters more than simple categorisations as "posh" or "period" is their "otherness." Each man is somehow removed from his family or society; he is different, by choice, type of work, or personality. He can never completely fit in polite society, even if he wants to—and the majority of the actor's characters choose their own path rather than conform to societal norms. Sherlock is the obvious example, but so is Tietjens, who struggles with maintaining a marriage with an unfaithful wife, for appearances' sake, or sharing an emotionally satisfying life with a politically charged "modern" mistress. The list continues: Peter Guillam, in the recent film adaptation of *Tinker Tailor Soldier Spy*, is a closeted gay man who becomes emotionally undone when he casts out his lover from their home in order to keep his sexuality secret from his fellow spies. Stephen Hawking's intelligence and debilitating neurological condition separate him even from other physicists. Major Stewart, as an officer commanding not only friends from similar social standings but ranks of enlisted infantry, must remain aloof and stiffly in charge, even if he would benefit from the counsel of his friends. Terminally ill James, whose friends cannot truly understand what he is going through, must decide how best to live or die.

Although Cumberbatch is more frequently being given lead roles in films or television series/miniseries—

or at least high-profile roles in A-list ensembles—his appearance varies as much as the traditional character actor as he shifts among characters, unlike most leading men, whose appearance seldom varies among roles. For example, George Clooney is always recognisable, even in films that attempt to make him scruffy (e.g., *O Brother, Where Art Thou?*). Cumberbatch, on the other hand, seems more likely to follow the pattern of Russell Crowe or Daniel Day Lewis in reinventing his appearance to suit a role. For *Sherlock* he maintains a very slim physique, through diet, swimming, and yoga, in order to match expectations for the consulting detective's long, lean look. Although he requested shorter locks for the second series, Sherlock's dark waves of hair are as much a trademark as his billowing coat. For *Star Trek* Cumberbatch worked with a trainer to bulk up as a villainous heavyweight. Plump Christopher Tietjens of *Parade's End* allowed the actor to eat heartily during filming in Belgium, whereas for earlier World War I drama *War Horse,* Major Stewart is whippet thin and ramrod straight. Hair colour is often changed—from the shockingly white-blond locks of Julian Assange in *The Fifth Estate* to the darker blond Peter Guillam in *Tinker Tailor Soldier Spy* to the more natural ginger of Victor Frankenstein or the more frequently chosen brown-to-black shades favoured by characters in the majority of films, plays, and series. At times his characters sport a moustache or wild sideburns. These superficial changes support the actor's characterisation but never replace it. His walk and posture vary by character, and some roles, such as terminally ill James in *Third Star* or ALS-stricken Stephen Hawking, require further accommodations to a character's physical abilities. If Cumberbatch is chameleon in appearance more than most actors, his altered physical appearance only emphasises the more subtle, internal conflicts taking place within each character.

When Cumberbatch is given a role written with enough depth and permitted enough screen or stage time for development, he excels in revealing the vulnerability of even the strongest characters, the difference between this character and what he or society deems completely "normal," and the lush inner life that propels his characters into sometimes questionable actions. Even when Cumberbatch has only a brief scene, as in *Four Lions* or *The Whistleblower,* that allows only one dimension of a character to be glimpsed on screen, the actor makes the most of the material. In *Four Lions*, his negotiator—a character not even given a name—is memorable because he is humorously inept; he is "other" to what a successful negotiator is expected to be. In *The Whistleblower,* Cumberbatch's American accent may startle fans, but Kaufman's loose-limbed confidence and come-ons clearly make audiences understand who he is and why Rachel Weisz's title character may be in deep trouble. Researching a role to find an "in" to playing him—to make him real, to find a hook for the audience as well as the actor, to determine nuances of inflection or gesture—and then incorporating that research into a unique performance is why Benedict Cumberbatch is offered role after role in increasingly high-profile productions. His guest roles on television or in short or independent films are well worth watching again, because the kernels of talent waiting to pop on a bigger screen are still evident in these early performances, several which are described in more detail in the following sections. (The truly breakthrough performances, such as *Hawking,* are analysed in Chapter 5.)

Television Movies or Miniseries, 2005-2010

After *Hawking,* Cumberbatch almost annually starred in a television movie or miniseries that kept him at least on the periphery of mass awareness: *To the Ends of the Earth* (2005), *Stuart: A Life Backwards* (2007), *The Last Enemy* (2008), *Small Island* (2009), and *Van Gogh: Painted with Words* (2010). Many BBC projects eventually made their way overseas, such as on PBS *Masterpiece* in the U.S., but none had the popularity of a *Sherlock* or received the number of American television awards as a *Downton Abbey.* As career vehicles they kept the actor comfortably employed and gave him the freedom to pursue roles in the theatre or films. In 2007, for example, Cumberbatch's work could be seen in the much-publicised *Atonement* as well as the television movie *Stuart: A Life Backwards;* on stage that year he could be seen in the Royal Court's *The Arsonists* and *Rhinoceros.* Similarly, in 2008, audiences could watch him in a very small role in *The Other Boleyn Girl,* as the lead in the nerve-wracking five-part miniseries *The Last Enemy,* or on stage again at the Royal Court in *The City.* Interspersed among these roles were radio or guest roles on television series. After the immediate acclaim for *Sherlock* in 2010, Cumberbatch's television work became far more limited to his television series, but he became the go-to narrator for BBC documentaries and special events (e.g., introducing the BBC's coverage of the 2012

London Olympics). Apart from television and a star turn in *Frankenstein*, Cumberbatch turned his career more toward film, with roles, small or large, in thirteen films between 2010 and early 2013, with the media announcing or speculating on at least four more film productions scheduled for 2013. It is no wonder that one fan site exasperatedly asked "Cumberbatch, could you stop picking up new projects already? . . . We're never going to get season three of *Sherlock* at this rate."[168] Although during this transitional period into international stardom Cumberbatch emphasises film, *Sherlock* nonetheless grounds him in television for the time being.

Television movies or miniseries prior to *Sherlock* permitted Cumberbatch to show a wider skill range and to play modern men as well as historic figures, much as his minor roles in Hollywood-backed films were doing during this time. In *Stuart: A Life Backwards*, Cumberbatch does not play the title character (that honour belongs to Tom Hardy, who later was memorably reunited with Cumberbatch on screen in *Tinker Tailor Soldier Spy* after both had become far more famous). Instead, *Stuart* is notable for the actor's low-key performance, in which he does not have to portray extremes of emotion but rather to balance the often chaotic, extreme actions of another character. This performance, however, illustrates how far Cumberbatch had come from playing merely pleasant, mild mannered young professionals in his earliest television roles in which he was given little to do but to look interesting or interested, deliver lines, and hit his marks. *Stuart* allows Cumberbatch to be the character through whom the audience meets, understands, and ultimately befriends homeless Stuart; his is a less overtly dramatic role but a performance that shows how subtly effective the actor can be as an "everyman" faced with an extraordinary opportunity to learn more about Stuart and thus himself.

To the Ends of the Earth, based on William Golding's novel, recounts the story of Edmund Talbot, who, in the early 19th century, sails for New South Wales to take up a job with the governor. During his chaotic voyage, he keeps a journal of his experiences. The role gave Cumberbatch the opportunity to develop a character who matures during the voyage and through encounters with a very different on-board culture. Of course, Cumberbatch fans may enjoy this role for the actor's brief nudity and sex scene. The role in this three-part summer 2005 miniseries earned the actor a second Golden Nymph (Monte Carlo TV Festival) award as best actor. (His first was for *Hawking* the previous year.) Perhaps what is more crucial to Cumberbatch the man, irrespective of his acting career, is a harrowing carjacking that took place while the cast was filming the miniseries in South Africa.

As recently as 2012, tabloids picked up this now-old news and sensationalised it in light of the actor's *Sherlock* fame. In the past few years, Cumberbatch has been asked to recall the kidnapping, but his retellings have become more direct and brief. Instead of playing up his role as a hero—Cumberbatch and two friends endured the ordeal—or using it to promote himself as an adventurer, tough guy, or even survivor, he has merely told the story without embellishment. The trio had gone diving in Sodwana Bay earlier in the day, but Cumberbatch wanted to head back to town that evening instead of early the next morning, not only to ensure he would be back in time for work but because he felt he was coming down with a cold. He suggested they "break a cardinal rule by driving after dark." When the car blew a tyre, Cumberbatch unsuccessfully tried to change it. While the friends waited for roadside assistance, six men carjacked them, robbing and threatening to kill them. Cumberbatch recalled being forced into "the execution position with a duvet over our heads to silence the shots," which never came. Feeling ill and disoriented, Cumberbatch tried to stand up while his friend, a South African who owned the car, was trying to negotiate with their captors. That was a bad move. Ordered into the car's boot, Cumberbatch heard his friends pleading for his life. When his captors returned for him, the actor lied that he was claustrophobic and likely to die. Eventually the captors tied up their victims and left them off road while they drove away with the car and credit cards. The trio made their way to the safe haven of a truck stop, where they waited for the police and production company.

Cumberbatch later wrote that "I wept as an African man's hand reached down to untie one of the remaining shoelaces on my wrist. I wrote as we waited . . . , sipping an instant coffee and smoking a cigarette that were the best of my life."[169] The actor's written account of this event, published prior to his casting as Sherlock, seems wildly different from the *Mirror*'s 2012 headline "Benedict Cumberbatch used Sherlock skills to survive armed kidnapping ordeal"[170] or the *Daily Star*'s "Sherlock Star Gun Scare."[171]

During the transitional period to stardom, mainstream global audiences, who are getting to know Cumberbatch, likely have not read pre-*Sherlock* interviews. For them, the kidnapping is a new story, and a shocking headline is likely to attract a great number of readers. Quotations or isolated facts from other old news stories have been exaggerated into full-length articles, especially when there is nothing truly new to report about the actor. Keeping his name in front of readers may sell advertisement space by attracting more readers or gaining more website hits, but even these "re-treads" remind headline-glancers of Cumberbatch's name and ingrain the actor a bit more into public consciousness.

Despite such real-life drama during filming, Cumberbatch also remembers more pleasant South African adventures, such as exploring the ocean and coast on days off. He once irreverently summarised his role in the miniseries as "a sort of rock and roll 1812 period drama about a young man's gap year. It's full of filth, dirt, discovery, sex, drugs, dancing, love, spiritual awakenings and massive sweeping changes!"[172] The role, filming locations and near-death experience make *To the Ends of the Earth* a crucial production in the actor's professional and personal history, but the way that Cumberbatch has failed to use what is now "old news" in his life to promote a heroic image of himself also says a lot about his nature and the way he is building a public persona.

Not all of Cumberbatch's miniseries were accompanied by such life-defining moments. The actor frequently received accolades for his work, such as a BAFTA best supporting actor nomination for *Small Island* and a Satellite nomination as best actor in a television movie or miniseries for *The Last Enemy*. His performances are solid; the stories, entertaining. None, however, had quite the star-making quality of *Sherlock*.

Something a Bit Different:
Van Gogh: Painted with Words

"If I succeed in putting some warmth and love into the work, it will find friends," artist Vincent Van Gogh wrote to his brother Theo, and actor Benedict Cumberbatch said in a docudrama based on the artist's letters. Certainly that is true of the BBC's *Van Gogh: Painted with Words,* broadcast in early April 2010, a few months shy of *Sherlock*'s July premiere in the U.K. Although Cumberbatch was well known and respected for his earlier film, theatre, radio, and television work, much of it for the BBC, he was far from a household name and just on the cusp of that big break. Nevertheless, an article touting overnight ratings proclaimed that "Benedict Cumberbatch's Van Gogh Fetches 960k," closely tying viewership with the actor's name. Perhaps because of *Van Gogh*'s subject matter, an early evening time slot, or other factors that ultimately determine ratings, the overnight ratings indicated that the drama had an average viewership of only 955,000, but the show gathered an audience throughout its eighty minutes, reaching a high of 1.61 million viewers in the last fifteen minutes.[173] The consolidated numbers later showed a total audience of 1.52 million; *Van Gogh* had an audience share of 8.1% on 5 April, a bank holiday that year. The numbers are respectable but not outstanding.

Despite this drama's ratings, Van Gogh is many fans' favourite (to date) role for the actor, not least because he is on camera most of the eighty minutes and showcases a range of emotions as Van Gogh changes from excitable young London art student to fervent clergyman to failed parson returning to art as salvation. Critics also praised Cumberbatch's performance. *The Telegraph* listed it as preferred viewing: "For the many who won't have been able to squeeze in to see the exhibition of Van Gogh's paintings and letters currently showing at the Royal Academy in London, this excellent drama documentary of Van Gogh's life and work comes as a superb replacement—with the added treat of Benedict Cumberbatch (*Stuart: A Life Backwards*) vividly bringing Van Gogh to impassioned, blue-eyed life."[174] Van Gogh's emotional highs, such as his enthusiasm for common workers or spectacular landscapes, to the deepest lows, as he accepts that he may, after all, be a mad artist, are given voice, but more importantly physical interpretation. The script consists solely of Van Gogh's letters, which Cumberbatch brings to life as he embodies the misunderstood artist. The "warmth and love" with which Cumberbatch imbues this role has indeed won this docudrama many more friends beyond its initial television audience. A subtitled YouTube video recording has received more than 13,000 views in a little more than a year, and clips or other tributes add thousands more to the YouTube files about this drama. Even better (and more official), *Van Gogh* still makes the rounds of international broadcasts.

When the docudrama arrived on New Zealand's Arts Channel in December 2012, both SkyWatch television magazine, with its advertisement of the Arts Channel, and television critic Jane Clifton highly praised Cumberbatch as Vincent Van Gogh. SkyWatch noted that Cumberbatch "portrays Vincent Van Gogh to perfection in this critically acclaimed docu-drama,"[175] whereas

97

Clifton wrote "From *Sherlock* to *The Hobbit* to *Tinker Tailor Soldier Spy*, he has displayed an astonishing range, despite his superficially limiting choirboy's face."[176]

The praise for Cumberbatch in this role is not surprising, but Clifton's introduction to the article indicates a difference in perception of the actor in this role *after* viewers have become familiar with his work through *Sherlock* or the other works the critic mentions. She wrote that "It's becoming a bit hard to find a good programme or movie that Benedict Cumberbatch is not in. His latest is *Van Gogh: Painted with Words*."[177] In contrast, the original British television audience watched Cumberbatch in this role prior to his fame as Sherlock. By defining *Van Gogh* as "latest, Clifton places it after *Sherlock*, so that New Zealand audiences (especially *Sherlock* fans) who might not have watched a program about Van Gogh may tune in simply because Cumberbatch plays the lead. Although the quality of the actor's work does not vary widely between projects, audiences in New Zealand who think of Van Gogh as a "new" role for the actor may expect an even greater performance than they may have otherwise or may be more critical of this BBC production in light of *Sherlock*'s production values and the actor's many awards for playing the detective. Viewers may look for aspects of "Sherlock" in "Vincent" or be more aware of the actor playing the role than the role itself.

In the essay "Reconceptualizing Screen Performance," Philip Drake explained that audiences evaluate a performance in light of their expectation of an actor or awareness of previous performances; audiences "bring their particular cultural capital, in terms of expectations, and memories of previous performances to the cinema [or television], and . . . are involved in a complex process of evaluation and ascribing cultural value to a particular performance."[178] At this point in Cumberbatch's career transition from actor to star, post-*Sherlock* audiences already consider Cumberbatch a television star and likely will compare performances they watch after seeing *Sherlock* to the actor's work on the BBC series. As is typical of actors in transition to stardom in one or more media, older roles are reinterpreted in light of Cumberbatch's body of work and his (to-date) most famous role as Sherlock.

What makes Cumberbatch's performance as Van Gogh stand out? This actor excels in revealing a character's inner life so that audiences can understand his thoughts and motivations; *Van Gogh*'s structure makes this task easier for both actor and viewer because Vincent explains himself aloud—speaking works the real-life Van Gogh penned in letters—and even breaks the "fourth wall" by looking directly at the camera while delivering key lines.[179] The effect is that Van Gogh confides in the television audience, a dramatic style that permits a more intimate understanding of the artist.

As is fitting for a drama about an artist, the actor's hands are in the spotlight and become a primary indication of the character's emotional state. Cumberbatch's Van Gogh talks with his hands. His finger stabs the air when he pontificates about religion. He rubs his nose as he thinks about the next phrase to write or reads from a book. He turns his pipe over and over in his hands and taps it on the table as he becomes agitated discussing his passions and his mental state after losing his job as a parson. He clutches his hands, thumbs incessantly rubbing against each other, as he talks about being rejected by the woman he loves. Wrists crossed as if Vincent is bound, his fingers flutter like a trapped bird's wings as he notes his father's displeasure with his son's "eccentricity." Some gestures provide continuity among early scenes when Vincent as a young man first explores the world beyond his home. Van Gogh's head is propped on his hand while he reads, a contemplative pose repeated in later scenes. Sometimes, while Vincent is lost in thought, he balances the point of his chin in his palm, fingers curling toward his mouth. He also chews his fingers at times while he reads. Because *Van Gogh* links a series of short scenes, many without dialogue, to convey important moments in the artist's life that narrator/writer Alan Yentob discusses in light of Van Gogh's paintings and artistic influences, Cumberbatch's body language is an important tool to illustrate the artist's changing moods. That the actor provides continuity among these short scenes and dramatises Vincent's emotional states with precise, natural hand movements makes this performance lovely to watch but also emotionally effective. Audiences come away with greater empathy for Van Gogh the man as well as a greater understanding of the method behind his madness.

The hospital scenes presented at the beginning of the docudrama introduce audiences to Van Gogh after his ear has been mutilated; the artist's earlier years are then presented as a flashback, which eventually brings the audience up to date again with Vincent's hospitalization. The rapid cuts among images of Van Gogh in a padded room (e.g., leaning against a wall, rocking on a mattress on the floor as he stares blankly) are offset by close-ups of Van Gogh's face swathed in bandages. As Vincent confides to Theo the horror of being in hospital after losing his ear, Cumberbatch's rough whisper and rapid eye movements that fail to make contact with the camera (or "Theo" and the audience) attest to Vincent's deteriorating mental state and his discomfort at being locked up. Tears leak from his eyes, and his voice becomes more manic as he talks about his hallucinations and nightmares. These effective scenes help audiences empathise with this fragile genius.

Although actors often work in less-than-comfortable conditions and are expected to be troupers—especially if they are not A-list stars—a filming blog provides insights into just what Cumberbatch and crew were dealing with in early December 2009 while the hospital scenes were filmed. Two photos accompanying the production blog are even more revealing of the actor's work in this role, which was filmed in December 2009 in Hunterston House in Ayrshire. The blogger bemoaned the cold: "it was Baltic, the catering van was 1st port of call for hot food and cups of warm tea, seemingly when you live in such a big old fashioned house as you can appreciate it's very hard and expensive to keep warm so you only heat the rooms you are living in." Photos of Cumberbatch between takes show him dressed warmly in leather jacket and grey woollen cap as he learns lines when, as the blogger described, he had a five-minute break to sit before the fireplace. In one photo, the actor sits doubled over, his face in his hands as he studies the script placed on the floor before him. Getting warm and being prepared for this mostly one-man show were clearly priorities on this day of shooting.

As has been true of every director or extra with whom I have spoken or filming commentaries published in the press, Cumberbatch has a good reputation as a professional who is well prepared on set and does whatever is necessary for the work (from carrying equipment to braving extremes of weather). This blogger concluded with a typical comment about working with Cumberbatch: he was "a delight to work with and a true professional, the amount of dialogue he had to remember was amazing; although he had a prompter, he rarely needed it."[180]

Three Key Indie Films: *Inseparable* (2007), *Wreckers* (2011), and *Third Star* (2010)

Similar to his television roles, Cumberbatch's pre-*Sherlock* film career occasionally included higher-profile roles mostly seen in Britain or small roles in higher-profile international films. *Starter for Ten* (2006) broadened Cumberbatch's resume and even brought him to the LA red carpet for the film's U.S. premiere. A brief role in *The Other Boleyn Girl* (2008), with some of his more important scenes relegated to the director's cut DVD, gained him a bit more international exposure because of the film's stars: Natalie Portman, Scarlett Johansen, and Eric Bana. Similarly, in *Creation* (2009), despite Cumberbatch's good work, audiences are more likely to recall star Paul Bettany's lead role as Charles Darwin. The same is true even in later films *Four Lions* (2010) or *The Whistleblower* (2010); Cumberbatch's roles amount to cameos, although he was not then enough of a household name to warrant a true "cameo" designation. Many of his brief roles became more notable more because of a film's somewhat controversial theme rather than as a vehicle for a breakthrough performance. *Atonement* (2007) was more important to his career because it provided him a standout role (even if it was a creepy one that many fans do not particularly like); the film received far more attention as a BAFTA, Oscar, and Golden Globe nominee or award winner.

However, leading roles in independent films truly allowed Cumberbatch to showcase his range before a different audience—critics and film aficionados attending festivals in major markets. As one author explained about film acting, "[t]he performances of great actors give us insight into . . . personal relationships and feelings by letting us see and experience their emotional impact."[181] Although tackling lead roles in television movies brought him to the notice of primarily U.K. critics and fans, indies allowed him to show what more he could do and allowed fans to see the full emotional impact of some devastating choices Cumberbatch's characters make. Fan word-of-mouth campaigns also helped spread news about and reviews of indies later available to a mass audience, whether online, on disc, or via special screenings. Social media and fandom have made many more people aware of Cumberbatch's fine work in starring roles in films made without the big budgets of major studios.

The following three films give Cumberbatch a starring role and show that he can carry a film of any length. These indies showcase the actor's chameleon ability to create engaging characters—often despite a dark side or deep flaw. They first help illustrate—on a cinema screen—Cumberbatch's ability to create dynamic characters who can be both bold and vulnerable and who can surprise audiences who might think they know how a "dying young man" or a "psychologically frightening husband" will be played. "The camera sees everything and demands absolute truth"[182] is emphasised in actors' texts, and in these roles, the camera demands Cumberbatch reveal the many layers of each often difficult-to-love character and become emotionally honest, even when such honesty illustrates a character's uncertainty, hidden darkness, or deepest secret.

Inseparable

Such is the case with one of the few short films Cumberbatch made prior to *Sherlock*. *Inseparable* (2007)[183] is an 11-minute canvas on which he paints two vividly different characters but creates the necessary dramatic thread to bind them. He plays Joe and Charlie, identical twins with polemically different lives. Light-haired Charlie likes a liquid lunch and gambling on dog races; when he loses, he is beaten for his debts. He looks dead-eyed at the world but still shows up when his far more affluent brother Joe calls a meeting. Joe has just received bad news—he is dying, and the brain scans shown in the background of the diagnosis scene suggest that he might soon be out of his mind. Of course, his solution to his problem already calls into question his sanity—he has a unique offer that can change his and Charlie's lives.

The premise is intriguing, and the filmmakers hope to make a feature based on the same premise. In 2011, independent site Sherlockology provided a review, aptly summarising the film as "a tremendous mood piece, almost wordless, that rests fully on the shoulders of Cumberbatch."[184] Sherlockology also listed links to the film's Facebook and websites, through which the filmmakers seek support in order to make this feature. White directed the short film (written by Matthew J. Wilkinson), which had a five-day shooting schedule in 2007. Filming took place "largely around Peckham: the hill at the beginning is Peckham Rye Park, the house is just around the corner from there, and the cafe is Starburger on Rye Lane. The dog track is the now disused but very beautiful art deco dog track in Walthamstow."[185] The short provides audiences with visually interesting locales and characters, but in only a few minutes, the plot can only tease audiences with an outline begging to be fleshed out.

White recalled that the film was already in production "when a friend recommended I check out Benedict in BBC's *Hawking*, for which he was later BAFTA nominated. His performance just blew me away, parts of which I still remember clearly a decade later . . . . So he was really top of the list, and it was incredibly fortunate that he was interested. His involvement then helped to get Nathalie Press on board. In hindsight, it all seems like it was plain sailing, but really I think we were just incredibly lucky."[186]

The performance is especially notable for the actor's range. Because much of the film has no dialogue, the actors, primarily Cumberbatch, must convey the story only through expression and body movement. The task is compounded when Cumberbatch must play two distinct roles and not only convince audiences that these men are very different, but that their genetic bond makes them truly inseparable. The highly controlled Joe wears crisp suits and glasses, his neatly trimmed dark hair in place, but his lack of control over his life is made clear as he falls apart emotionally. When the doctor explains the prognosis, Joe merely purses his lips, removes his glasses, and carefully turns over the paper the doctor hands him. He perfects a blank stare—one very different from the life-deadened close-up of Charlie a few scenes later. In the privacy of his car, however, Joe angrily swears and cries, his shaking hand and quickened breaths illustrating his devastation.

Charlie's physical presence distinguishes him from his brother. When he arrives at their meeting, his staggering gait is vastly different from Joe's assured step. Charlie's fringe falls across his forehead, establishing his unkempt look. In a later scene, the brothers stand naked before each other—mirror images of one incomplete man. Both characters have squandered potential—Joe due to a terminal illness, Charlie due to poor life choices. In close-ups of Cumberbatch's face, as first Charlie, then Joe, the actor must convey the bond between the brothers but clearly differentiate them. On film, the scenes showing the brothers together are seamless, but, of course, achieving this result required Cumberbatch to play each role separately and "react" to what he had previously done as the other brother.

White noted that "Ben made everything very easy for me as a director. He's very bright, knew both parts extremely well, [and] had a very clear idea in his head on how to play the roles. The biggest challenge for us was getting a smooth flow in the conversations between brothers. You have to remember that the other side of a conversation by necessity ends up being shot 20-30 minutes later, as he has to be re-dressed and make up changed into the 'other brother'—so during his performance, he's having to react to lines that are just his memories of how he played the other side, [which is] no mean feat."[187]

Wreckers

During my PopMatters interview with director D R Hood in December 2011, [188] she discussed *Wreckers'* long road to the cinema. In May 2009 she began the 20-day shoot, with reshoots and Automated Dialog Replacement (ADR) occurring in January 2010. *Sherlock* filming also began early in 2010, and by the time *Wreckers* debuted at film festivals worldwide, Benedict Cumberbatch was already well known to television audiences for playing Sherlock Holmes. His schedule became increasingly busy, so much so that he was absent from the red carpet when the film opened at the London Film Festival in autumn 2011. He no longer was the "hungry young actor" Hood had cast for her film and had many more demands on his time. In December 2011, however, the actor participated in a Q&A at the Curzon theatre in Soho,[189] which provided a number of insights into Cumberbatch's role.

Although *Third Star* was released before *Wreckers* and is thus often considered to be Cumberbatch's first lead in a feature, *Wreckers* was filmed a few months before *Third Star*. David is an interesting choice of role; he initially seems a devoted, benign young husband to equally in-love Dawn (Claire Foy), and the couple has moved from London to the small town where David grew up. The arrival of his brother Nick (Shaun Evans) brings up many old wounds, including discussion of physical abuse, and some scenes heavily hint at incest. David's version of his past seems increasingly dark in light of Nick's reminisces to Dawn. As the story progresses, David displays fits of temper and violence, and Dawn eventually begins to learn some hard truths about her husband. They become expert at constructing the dream life they want so badly, even if it is built on the carefully crafted lies they tell each other.

Hood's director notes indicate her fascination with the way "people hide things and lie to each other about the things that are most vital to them, even though they love each other. For shame or fear. I wonder how long people can live with lies. In films, lies often emerge in a climactic scene, but I wanted to see what would happen if they were kept hidden."[190] To capture Dawn's growing unease with her marriage, Hood "wanted a very wide landscape to shoot in, mixed with close, intimate, shots of our actors to give a feeling of Dawn's isolation . . . . We found the Fens a perfect place to evoke those contrasts."[191]

An interesting part of the Curzon discussion underscores the differences between the actor's, director's, and writer's roles in filmmaking. After shooting wrapped, the director changed the order of scenes as they were listed in the script to, in effect, create a slightly different story than the one the actors envisioned when they read and shot the script. Hood has commented that "Dawn doesn't want to really 'see' what is going on between the brothers. Because she is our perspective on the film, we found in the edit and in test screenings that we can also make our own story about them. There was a more closed ending possible to the film, but with Benedict playing David, my editor Claire Pringle and I chose something more open because we believed both the plausibility and the ambiguity of David's character, and that Dawn wants to love and stay with him."[192]

Hood has described Cumberbatch's performance as unsettling but intriguing: "the character of the husband could've been much less sympathetic. He could've been much more aggressive. Because Benedict plays him with this marvellous ambiguity, people are responding to that. They are unsettled by it, but they like it. It's much more interesting than 'I married a psycho.'"[193]

David is a frightening, mesmerising character who is sinister in a far different way from Cumberbatch's previous role as a paedophile/liar in *Atonement* or far-future role as a terrorist in summer blockbuster *Star Trek: Into Darkness*. Two scenes stand out to show David's conflicting emotions and ability to manipulate Dawn, and, by extension, the audience.

In the film's bookending scenes, David and Dawn play with their infant son. The audience's first glimpse of the couple is idyllic. David coos "my son" and smiles as he carefully lifts the child while the family reclines on the grass. Without the context of the intervening scenes between this first image and its "correct" timeline placement at the end of the story, the audience is likely to be enchanted with the new father. Soon after the idyllic introduction to David and Dawn, audiences begin to see Dawn's growing frustration with her inability to become pregnant, and viewers question whether the introduction was a fantasy or dream sequence. By the film's conclusion, after David's dark side has been illustrated, the "happy family" illusion seems questionable. In the concluding bookend, David carries the baby, again lifting him into the air, as the couple walks down a wooded path in spring. However, the audience may now wonder whether David can be a good spouse or parent. Adoring daddy David must now be interpreted as a much more complex and less lovable man, but audiences may also understand just what Dawn sees in her husband. Cumberbatch is extremely convincing in these bookends as a loving, devoted parent and can almost make audiences forget that he is equally convincing as a violent, manipulative man in the scenes in between.

David's character (like the film's plot) is often ambiguous enough that audiences may choose, like Dawn, to deny or downplay obviously troubled brother Nick's version of his and David's childhood—at least until audiences first see David's explosive temper. As part of her attempt at a rural lifestyle, Dawn raises chickens, but she must be careful to keep them penned so that the family dog will not slaughter them. One day Dawn finds an open fence and dead chickens. Nick denies having anything to do with the killing, although David implicates his brother. Given recent dissent among the three, Dawn begins to wonder whether David might have opened the fence. Her hinted accusation angers him, and Dawn retreats to the house. Furious, David slams his palm against the locked door and yells for Dawn to open it; he brutally kicks the frame when she refuses. David's swift, fierce anger completely changes the way that

110

audiences understand the character and indicate just how much David has been hiding.

Cumberbatch makes both contrite, sometimes vulnerable David and his violent alter ego believable. The character's definition of "love" requires total possession of the love object, leading to emotional, and possibly physical, abuse. Such a character may be intriguing to play or watch, but David could be an effective character without audiences thinking of him as "lovable." However, Cumberbatch makes audiences want to give David the benefit of the doubt or another chance. The "happy family" conclusion to *Wreckers* seems plausible, given the way David carefully handles the baby and seems to love him; Cumberbatch makes audiences believe in David's possible redemption.

Third Star

Cumberbatch could have played any of the four characters who take what most would call a doomed camping trip to Barafundle Bay on Wales' southern coast. He ended up with the role of James, a terminally ill young man who knows, on his 29th birthday, that he will not live to see 30 candles on his cake. His wish is to visit his favourite place on earth, and with the help of three friends, he sets out what seems to be a well-planned adventure. Of course, not all goes according to plan, and after a series of mishaps, James is left without the strangely effective wheelchair-cart devised to transport him on this journey and, even more critically, his pain medication. The little group is truly isolated, having also lost their only mobile phone, but they become determined to reach the bay. James, however, has an ulterior motive for this buddy road trip and relies on his friends to help him choose how to live the rest of his life.

Third Star is another interesting choice as a first leading-man role. Although *Third Star* was filmed a few months after *Wreckers,* it was released earlier, and many people thus think of this film, not *Wreckers,* as Cumberbatch's first film lead. Scriptwriter Vaughan Sivell, who worked closely with the cast throughout production, initially questioned whether Cumberbatch should play James, even though he clearly could handle the role, but Sivell feared that, "having become well known for playing Stephen Hawking so brilliantly, he would be perceived as some sort of a 'rent-a-cripple.' But there was something I needed in James that so few people could portray."[194]

Cumberbatch has protested the distillation of a performance into the amount of effort going into changing his physique in order to play a character, saying "I've always been a bit po-faced about [the idea] that all you need to do to be put in the hallowed halls of method acting with Marlon Brando and Robert De Niro is put on sh--loads of weight. Come on! . . . The effort involved deserves some credit, but it doesn't make a performance."[195] Yet for this role, as he has done for others, the actor ensured that James looked appropriately thin and wan. To achieve the right look, Cumberbatch "dieted, ran the cliffs and swam in the cold sea." The actor also wanted to shave off his hair, but contractual obligations to *Sherlock* prevented him doing so. Sivell was impressed with the way that the actor also was technically accurate in the role, noting that, as another part of his preparation, he would "delve into the meaning of every line in rehearsals, and then plot the effect of his illness on his body and mind as it would be in each scene (shot in the wrong order), while all the while being a joy to be around."[196]

Director Hattie Dalton was equally pleased with the cast and the film when I interviewed her in May 2011, soon after *Third Star*'s London release. (The film had previously debuted in 2010 at international film festivals.) "[I]f the film was only about death and dying, I wouldn't have been so interested. It's more about friendship and living. A young man in his prime, full of the simple regrets of not having lived his life as he always imagined he would, is the most important theme and what interested me most. We all have to face death at some stage, and I think it's important to ponder whether we are living the lives we want to live."[197]

The film is uplifting in an irreverent way, in large part thanks to what Sivell termed James' winning combination of hero and pompous dick.[198] Being flawed but still lovable makes James a character who inspires loyalty in his friends, enough so that they support him even when they disagree with his choices. Cumberbatch explained that "I've been very privileged to be around a couple of people who were dying . . . and it's incredible what affirmation there can be, what clarity of mind there is at the last point."[199] Bringing that sensibility to his performance as James elevates *Third Star* from being merely a weeper or a buddy travel film to a story about the transcendence of friendship and the quality of life.

Although Cumberbatch is highly watchable in every scene, one in which he has little activity and no dialogue until the very end still provides an emotional highlight. Author Paul McDonald explained that a "starting point for the study of film acting is . . . to analyse the signification of the body and voice in those fragmentary moments when the actions and gestures of the performer impart significant meanings about the relationship of the character to the narrative circumstances."[200] A "small" scene offers one such moment when the audience understands that James is having more difficulty coming to grips with his impending death than even his closest friends realise; despite his bravado—and even fleeting revelatory moments of great weakness or pain—he seems to be holding up well. However, Cumberbatch lets the audience see James' fear and sense of loss in one of the film's quietest moments. James is shown on camera stretched out in a field, deep in thought. He idly plays with a piece of grass. A plucked blade of grass may help audiences recall the film's opening scene, when grass in a cemetery is being mowed down as symbolic of James being cut down in the prime of life. In the later scene, James is the one who is laid out in the field, apparently toying with the tall grass absent mindedly, but Cumberbatch's action has far greater symbolic meaning. As the camera zooms in, a single tear tracks down James' cheek. Everything he is thinking is evident in his expression and that lone teardrop. When one of his friends checks to see if he is all right, James' voice is slightly husky when he replies that he is fine, but the emotion in his voice is not strident enough to attract his friend's attention. James silently and heartbreakingly is saying goodbye to his life, and audiences understand the inevitability of his death but also its poignancy in quiet scenes like this.

A variety of television roles, small parts in Hollywood movies, and leads in indie films paved the way for Cumberbatch's trek to big-budget films helmed by some of the world's most prestigious directors. In some ways, Cumberbatch's lengthy resume of fine performances discussed in this chapter helped him not so much to improve his craft as to show what he can do. They moved him from being a juvenile lead to a leading man. One or more of these performances caught the eye of producers, directors, or writers who knew that they just had to have Cumberbatch in their cast. Steven Moffat and Sue Vertue, Steven Spielberg, and Tom Stoppard all would later claim that, when it came to casting their own projects, they remembered seeing Benedict Cumberbatch in one of these earlier roles. The rest, as they say in Hollywood, is history.

Chapter 4 Recent Radio Roles

"I like the idea that you can change a mood and create intimacy with just your voice and a microphone . . . . It's part of my craft. You can't rush [a reading] or it won't make sense, but you can't go too slowly or your risk treating the audience like they're morons."[201]
Benedict Cumberbatch, 2012

When Benedict Cumberbatch joins the cast of a new radio play, the news makes entertainment headlines. Not only Neil Gaiman fans began looking forward to BBC radio 4's *Neverwhere* when the impressive cast (including James McAvoy, Christopher Lee, Anthony Head, Bernard Cribbins, and Natalie Dormer) was announced in December 2012.[202] In some parts of the digitised world, radio is not considered as significant an entertainment medium in comparison with the realm of the highly visual means of storytelling. Audio plays require an audience's full attention before listeners can follow the plot or envision the characters, even when, in the case of *Neverwhere,* the actors' voices and stunning aural effects make visualisation easy. (Some websites referred to *Neverwhere* as an "audio film.") Even with less well-known casts or smaller budgets, the BBC's radio plays continue to appeal and have gained an audience of international listeners who go online to hear their favourite actors.

In a review overflowing with praise for *Neverwhere, Telegraph* reviewer Gillian Reynolds reminded audiences that radio is "inventive, creative, rustling with sounds that make new worlds come alive.

Evidence? Think of *Neverwhere"* and in particular praised actors well known for radio, as well as television, theatre, or film: "Did I say the cast was stellar? But then radio casts often are. Think of Cumberbatch in *Cabin Pressure* and *Rumpole*. Think of Anthony Head in *Bleak Expectations*. Think of Bernard Cribbins in anything. They were all here, alongside Romola Garai, David Schofield, Christopher Lee, Andrew Sachs, Sophie Okonedo and Hollywood's new sweetheart himself, James McAvoy, in the lead role."[203]

Throughout his career with the BBC, Benedict Cumberbatch has been heard nearly as often as he has been seen, and his performances on BBC Radio 3 or 4 span the comedic wit of multiple-series *Cabin Pressure* to the much heavier historic dramas based on the lives of the famous, such as poet T.S. Eliot (*Tom and Viv*) or physicist Werner Heisenberg (*Copenhagen*) to a recurring role as young Rumpole in the venerable *Rumpole of the Bailey* series. Whether as part of an ensemble or the lead, Cumberbatch's radio range is impressive. The following list,[204] although not a complete itemisation of all radio roles, indicates the number of Cumberbatch's performances on BBC Radio 3 and 4, as well as the prevalence of his malleable, memorable voice in radio dramas. The original broadcast date, if available, is included; several plays have been rebroadcast at least once.

Original Broadcast Date	Play
2004	*The Recruiting Officer*
5 June 2004	*The Biggest Secret*

Original Broadcast Date	*Play*
11 August 2004	*Kepler*
	(playing Johannes Kepler)
28 August 2004	*The Odyssey, Part 1*
29 August 2004	*The Odyssey, Part 3*
1 May 2005	*The Raj Quartet, The Day*
	of the Scorpion, Part 4
8 May 2005	*The Raj Quartet, Part 5*
21 September 2005	*Seven Women and the*
	12-Pound Look
2005	*The Cocktail Party*
5 May 2006	*The Possessed*
26 October 2007	*Fame and Fortune*
14 April 2008	*Good Evening*
	(playing Dudley Moore)
1 May 2008	*Chatterton: The Allington*
	Solution (playing Thomas
	Chatterton)
16 February 2008	*Spellbound*
8 August 2008	*At War with Wellington*
11 August 2008	*The Pillow Book*
24 September 2008	*Last Days of Grace*
27 December 2008	*Tom and Viv*
	(playing T.S. Eliot)
19 May 2009	*Rumpole and the*
	Penge Bungalow Murders
9 August 2010	*Rumpole and the*
	Family Pride
10 August 2010	*Rumpole and the*
	Eternal Triangle
1 March 2012	*Rumpole and the*
	Man of God

Original Broadcast Date	Play
2 March 2012	*Rumpole and the Explosive Evidence*
18 December 2012	*Rumpole and the Gentle Art of Blackmail*
25 December 2012	*Rumpole and the Expert Witness*
13 January 2013	*Copenhagen*
16, 18-22 March 2013	*Neverwhere*

In addition to acting in radio plays, Cumberbatch served as narrator for other stories, and, off radio, has leant his dramatic readings to audiobooks and a videogame (*The Nightjar*, 2011). Because this book cannot include, for word limits, a description, much less analysis, of his many audio-only roles, two representative roles are discussed. They involve dramatisation, not the "mere" (if enthralling) reading of a classic text, that span the actor's rise to fame via television in *Sherlock* or recent high-profile film roles. Cumberbatch has been part of the cast of *Cabin Pressure* since July 2008 and played an integral role in *Copenhagen* in January 2013. These roles well illustrate the actor's range of vocal expression in comedy or drama.

Cabin Pressure

In 2008, John Finnemore, who writes the *Cabin Pressure*'s scripts as well as plays Arthur Shappey, introduced the radio series and the first of its stars this way: "*Cabin Pressure*, it's about the pilots of a tiny charter airline, and very excitingly it stars Benedict Cumberbatch, from *A Life Backwards*, *Hawking*, and

119

Atonement."[205] Since then, BBC Radio 4's four series of *Cabin Pressure* steadily gained a following and earned nominations or awards for writing and as favourite radio series. Within the saga of beleaguered single-plane airline MJN and its bickering family of employees, Cumberbatch's unpaid pilot Martin Crieff struggles to maintain his dignity amidst mishaps. He financially supports his passion for flying by operating a moving service. What Martin lacks in sharp wit he more than makes up for in sincerity.

Despite the series' popularity, one entertainment news outlet's announcement of the series, entitled "Benedict Cumberbatch Not Too Big for Radio 4 Sitcom," indicated Cumberbatch's continuing participation in this show is something of a miracle, given his stature not only within the BBC but as a hot property worldwide. The cutline beneath an accompanying photo read "Despite Benedict Cumberbatch's huge roles in *Sherlock* and a series of films, the star has kept himself grounded."[206] At least MJN airline has not been grounded as a result of Cumberbatch's celebrity. As *Cabin Pressure* publicised new episodes to be recorded in December 2012 and early January 2013, the programme increasingly revolved around Cumberbatch's schedule and its publicity reflected this actor's exponentially increased appeal to a worldwide fan base.

When the fourth series of *Cabin Pressure* was announced, Finnemore both thanked fans clamouring for tickets to be in the audience during a recording and warned them about possible pitfalls in securing a seat. As an addendum to information about registering for a ticket lottery, he wrote, "Oh, one other thing—the ticket unit tend to issue more tickets than there are seats, because often people with free tickets don't turn up. Last series, this lead [sic] to a lot of people with tickets being turned away at the door, which I absolutely hate. I've asked them very nicely not to over-cater by much this time round, and I hope they listen. But even so, do bear in mind getting a ticket doesn't guarantee entry. If it was me, for instance, I would think twice before travelling a long way to see it."[207] The last line seems directed to Cumberbatch's international fans who tend to fly from places like North America, Australia, or Japan in hopes of seeing the actor. Such ticketing problems were not prevalent during the first two series' recordings, when Cumberbatch was less well known outside the U.K., but the success of *Sherlock* dramatically increased fans' interest in tickets, especially when they are free. Such interest in everything Cumberbatch does professionally further illustrates the shift in his celebrity since 2010.

The actor's fame is even occasionally tweaked within *Cabin Pressure*. *Sherlock* fans relished an insider reference to another British sleuth during the "Paris" episode, when Arthur exclaims to Martin, "Wow, Skip! You're just like Miss Marple!" Finnemore reported that "Benedict was an incredibly good sport about it all, especially given the audience was full of *Sherlock* fans. Though he did give me quite a look at the first read-through."[208]

Finnemore's blog provides insights into the series' filming, such as adjustments made to two episodes being recorded the same week in 2011. On the day before "Newcastle" was performed before an audience, "we got the call from Benedict's agent saying she was terribly

121

sorry, but he simply had no voice left at all (you can hear he's suffering a bit in some of the other episodes). So hooray for the tremendous Tom Goodman-Hill, who I think does a terrific job of being a Martin that's not just a pale copy of Benedict's, but on the other hand doesn't feel like a jarring leap away from his. And hooray for Benedict, Roger (Allam) and Stephanie (Cole) for very decently agreeing to re-record Martin's scenes in the next episode, 'Ottery St. Mary,' so that Ben-Martin could appear in five out of the six episodes. Isn't everyone great?"[209] An entry about the "Ottery St. Mary" episode explained that having additional time between two recording sessions for this episode, to circumvent Cumberbatch's illness, ended up helping scriptwriter Finnemore: "This was the other episode recorded the week Benedict was ill. However, the cast all very kindly agreed to re-do the Martin scenes at the end of the third recording . . . [w]hich meant I got to hear the script performed as if for real, in front of an audience . . . but with two weeks to improve it with rewrites and cuts, which was an incredible luxury."[210] Cumberbatch's influence resulted in at least a few other changes to the way scripts were performed. Finnemore noted that, in "Paris," continuing the French accent used in part of Martin's polar bear lecture by "doing the credits in the accent was entirely Benedict's idea!"[211]

Given fans' adoration of Sherlock's deep voice and Cumberbatch's darkly silky line delivery for Jaguar, for example, Martin Crieff's higher voice may come as a surprise to listeners, although the sound is appropriate for his indignant outbursts when he feels he is not receiving the respect due to him as captain or—equally frequently—when MJN is in trouble and Martin must stutter-stumble his way toward a solution. Because the radio programme relies only on vocalisations and minimal sound effects to tell a half-hour story, the actors have to be especially expressive so that radio, online, or CD audiences can "see" their emotions played out and recognise that their characters are more than two dimensional. Although the actors' delivery often emphasises one-line jokes or the humour inherent in the plot, the cast also must make their characters more than just vehicles for comic relief. Cumberbatch excels at finding the right comedic beats in dialogue to highlight the humour without obviously punching up a line. Because Martin often tries too hard to impress or does not get a joke immediately, other actors may have been tempted to make Martin a vocal caricature of a beleaguered pilot/ group leader who usually is the butt of a joke. Cumberbatch finds the humour in Martin's lines but also fleshes out a sympathetic character.

The series four episode "Wokingham" especially well illustrates Martin's relationship with his mother and siblings (with whom he is quite competitive but to whom he usually is made to feel inferior) versus his often cantankerous but surprisingly supportive relationship with his MJN family. When Martin's mother suffers what is "*not* a heart attack," he and siblings Caitlin and Simon look after her. Simon's idea of showing affection is to bear hug Martin, lift him up, and "fly" him around while he feebly protests but cannot free himself. When his co-workers visit the Crieff family, they "casually" mention the way Martin saved the day during an emergency, as well as the exotic locations where they have flown. Of

123

course, fans know that these adventures sound amazing to outsiders, who do not know about the airline's many problems. For once, Martin comes across as the most impressive of Mrs. Crieff's children, and his self-esteem gets a boost from the co-workers who normally find their own ways to needle him.[212] With such an episode, the other regular characters revolve around Martin (Cumberbatch), whose role not only is enhanced but given depth through more backstory. As Cumberbatch voices him, Martin can be worried about his mother, annoyed with his siblings, petty in one upmanship, but also endearingly self-doubting and grateful to his co-workers, all within a few minutes.

Cabin Pressure allows the actor to play comedy, which, between 2010 and 2013, has been increasingly rare. (Even an announced role in a Monty Python film rumoured to begin filming in 2013 would include Cumberbatch as a straight man.[213]) If anything, Martin Crieff seems to be a descendant of Cumberbatch's Patrick Watts in the film *Starter for Ten* (2006), which offered brief moments of broad comedy in his scenes as the beleaguered college quiz coach who clashes with his team and ends up losing control. Martin Crieff may be a smaller role in a less commercial medium than Cumberbatch's other continuing series roles (although the 2013 episodes were far more Martincentric than those in previous years), but it also allows him to play comedy, retain his "Britishness" as an actor, and reassure fans that he has not become too important for radio or ensemble roles.

The so-far-unresolved cliff hanger to series four left fans with the feeling that, despite all news articles to the contrary, maybe Cumberbatch has played Martin for the last time. In "Yverdon-Les-Bains," Martin Crieff has an excellent job interview and—the cliffhanger—must decide whether to move on. In response to fan criticism (and much wailing), Finnemore blogged this reply: "Look, I don't mean to be an insensitive bastard, but . . . what's so sad? . . . Martin got the job! He got 100% on the tech exam . . . and he did a big ol' hero's speech . . . . Yes, he has a big decision to make, and it has potentially sad consequences . . . but he hasn't made it yet, so we don't know which potentially sad consequences to be potentially sad about."[214]

If series four, featuring Cumberbatch more than previous series, is the finale for the actor in this role, Martin Crieff has made an incredible journey. He has grown from a character with highly questionable people or piloting skills to a pilot capable of getting a job with a real airline and being able to pass the technical test and interview that would have been his undoing a few years earlier. What is more telling about the series' future is Finnemore's conclusion to this blog, which illustrates that, despite Martin's popularity, *Cabin Pressure* is an ensemble series that does not have to rely on or revolve around one actor on the verge of international celebrity. Finnemore wrote that "although I'm afraid I can't comment on the future of the show at the moment, partly because it's not only up to me, I will say this much, because to be honest I thought it was totally obvious, and I'm amazed there's any ambiguity over it: It is not and never was my intention that Yverdon should be the last ever episode of *Cabin Pressure*."[215]

In 2013, Cumberbatch may soon be making another "head/heart" decision when it comes to the radio series. If radio roles like the more commercial, star-studded cast of *Neverwhere* become the type of high-profile radio dramas Cumberbatch prefers to make in future (if, indeed, he sticks with the very British programming of BBC radio), then *Cabin Pressure* may be viewed as his "breakthrough" radio role that led to radio stardom, especially in a much-touted serial like *Neverwhere.*

Copenhagen

At the opposite end of the comedy-drama spectrum from *Cabin Pressure* is *Copenhagen,* which was broadcast by BBC Radio 3 in January 2013, coincidentally on the same day that Cumberbatch fans also followed the actor's every move on the Golden Globes red carpet in Los Angeles. The weekend of the *Copenhagen* broadcast seemed expertly timed to showcase all of the actor's talents—as a best actor award nominee for *Sherlock,* a celebrity gaining more attention than ever in the U.S. media, a British actor abroad being recognised in LA at the BAFTA tea party, and a star of a new BBC radio play. Red carpet interviews also afforded Cumberbatch the opportunity to further tease fans with hints about his role in *Star Trek.* All these events ensured that the name Benedict Cumberbatch would be prominent in the media, especially in the U.S. market, but it provided *Copenhagen* the enviable opportunity for additional press.

As with all Cumberbatch's radio roles, fans and critics often emphasise his deep voice that seems made for radio and voiceovers. A *Montreal Gazette* blogger wrote that fans "often swear that they'd be happy to listen to him read a telephone book. Well, *Copenhagen* is for them because it's two hours long and there's lots and lots of talking. . . .Cumberbatch is a talented mimic (you should hear him imitate Alan Rickman!), but he doesn't try to put on a German accent or anything."[216] However, *Copenhagen* also upped audience perception of the actor as "brainy" as well as sexy voiced—attributes that certainly helped fans connect the actor's role as physicist Heisenberg with his more famous role as quick-minded Sherlock, despite the two being far different. The article's title encourages fans to listen to Cumberbatch "talk in a brainy way about nuclear physics." Undoubtedly many fans listened online simply because of this combination of brains and sex appeal.

Playing Werner Heisenberg (perhaps best known for the Uncertainty Principle) is far more than an opportunity for Cumberbatch to speak with his "sexy" voice. The way he uses his voice as an acting instrument underscores a talent far greater than his comedic timing in *Cabin Pressure,* recurring role in the *Rumpole of the Bailey* series, or even the range of tones and pace heard during an episode of *Sherlock.* Scientific drama *Copenhagen* might seem on the surface to be boringly dry—a three-person play analysing a pivotal World War II meeting between Danish scientist Neils Bohr (Simon Russell Beale) and the younger scientist he mentored and befriended, Heisenberg. Their meeting, the topics which have been left for historians' speculation, is re-enacted and recounted not only by these two, but also by Margrethe Bohr (Greta Scacchi). Because the three are literally speaking from beyond the grave—they note that, after death, they can look at their lives more objectively—they share their inner thoughts with the radio audience and discuss among each other their feelings and motivations surrounding the meeting.

Heisenberg could be perceived historically by Britons as a potential villain in this story; he was working in his native Germany for the Nazi government on what could become a nuclear weapon. However, as written by Michael Frayn and directed by Emma Harding, *Copenhagen* explains Heisenberg's own uncertainty about the decisions he might have to make as a scientist: to work on a project that could help destroy the world or to steer the project in a direction that would prevent Germany from developing a nuclear weapon. He worried whether the U.S., with its own German scientists, would develop a weapon used to destroy his homeland and family. As played by Cumberbatch, Heisenberg is placed in an impossible position morally and scientifically, and the actor's range of emotions, revealed only through his voice, breathing, and pace of dialogue, convey Heisenberg's frustration and desperation. Even the sound effects are minimal in this play; the crunch of footsteps on gravel, for example, is the audio cue that Heisenberg and Bohr have left Bohr's house for a walk. The actors' conversations are often so intense that the dialogue must be timed perfectly so that they do not run over each other's lines, but there is no hesitation or pause in the interaction. As a display of effective vocalisation and the power of radio, *Copenhagen* is one of Cumberbatch's most impressive projects.

The play brilliantly illustrates uncertainty in its many forms—the future, the longevity and shifting nature of a close friendship, and the probable consequences of the possible actions of others. The complex characterisation and scientific subject matter likely appealed to Cumberbatch, who, especially at this time of his career, can choose what he wants to do among a variety of projects fitted into a very tight schedule. In her director's blog, Harding wrote that "a drama about the uncertainty of a character's motivation presents an interesting dilemma to actors and director, who are more used to asking 'why am I doing what I'm doing?' and making a decision one way or another. Fortunately, I had a terrifically bright and engaged cast . . . who were more than capable of taking on these mind games."[217] Given Cumberbatch's penchant for "homework" prior to taking on a role, Harding's decision to bring physicist and broadcaster Jim Al-Khalili to the cast's read-through must have been extremely helpful in becoming comfortable with the concepts and terminology Heisenberg would know intimately.

Cumberbatch made the role his own, not a re-interpretation of other actors' performances when the play was previously produced for theatre. He admitted to the *Radio Times* that "I'm probably going to piss a lot of people off who want to hear it the way they last heard it. There's no way I can impersonate that."[218] The cast photos, taken at Broadcasting House around the recording session, show a serious Cumberbatch casually attired in grey trousers and jacket, his blue-grey shirt opened at the neck, leaning against a pillar, hands behind him, or standing with hands in pockets[219]—an actor at work, not at a photo op or fashion layout or in character as Heisenberg. The images belie the fun that Cumberbatch described during rehearsals, when he, Scacchi, and Beale often had "a giggle" as they learned to pronounce names and get the pacing just right. Despite Cumberbatch's joking with the *Radio Times* interviewer about rehearsals and the difficulty of learning such a script, the actor also eloquently summarised the play's meaning: "The way atomic physics works is a metaphor for these three people trying to understand their motivations looking through the mists of time . . . . Science has come from the human, not the other way round. Our idea and understanding of it is through our sensory filter. Whether that be a process of mental theory or observable, experimental, tenable science, it's a beautiful metaphor for these three people trying to understand each other—and then you've got war splitting everything apart."[220]

Copenhagen begins with Heisenberg talking from beyond grave, pondering the meaning of his life. (Aurally, this beginning may remind fans of a similar voiceover at the beginning of *Third Star*, when Cumberbatch's terminally ill character also grows philosophical about his life.) The softly spoken introduction lures the audience forward to hear the actor's voice and gain entrance into the world of Heisenberg and Bohr.

In a comparison of roles similar to Heisenberg, Cumberbatch's real-life conversations with Stephen Hawking, both in preparation for playing him in *Hawking* and as recently as the premiere of Hawking's documentary series, *Stephen Hawking's Grand Design*, also inform his performance. The Heisenberg role may

130

remind filmgoers of the actor's 2011 role as "watched" spy Peter Guillam in *Tinker Tailor Soldier Spy*, because Heisenberg also is carefully monitored by the German government during his visit to Bohr. Although Cumberbatch's many previous roles may make aspects of Heisenberg (or any of Cumberbatch's successive roles in a given genre) a bit familiar, the actor ensures each performance is unique. Although Heisenberg may be as scientifically smart or emotionally frustrated as other characters he has played, Cumberbatch makes Heisenberg a sympathetic, haunted man that audiences can easily understand and empathise with—and he creates this complex character solely through his voice.

Some vocal highlights of this role include the following:

• Heisenberg's uncertainty about what to say to maintain his friendship with Bohr, given the strains of war. (Jewish Bohr lives in Nazi-occupied Denmark; Heisenberg in his native Germany.) About fifteen minutes into the play, after a great deal of introductory narrative by Heisenberg, Margrethe Bohr describes the Heisenberg visiting her wartime home in Denmark as "shy, arrogant, and eager to be loved," a man seeming much younger than his nearly 40 years. Cumberbatch vocally portrays such a man by changing the cadence, emphasis, and amount of emotion from the way he spoke during the opening narrative. He speaks more slowly, as appropriate to small talk, hesitates when the conversation becomes difficult, and huffs to indicate an attempted joke. As the conversation becomes yet more difficult when Heisenberg tries to establish safe, non-

131

scientific, non-war-related topics of discussion, the actor's pitch is higher, his tone uncertain; he stutters as he searches for the right words.

- Word repetition given specific, different emphases: Cumberbatch highlights the word *friends* throughout his impassioned speech to convince Bohr to work with him, but the context, and hence the way the word is spoken (e.g., sincerely or facetiously) changes with each repetition. Similarly, he later says *again* four times— each time with a different emphasis—when he comments on the Bohrs' marriage and the way they fail to discuss the loss of their children.

- Changes in speaking rate to reflect the character's commitment to and passion for science: Cumberbatch's voice becomes clipped—impatient, harsher, faster—as Heisenberg discusses science and tries to clarify the type of contact he wants to establish for Bohr in Germany. By discussing the cultural institute sponsoring his scientific research (not the Nazi party), Heisenberg hopes to establish a way for Bohr to continue to work with him. Similar to Victor Frankenstein's impassioned explanation of his work to his much younger brother in *Frankenstein,* in *Copenhagen* Cumberbatch rapidly and unerringly describes his scientific theory to Bohr; Heisenberg is impressive not only for his knowledge but because his thorough explanation is spoken without hesitation or pause. This speech flows freely and simply must be absorbed by the audience. In contrast, when Heisenberg heavy-handedly wants to suggest to anyone recording his conversation with Bohr that he only wants to take an after-dinner walk with his old friend, Cumberbatch punches words in the line "You don't feel like a *stroll*, for *old time's* sake?" Heisenberg's exasperation at his inability to explain his "official" reason for his visit is clear in this invitation; the scientist wants to talk with his friend privately. In a later scene, about 43 minutes into the play, Heisenberg admits the potential destructive application of his work. He slowly says, "If we could build a reactor, we could build bombs," and "My (pause) one (pause) hope (pause) is to maintain control." By speaking slowly and dramatically pausing between words, Cumberbatch not only suggests the enormity of Heisenberg's moral dilemma—or scientists' responsibility for what they create—but makes Heisenberg a very human, not merely historic, character.

Just as the play began with Heisenberg, so it ends with his words, "uncertainty at the heart of things,"[221] a fitting dramatic close to the play and a testament to the universally understood, eternally relevant subject matter. That Cumberbatch makes this final line poignant and haunting helps the play stick with audiences long after the two-hour broadcast.

Chapter 5 Turning Point Performances

"Every single element of this role appealed,
although it was daunting as well." [222]
Benedict Cumberbatch, 2004

"For me, every single job is a new beginning,
a new starting point where you can learn again
and begin again." [223]
Benedict Cumberbatch, 2012

A "turning point" performance often is categorised
only years afterward, when an actor's career takes a
sudden turn—for better or worse—after that production.
Cumberbatch's career has had quite a few possible
"turning points" that won him acting nominations or
awards, gained him a broader audience primarily in the
U.K., and showed that he could carry a production. Some
turning point productions discussed in this chapter, such
as *Parade's End*, illustrate a turning point in the actor's
international status or degree of celebrity. This type of
performance does not have to be a true breakthrough, as
discussed in Chapter 7, but one that nonetheless has
special significance to an actor's career.

Hawking is perhaps the first of a series of
television roles that brought him to national attention and
led to more work on television and film. His lead roles in
miniseries *To the Ends of the Earth* and *The Last Enemy*
gave him additional exposure and critical kudos, but
again, primarily in the U.K. Although the actor's work is
exemplary in these productions, and Cumberbatch has
been proclaimed to be on the verge of stardom after each

134

of these noteworthy, increasingly higher profile roles, he nonetheless seemed unable to capitalise on the momentum of good reviews or awards. He has consistently worked, far more than most actors his age, but until *Sherlock,* he was not nearly so well known outside the U.K. or did not benefit as often from having directors and scriptwriters seek him out for a role.

Television series and films often reach different audiences, and Cumberbatch's number of film roles in big movies—such as Steven Spielberg's *War Horse,* J. J. Abrams' *Star Trek,* Peter Jackson's *Hobbit* trilogy, Brad Pitt's *Twelve Years a Slave,* George Clooney's *August: Osage County,* or Dreamworks' *The Fifth Estate*— ensures that mainstream audiences around the world are more likely to view one or more of his performances. He may play the villain or be relegated to a small, if memorable role, but his presence is increasingly being felt in the cinema, which, in turn, gives him more clout in negotiations and more control over the types of roles he is asked to consider. These types of roles can earn him more money to reflect his increased status. He is less likely to be pigeon-holed as a certain "type" because he plays characters in so many genres.

The roles discussed in this chapter have, to date, been turning points in the way those in the entertainment industry perceive Cumberbatch and the amount of attention these projects have gained the actor. Listed in chronological order by broadcast or release date, each of the following has helped establish Cumberbatch as not only an excellent actor—perhaps the best to come along in years—but also one who can retain control of a high-profile, highly creative career that allows him to show ever larger audiences exactly what he can do as an actor.

Hawking (2004)

The BBC publicised its biography of Stephen Hawking as the story of "a bright and ambitious 21-year-old PhD student at Cambridge University, [who] is diagnosed with the debilitating motor neurone disease and given two years to live. Against the odds, he goes on to achieve scientific success and worldwide acclaim."[224] Cumberbatch summarised the premise of *Hawking* as "a story of hope, without a doubt, and a story of grace under pressure, how to conquer adversity and how a situation like that can be used for the positive. He's a small person with an incredible brain in a very fragile body, thinking incredibly huge thoughts."[225]

His audition separated him from other actors being considered for the role. "The voice, funnily enough, I picked up very quickly, and apparently I was the first in the audition to give it a crack. It was quite clearly written in the script—it's slightly like the atonal palate of a deaf person because the soft palate goes, the atonal variation goes, the tongue loses its elasticity so it's very vowelly, the consonants go," the actor seriously explained to an interviewer before joking that this voice was similar to his when he suffers a hangover.[226] As he often does in interviews, Cumberbatch goes into depth in explaining a character or his process but then self-deprecatingly adds a joke, as if he worries that he may be too serious for his audience. His responses, however, illustrate to non-actors exactly how a professional approaches an audition or develops a character.

To prepare for the role, he met Stephen Hawking, read books about his work, and worked with a LAMDA movement coach. With only one week of rehearsal before shooting began, the actor felt that "[e]very day, there'd be something else I'd get a bit more right and feel more confident about." One of the most fearsome tasks involved quickly writing equations across a chalk board. For his homework before filming scenes of the student scientist explaining his work with such equations, "a fantastic pupil of Stephen's" who worked on the production "drew stuff out for me to have a look at the night before."[227] On screen, Cumberbatch succeeds in illustrating Hawking's thought processes and his theoretical brilliance.

Although the memorisation of scientific theory may have daunted the actor, other scenes, beyond the mastery of movement or maths, reveal less showy but highly impressive aspects of his craft. During Hawking's 21st birthday party, the young man slips away with the woman who one day will become his wife, and the two stretch out side by side on the lawn to look at the night sky. Hawking amiably discusses the physics of stars. The romantic idyll is shattered when, deciding it is time to return to the party, Hawking makes the horrific discovery that he cannot stand. Cumberbatch's voice conveys quite an emotional range, from discovery, to embarrassment, to fear, to panic.

After a series of painful tests, Hawking confronts his doctor and demands to know the results. He refuses to wait until his parents arrive to hear the news and therefore is standing alone in a hospital ward while the doctor explains the progression of motor neurone disease.[228]

Cumberbatch's/Hawking's face reflects the scientist's realisation that his brain will survive untouched, but the rest of his body will shut down. Hawking takes a step back when he understands the implications of the prognosis. As in other performances, Cumberbatch excels in the ability to reveal a character's thoughts and emotions in key scenes that often lack dialogue. *Hawking* is the first widely seen performance to show this particular aspect of Cumberbatch's talent.

Sherlock (2010-)

Sherlock, like *Hawking*, requires Cumberbatch to memorise the complex dialogue of a genius scientist. Unlike *Hawking*, this more recent role has prompted speculation about similarities between character and performer. Although media articles sometimes try to match Sherlock Holmes' behaviour or personality to Cumberbatch's, the actor sees few real comparisons. "Because I talk a lot, probably because I'm nervous, I get pinned into the same mania bracket," he told *The Independent* in 2012.[229] Yet he also admitted that he "practices" being Sherlock when he tries to decode information about the people around him, simply by observing their appearance and actions when, for example, he rides on trains and has time to watch his fellow travellers.[230]

He takes the role of Sherlock seriously. During a December 2011 Q&A following a *Sherlock* screening, Cumberbatch made good on his promise to a young boy to let him ask the first question. How can someone become a detective like Sherlock? Cumberbatch thoroughly provided a plan, choosing his words and pace carefully so that the young man could absorb the information. The response was lengthy enough that *Sherlock* co-creator Mark Gatiss exclaimed "That was a real answer!"[231] But of course. Cumberbatch's fans or a Sherlock Holmes apprentice expect nothing less.

For all that Cumberbatch fans seem to love Sherlock, the character sometimes is less than lovable. Although in the first episode, "A Study in Pink," Sherlock describes himself as a "high-functioning sociopath,"[232] the actor who portrays him does not believe that Sherlock is a damaged man but instead is "an adolescent that is being repressed from childhood purposely in order to try and become the ultimate, calculating deduction machine. And he can't actually do that . . . . [He is] somebody who had to let vulnerability into his life, as he sees it, which is emotion, a moral compass of some sort, honour, defending your friends and what you hold dear, and actually being on the side of the good guys."[233]

Sherlock evolves during each series, as the writers allow him to expand his humanity and moderate his behaviour because of John Watson's pervasive influence. Similarly, Cumberbatch's interpretation of the role becomes richer each series as the writers give him more to do and as he returns to the role after some very long hiatuses. When returning for the second series, Cumberbatch worried that, after receiving praise, nominations, and awards for the first, he might be performing a parody of his original work. Not to fear—as the premiere episode of the second series, "A Scandal in Belgravia," illustrates, cast and crew exceeded their and audiences' high expectations. Although *Sherlock* is best viewed as a complete collection of episodes, even though each one can stand on its own merits, "A Scandal in Belgravia" provides a useful example of both the high quality of the production and Cumberbatch's self-critical commentary about his work. Because this episode has been the most nominated and awarded episode of the first two series, I chose it as the representative episode of all that is remarkable about *Sherlock*, and the following lengthy plot and character discussion indicates the emotional highs and lows and physical requirements facing the cast, particularly Cumberbatch.

The Woman. The Hound. The Professor. These tweeted hints from Mark Gatiss revealed which canon stories would be updated for the second season of *Sherlock*. The hints eventually grew into three ninety-minute episodes: "A Scandal in Belgravia" (based on Sir Arthur Conan Doyle's "A Scandal in Bohemia"), "The Hounds of Baskerville" (updating possibly the most famous Sherlock Holmes story, "The Hound of the Baskervilles"), and "The Reichenbach Fall" (a reference to the site of the final confrontation between Professor Moriarty and Holmes in "The Final Problem"). Fans might better summarise these *Sherlock* stories by some of their favourite scenes: The Sheet. The Terror. The Fall. The visual delights and symbolism of The Sheet (Sherlock's wardrobe when he visits Buckingham Palace) endear it to fans and illustrate some cultural differences between British and American audiences. The Terror of the Hound goes far beyond a monstrous canine and makes Sherlock question the very foundation of his belief system—the evidence he sees and can analyse. Finally, the Fall dramatises not only Sherlock's final encounter with Moriarty but the modern dilemma of celebrity and the media's destruction of those they helped elevate. Although these keywords highlight important characters or scenes in the second series of *Sherlock,* each detailed, witty, carefully crafted episode cannot be reduced to a few words. Even "episode" might not accurately describe each story within the series.

During an online chat that PBS held with *Sherlock* co-creator Mark Gatiss, I asked what he learned from making the first series' episodes that was most helpful in making the second. Gatiss replied, "the importance of treating them as movies on TV, really. [Ninety-] minute adventures demand a certain scale of storytelling. It's very exciting and quite liberating to move at that kind of pace but it absolutely eats up story! The reaction was so incredible, though, that we all felt very excited about coming back for more."[234] Even while feeling the pressure to make successive batches of episodes just as exciting and high quality as the first, co-creators, cast, and crew upped their game. By mid-2012, when the second series had finally made it around the world, *Sherlock* already was winning more awards.

"Critically acclaimed" and "award-winning" are frequently used descriptors. *Sherlock* has won BAFTAs for editing and sound at the television craft awards, held separately from the acting awards. Steven Moffat, the series' co-creator and scriptwriter of "A Scandal in Belgravia," won a BAFTA for writing this episode and received a special BAFTA at the 27 May 2012 television awards for "outstanding creative writing contribution to television." For series two, Benedict Cumberbatch was nominated as best actor (as well as for an Emmy and

141

Golden Globe, all for this representative episode), and Martin Freeman (John Watson) and Andrew Scott (Jim Moriarty) competed for the best supporting actor statue. The previous year Freeman was the award winner; in 2012, the award went to Scott.

Quality, if not quantity, is another keyword to describe *Sherlock*. Gatiss, sounding remarkably like his *Sherlock* character, Mycroft Holmes, chuckled deviously when he said that he wants to keep the audience wanting more.[235] Whether dubbed a miniseries, movies, or episodes, series two illustrates just how *Sherlock* has grown even stronger in writing, characterisation, production values, and acting.

Whereas the first series introduces Sherlock and John and establishes their friendship, the second series—which quickly moves the story forward about six months—further establishes their relationship. Although they are still learning about each other, they have settled into a routine, absurd as it may look to the rest of the world. Thanks to John's popular blog and Sherlock's publicised crime-solving deductions, their business is a success. Being a consulting detective has never been so lucrative, and, true to the Conan Doyle texts, Sherlock does not even have to leave home in order to unravel mysteries. Clients now seek him, and he can choose which cases interest him most.

But that is not the only change at 221B. Among the detritus of dozens of lab tests and documents for research, a far more important experiment is under way: to see which of Sherlock's deepest emotions can be excavated and how far his emotional range can be expanded. John may think of his influence on his flatmate in nonscientific terms, but he seems determined to prove to the world (or at least Mycroft Holmes and Scotland Yard) his hypothesis that Sherlock is very human, if unique. The detective simply needs a nudge—probably more of a shout and a shove—in the right behavioural direction. John accepts his role as arbiter of what is socially acceptable or "a bit not good." Sherlock is far from unfeeling, and his emotional range exceeds cursing forensics specialist Anderson or scowling at brother Mycroft. He laughs or languishes, loves and loses, and, in "Scandal," such emotions are stirred by Irene Adler.

The Woman is what Conan Doyle's Holmes calls Adler, the only woman to match wits with him. In the original story, "A Scandal in Bohemia," Adler blackmails foreign royalty and battles Holmes, whose client seeks the return of a scandalous photograph. In the end, she escapes into marriage, and Holmes possesses the photograph. In Moffat's episode, Adler blackmails a female relative of the British monarchy, almost beats Sherlock intellectually and emotionally (but does whip him with a riding crop), and is far from marriage minded regarding any man. When she turns her thoughts to Sherlock, neither of them escapes unscathed.

Adler fascinates him. During their first meeting, Sherlock's thoughts about his companions are printed on screen as he deduces facts about them. John's shoes indicate that he has a date that evening, and the bags under his eyes clearly point out a late night with friend Mike Stamford. When Sherlock looks at Irene, he is unable to learn anything about her. Question marks surround her as he tries to make any deduction. Irene is the only person he cannot immediately interpret, which

143

both attracts and repels him. Some viewers think that Sherlock has met his match, but he is truly looking at his reflection, his counterpart—what he could possibly be if he, instead of Adler, worked with Moriarty and could bring down a nation, despite brother Mycroft's machinations. Sherlock and Irene may challenge each other to an intellectual duel, but the weaknesses that they also bring out in each other ensure that they are scarred by their encounters.

Indeed, Irene is a great deal like Sherlock. Cumberbatch explained that the detective is attracted to Adler because she is "incredibly smart, quick thinking and resourceful . . . . She's got a lot of attributes that mirror his. She doesn't suffer fools gladly."[236] Both are narcissists who enjoy playing mind games. Whereas Sherlock's greatest "game" to date has resulted in a stalemate with Moriarty, he frequently tackles the mysteries of a murder with gusto and eagerly proclaims "The game is on!" as he heads to a crime scene. Adler's mind games go a little further, sometimes assisted by that riding crop. As a dominatrix, Irene knows what her clients need, and she is ideally suited to help them discover the truth about themselves. She revels in the power her sexuality provides and plans to use it to bring down the British government; she possesses a locked mobile phone that contains government intelligence. If Irene does not get enough money to bankrupt the country, she plans to turn over the information to other interested parties (i.e., terrorists) who can pay her price. She works with Moriarty because he enjoys destruction for its own sake; taking out the Holmes brothers at the same time is just a perk.

144

The addition of new player Sherlock intrigues Adler. She wants to be the one to unravel his mind and his reserve, especially if she can do so across a convenient piece of furniture until he "begs for mercy, twice."[237] She bares her body to him at their first meeting; she wants him to bare his mind to her. Sherlock, however, proudly and stubbornly refuses to surrender. Nevertheless, Irene does manage to capture his attention for months at a time. Even after he identifies a tortured woman's body as Irene's, she still dominates his mind and heart. Sherlock may coldly define love as a chemical reaction, but he does not delete the equation from his mental hard drive. The Woman has a profound effect upon his self-esteem and self-awareness.

Irene Adler may be Sherlock's "evil twin," but John Watson is the Yang to his Yin. They create a perfect balance when they work together, and as partners they are highly efficient. When Irene has John kidnapped so she can confront him in an abandoned building (actually the Battersea Power Station), she accuses him of jealousy. "Once and for all, if anyone still cares, I am not gay!" John protests. "I am," Irene reminds him. "Where does that leave us?" she asks honestly. John clearly loves Sherlock—or else he would not threaten Irene into telling his friend the truth about her whereabouts. He does not want Sherlock to continue to pine for the woman he thinks is dead and threatens to track Adler wherever she goes until she stops toying with his friend. That neither of them is sexually involved with Sherlock does not lessen the depth of their feelings for him.

Perhaps the love that fans most enjoy watching, if fan fiction and website commentaries are reliable indicators, is that between Sherlock and John. To Cumberbatch, this warehouse confrontation between Irene and John is the most loving scene of all. "It says everything about their relationship, what the love is, the care is . . . . It's everything they don't say to each other but [John] can say [to Irene], thinking that he's not there. That's where the romance is a beautifully British affair, its remarkably understated subtlety and nuance."[238]

Although The Woman is an important player in this story of intrigue and double crosses, she is more importantly a catalyst for The Man—Sherlock. Before the BBC broadcast this episode in January 2012, television critics badgered Moffat and Gatiss for details about Sherlock in love. Gatiss finally corrected them—this is the story of Sherlock *and* love.[239] One of the most important lessons Sherlock can learn is that Love surrounds him, if he will only observe and not merely see.

Love is All Around

So many of Sherlock's inner circle show their love for him in this episode, and Sherlock even reciprocates in his own special way toward Mrs. Hudson. She withstands a rough interrogation by CIA agents and cleverly conceals evidence Sherlock needs for this case. She also shrewdly struggles enough as the agents drag her upstairs to 221B to leave a trail Sherlock can follow. Upon finding scrapes and gouges in plaster by the staircase, Sherlock's eyes narrow, and his expression becomes coldly calculating and malevolent. After disabling the agents and gaining the upper hand (and one of their guns), Sherlock makes sure Mrs. Hudson is safely out of sight and being comforted by John before he throws the CIA agent who dared to touch his landlady out the window. Sherlock's methods are unorthodox and cruel— the agent survives more than one upper-storey fall—but they also leave no doubts as to the extent Sherlock will go to protect those he loves. He may never say the words, but his actions illustrate his intent. Beginning in the first episode of series two, Sherlock takes dire action to ensure his friends' safety, foreshadowing events that take place in "The Reichenbach Fall."

Although Mrs. Hudson protests being anyone's housekeeper, she has become a surrogate mother who plies Sherlock with food when he is depressed and keeps 221B tidy. Because the detective often refuses to eat during a case, a scene in which he visits Mrs. Hudson reveals the depth of their bond. Once the CIA agents have been disposed of, Sherlock checks on Mrs. Hudson. After politely wiping his feet on her doormat, Sherlock opens her fridge (a bit of business Cumberbatch added) and helps himself to a snack before hugging her and praising her for her quick thinking under duress. He feels comfortable enough to make her kitchen his, but he also acts like a respectful, affectionate son.

Gatiss praised the actors' "warm, wonderful relationship" on screen and described Una Stubbs (Mrs. Hudson) as "beyond a national treasure." Moffat admitted that he included more examples of her motherly touch after the first episode because Cumberbatch was always giving her hugs and kisses on set.[240] During the Q&A session following the BFI's screening of "Scandal," Cumberbatch gave a shout-out to Stubbs, who was sitting quietly in the audience. She teared up when he explained that she has known him all his life, because she and his mother are long-time colleagues and friends. When Cumberbatch prepared a birthday present for his mother, locating clips of her early work for a personal tribute, he also came across Stubbs' early commercials and roles, which he then brought to work to share.[241]

"Scandal"ous Nudity

Fans who like Cumberbatch's physique may want to see more of Sherlock "in the sheets," but sex scenes are far from likely. Many people may love Sherlock, but no one (on screen at least) has got him into bed, unless to help him sleep off the drug with which Irene Adler injected him. Although Sherlock in the sheets is out of the question, Sherlock in a sheet becomes a highlight of this episode. Sherlock works on a case by Skype before being summoned to Buckingham Palace. John is quite literally doing field work, carrying a laptop around a rural crime scene so that Sherlock can analyse clues via webcam. The detective sits in the living room, wearing nothing but a high thread count, when two intruders command he get dressed and accompany them. Ever contrary, Sherlock sees no need to bother with clothes, even though he can deduce where he is being taken.

John soon is beside him in a very posh sitting room at the palace. A quick glance at his flatmate piques John's curiosity. "Are you wearing pants?" he asks matter-of-factly, instead of being surprised or scandalised. "No," Sherlock admits. They wait a beat and burst out laughing. They cannot control their giggles when Mycroft disapproves of both Sherlock's attire and their less than serious demeanour. "They are so bonded as friends, and they have such a good time," Moffat enthused. "That's how they'd look to other people, like a couple of schoolboys."[242]

Even when Sherlock is introduced to the Queen's Equerry, who sympathises with Mycroft because of his embarrassing little brother, Holmes the Younger refuses to conform. In a tiff, he haughtily stalks off with as much dignity as he can exude while wearing a sheet. Mycroft conveniently steps on a corner as Sherlock attempts to leave, and the sheet slips dangerously. Viewers are gifted with a glimpse of Cumberbum as Sherlock quickly attempts to regain control of both the sheet and the situation.

Not all takes for this scene went smoothly. Gatiss gleefully admitted that once, when he stepped on the sheet and Cumberbatch continued forward, the mummified actor simply fell over, face to floor. Ever sympathetic, Freeman and the crew laughed. "I overstepped my sheet's limit and just fell. Fell over like a tree. I was dedicated to the moment," Cumberbatch insisted but also recalled that, because of his nude scene in *Frankenstein*, "I've had quite the year falling over with little clothes on."

About a hundred British viewers, however, were not so blasé about nudity, not only Sherlock's but a longer nude scene involving Irene Adler. The BBC received complaints that the pre-watershed (i.e., family viewing) time is no place for "raunchy entertainment." Ben Stephenson, controller of drama commissioning, told *The Guardian* that, although the complaints would be taken seriously, they were a minority (100 complaints out of around 10 million viewers). Furthermore, *"Sherlock* is

149

cheeky entertainment that takes risks."[243] Talking with the Television Critics Association in California, Cumberbatch added that "there's an awful lot of support for the way that we did [the scene] and the taste that we did it with. And if it creates more interest in the program, thank you very much for that."[244] PBS did not report any complaints when the episode was shown in the U.S.

Character Growth and Foreshadowing the Fall

Sherlock's emotional growth across the second season episodes accelerates in "Scandal" and escalates exponentially in the next two stories. Not only does Irene Adler play him as well as Sherlock plays the hauntingly beautiful violin solo he composes in her memory, but she forces him to see himself as Mycroft often does: the black sheep younger brother who can disgrace their family and perhaps the entire nation. When Mycroft describes the sad, lonely man who succumbs to Adler's charms and threatens national security, Sherlock berates his brother for not identifying likely weak links in the Ministry of Defence. He is stunned to be named the security breach and, from that moment, seeks a way to redeem himself (which he does by the end of the episode).

Accustomed to being the cleverest person in the room, Sherlock shockingly comes in third—at least for a while—when he shares that room with Mycroft Holmes and Irene Adler. Audiences who expect Sherlock to immediately solve puzzles on demand come to understand that the consulting detective may not always be able to discern the truth or to unravel every mystery without causing some collateral damage; the stakes only get higher with each successive episode in series two.

Moffat also reminded viewers that when "you take John out of the equation, . . . Sherlock is immediately more vulnerable."[245] When Sherlock acts alone, as he does in many scenes in this episode, he loses the benefit of John's counsel. Beginning with "Scandal," Sherlock becomes more emotional and makes decisions that end up hurting someone close to him.

Hurting himself is also more of a tangible concern in "Scandal." Although Conan Doyle's Holmes has a bohemian outlook that sometimes manifests itself in experimentation with cocaine, and his Meerschaum pipe is legendary, modern-day Sherlock wears nicotine patches in an early episode and, even if his flat is not drug free, he is. As Sherlock loses a bit of his emotional control in the second series, he returns to some bad habits. Cigarettes start him sliding down a slippery slope in "Scandal," an addiction that becomes exacerbated in "The Hounds of Baskerville," an episode when Sherlock also mentions looking for something "seven percent" stronger.[246]

When Sherlock accepts a low-tar cigarette from Mycroft to assuage his shock and grief at Irene Adler's death—on Christmas Eve, no less—John Watson quickly receives a call that a Danger Night may be in store for them. (Interestingly, this scene was deleted from the PBS broadcast as one of the many edits required to trim eight minutes for *Masterpiece Mystery!* The result is that Sherlock's possible drug use is not mentioned in this episode, leaving American viewers with the image of a cleaner cut, or just "clean," character.)

The smoking scene also proved perilous for Cumberbatch, who had to light up for several takes. He suffered nicotine poisoning, which was unpleasant enough on its own, but insomnia also made it difficult for the actor to deliver a long, complicated monologue the next day. "It was a bit of a disaster," Cumberbatch recalled. "We came back to it the next morning, and I nailed it first time. It's a beautiful thing, but it took an awful lot of work, and [Freeman and Pulver] were both sensationally patient . . . until I got it right." The actor appreciates Sherlock's "team of carers around him, this network," but he likewise has a support network among cast and crew.[247] Although Cumberbatch's confidence and security in the role increased from series one to two, Sherlock instead grows more vulnerable to attack, from enemies or narcotics, as he becomes more emotionally open.

The Sound of Cumberbatch's Music

Eos Chater is a violinist in the classical crossover string quartet Bond; her honours degree was granted by the Royal College of Music in London. She also is Cumberbatch's violin teacher. Cumberbatch questioned her about correct playing technique but also wanted to ensure Sherlock handled the instrument convincingly at other times. Chater reported that the actor asked "How would you lift it to your chin?", "How would you play around with the bow?", "Which way would you put it down on a chair?"[248] After only a week of instruction, Chater said that the actor "had a surprisingly good sound." When he plays the violin, Chater noted that the actor "only has to be able to fake it. . . . it doesn't have to be pitch-perfect. But it does. Because he's Benedict." On set, Chater encouraged her pupil but suggested "some tweaks—Benedict smiles, 'was that ok?' (it was) and then when I give a tip he consumes it entirely. Information is his quarry and it shall not escape him. No wonder he's such a good Sherlock."[249]

Being good enough to fake Sherlock's virtuosity falls short of Cumberbatch's goal for his musicianship. While watching himself during the DVD commentary's recording session, he dissected his musical performance just as harshly as his acting. "Oh, God. I can see every bow that's wrong with this," he complained as Sherlock picks up the violin and plays "God Save the Queen."[250] While he played a specially muted violin, his teacher simultaneously played the same song; he mirrored Chater's moves during filming. Cumberbatch explained that he "can play about three or four pieces on the violin" but hoped to have more practice time before the next series' filming.[251]

Cumberbatch's Self-Evaluation of His Performance

As the narrators of the *Sherlock* DVD commentary introduce themselves, a distinctive voice announces "I'm Benedict Cumberbatch, and I *am* the Sherlock." His confidence, as well as a revealing "the" suggesting his place in the current pantheon of adapted Holmses, underscores the actor's newfound comfort with the role and the level of critical acclaim and celebrity it provides him. Still, the actor seems to be keeping his fame in perspective: "If you start worrying about the legends, the fans, the cult following, it's too much to take on. You have to concentrate on problem-solving as an actor."[252] (Concentrating solely on filming proved even more difficult when series three began shooting in public

153

locations in Wales and England. Fans often showed up and stayed, despite frigid weather. When possible, Cumberbatch stepped outside to say hello, but he also reminded fans that he had to go to work and needed to concentrate on upcoming scenes. At times he sent apologies for being unavailable or visited briefly with fans on his way to or from location.)

Cumberbatch is a fascinating combination of self-effacing honesty and self-deprecating humour with a clinical acceptance of his talent and plenty of drive to be a bona fide movie star. He accepts the fact that all eyes are on him when he enters a room, but he remains cordial to everyone, from hyperventilating fans to venue staff to his colleagues. When he arrived at London's BFI for the first public screening of "A Scandal in Belgravia," he waited patiently in an aisle, amid hundreds of fans and press, until he could be seated in the row behind Moffat, Vertue, and Gatiss. He, along with everyone else in the theatre, remained riveted to the big screen as "A Scandal in Belgravia" began. At various points in the evening I looked across the aisle to watch his reaction to important scenes, such as that now-infamous one with the sheet. He did not visibly react to the audience's laughter or "awwwwwws" but occasionally leaned forward to say something to his colleagues. When the lights came up and the audience enthusiastically applauded, Cumberbatch looked a bit relieved. While the stage was set for the Q&A, he, Moffat, and Gatiss gradually made their way to the front of the auditorium. Cumberbatch gave his on-screen sibling a one-armed hug and kiss on the cheek before everyone went on stage, where the attention, and most questions, were primarily directed to him. He is not self-conscious, whether on stage or seated with a crowd of fans in the auditorium, but neither does he seem to turn "on" his personality just before a press event.

Cumberbatch joked that he lost weight during the screening because he was sweating out the audience's verdict. He need not have worried—the crowd was highly pro-*Sherlock* and had fought hard to be in that room. Moffat acknowledged his worry that the audience would think the episode over before the final scene with Irene Adler, but the transition into the final scene was clear enough that the audience responded just as he had hoped they would.

Surprisingly, the svelte Cumberbatch criticised his appearance, especially his weight, during the post-screening Q&A, as well as on the DVD commentary. He noted that his face looked bigger than expected on screen and admitted he had been eating more prior to filming, never good "as an actor and possibly as Sherlock, who doesn't eat and gets his nourishment possibly from air." At the BFI screening, he assured audiences, and perhaps himself, that he would not seem quite so big on television, unlike on the gigantic screen in the auditorium. On the DVD commentary, he ruefully said that his face "expands" between his appearance in the last scene filmed for "The Great Game" and the continuation of that scene filmed more than a year later. "And now we age 18 months," he announces as the first new scene in "A Scandal in Belgravia" begins.[253]

Perhaps Cumberbatch was sensitive about having a more muscular build, courtesy of roles he was filming around the *Sherlock* screenings. During filming of "The Reichenbach Fall," he was gaining weight for his next role as the much heftier Christopher Tietjens in *Parade's End*. At the BFI screening, the actor was fit but larger than fans were used to seeing him. He admitted ruefully that he was "hitting the doughnuts" beginning around the time of the final series two episode. Similarly, he told a Los Angeles reporter that he was constantly eating—if a balanced, healthful diet—and working out two hours a day to build muscle for his *Star Trek* role. Since arriving in LA, he had gone up two suit sizes.[254] Although Cumberbatch has been known to change his build and lose or gain weight for roles, he seems most concerned about Sherlock's appearance and the continuity between episodes or scenes—or apparent shifts between what is expected of the extremely thin detective and the actor who plays him, who may also be juggling other roles before or after the episodes finish shooting.

Cumberbatch is that proverbial consummate professional, and his attention to detail and concerns about his performance—whether appearance or nuance of a gesture or line—make his self-critiques endearing to fans and understandable to a wider audience. Here is an actor in love with his craft, not himself, and he constantly strives to improve his work. Playing Sherlock takes a great deal of mental and physical preparation.

At both the PBS and BFI screenings, he mentioned his choice of physical activity to get the long, lean lines of the great detective. Cumberbatch swims to develop Sherlock's body type. According to one fan who ran into the actor as he checked into a downtown Cardiff hotel, where he would stay during filming some first-series episodes, Cumberbatch made sure he could use the hotel's pool and then dutifully swam "thirty lengths" which the actor said he had completed "really fast and really badly, but it was enough."[255]

During interviews, whether the formal type with journalists or the informal ones in hotel gyms or outside stage doors, the actor seems sincere, if guarded, knowing exactly what and how much to say. His reactions in Q&As, such as those for "Scandal," tell a lot more about the public man, not the "product" being sold to potential *Sherlock* viewers or casting agents. When Moffat told the New York City audience that it is not important to know Sherlock's background in order to understand the character portrayed in these episodes, Cumberbatch pulled back and grimaced, not attempting to school his immediate response to Moffat's comment.[256] The actor is well known for his preference for research and knowing as much as possible about a character's backstory. Even if he seems to take his cues to Sherlock's personality from Moffat and Gatiss more than Conan Doyle, he clearly wants to ensure consistency of characterisation and in-depth understanding of the role.

When Cumberbatch becomes invested in a role, he throws himself into it, intellectually and physically. Perhaps for that reason, he was perturbed when, standing behind the screen during the New York preview of "Scandal," he noticed that some scenes had been edited. He mentioned the edits to producer Sue Vertue, who is responsible for editing scenes so that episodes fit the parameters of PBS' allotted time for *Masterpiece Mystery!* On stage later, Vertue commented on Cumberbatch's response, and the actor reiterated that the entire episodes should be seen. He said something similar in a *New York Times* interview, choosing the word "desperate" to describe his desire for U.S. audiences to see *Sherlock*. Unfortunately, that one line, emphasising a different connotation, became the headline for newspapers that picked up the story. "Benedict Cumberbatch 'Desperate' for 'Sherlock' U.S. Success"[257] and similar headlines made the actor's comment seem self-serving, rather than placing it in the context of his pride in the whole production and everyone's contribution to the show's high quality. Certainly Cumberbatch is profiting from the global exposure *Sherlock* brings him, but at the BFI screening, for example, he genuinely seemed interested in promoting the episode and was pleased—upon seeing the final cut for the first time, and in a very public setting—with the result of everyone's collaboration.

Despite praising the composite result, the actor sometimes criticises his acting decisions. With hindsight, he would have taken a different approach to a transitional scene that begins in Irene Adler's home but then shifts to an outdoor location representing Sherlock's description of a distant crime scene. During the interior shots, he is wide eyed—a deliberate choice. When the setting shifts outdoors, he narrows his eyes to reflect the setting change, even though Sherlock is only "outdoors" in his mind as he describes the crime scene. The actor disliked Sherlock's frown and "troubled look," which did not seem appropriate for the scene when the exterior and interior shots were edited together. "But that's me perhaps," he suggested. "I have an awful lot of other things I wish I had or hadn't done." By opening his eyes wider, he was "trying to wear a mask of impregnable neutrality" in front of Adler. His eyes appropriately matched the shift from indoors to outdoors (that is, it would be natural to squint a bit in sunshine), but then he did not like the resulting facial expression. Gatiss disagreed, telling Cumberbatch that "you can't go down that road," because then why would Sherlock's hair, blowing in the outdoor breeze, be moving inside the house?[258] The shift in setting is only within Sherlock's mind and explained through his dialogue in Irene's living room. The hair problem did not bother Cumberbatch—that is something he could not control—but his eyes are well within his physical control and part of the persona he consciously developed for this scene. Of course, casual viewers likely do not notice the slight slant to his eyes as the scene shifts location, and the fans who carefully listen to the DVD commentary might not pick up its significance to the scene—but such details are clearly important to the actor, not because of vanity or the desire to show off his knowledge of acting.

The scene that Cumberbatch someday hopes to show his grandchildren is the slow-motion filming of an action sequence when Sherlock figures out the combination to Irene's safe while American agents are holding Adler and Watson at gunpoint. The detective realises the safe is armed with its own weapons system, ducks out of the way, and fights to disarm one of the gunmen. The action and filming style are very James Bond.

"I'm a sucker for picking things up and twiddling them," Cumberbatch commented about the way he handled the gun in this action sequence. "I must calm that down next time." From that point in the commentary, he noticed every time that he fiddled with a prop and found it distracting. "Another twiddle. I've got to stop twiddling," he reminded himself as he watched a dramatic scene when Sherlock sprays cleaning fluid in an assailant's eyes. He reported yet another twiddle a few scenes later, when Sherlock flips his bow before playing the violin.[259] Although actors often receive a director's notes to improve or simply take another approach to a scene, Cumberbatch's fans get the idea that no director could possibly scrutinise the actor's performance as much as he does himself.

According to Danny Boyle, Cumberbatch's director for *Frankenstein,* and *Sherlock* co-creators Moffat and Gatiss, the actor appropriately applies what he learns for one role to other characters or situations. "Go ahead and say it," Cumberbatch groused on the "Scandal" DVD commentary. He clearly has heard the comment Gatiss and Moffat seemed eager to make about the scene when a drugged and barely conscious Sherlock half-falls out of bed and attempts to stand upright. "It's not supposed to be" the Creature, the actor insisted. Nevertheless, his current colleagues and former director Boyle equally insisted it is, even if the stumbling movement had become so ingrained after months of falling out of a sling-like "womb" on stage in *Frankenstein* that a similar action in *Sherlock* triggered the actor's muscle memory. Boyle told the *Radio Times* about "a couple of things [Cumberbatch] put in ["Scandal"] that were direct mimics of Frankenstein's creature. Those of us who shared it all, we spotted them . . . .When actors are on a roll, it's a continuum. They channel everything incoming that's useful. Everything feeds into everything else."[260]

Frankenstein may have influenced Sherlock, but the Great Detective and an internationally popular television series have a more potent influence on Cumberbatch's fame and burgeoning film stardom. Perhaps Boyle's concept of one "feeding" the other is inappropriate terminology, considering Cumberbatch's heavy concern with Sherlock's physique. Nevertheless, the actor should be feasting on the praise being heaped upon him by fans and television critics alike.

Frankenstein (2011)

Cumberbatch often suffers for his art. For all the awards and critical praise given him for his performance as scientist Victor Frankenstein and his clever, sly Creature in the Danny Boyle-directed National Theatre presentation of *Frankenstein,* the actor seemed to receive an equally long list of injuries, as well as sometimes having to cancel a performance because of illness (such as food poisoning). He apologetically promised *Sherlock* fans who attended the PBS screening of "A Scandal in Belgravia" and the following Q&A session that, should the play eventually come to Broadway, he would do better not to miss performances.[261] In an interview for *The Big Issue* in 2011, Cumberbatch, described by the writer as "exhausted and battered," worried that his body might not return to pre-play condition because of "wrists turning into ankles, . . . joints coming out of my f---ing hips," neck problems, failing voice, plantar fasciitis in his left foot, cuts, concussions,[262] and scars on his forehead from the prosthetics required to play the Creature.[263] "It's great," he still enthused, "but there's a limit to us humans."[264] Perhaps as consolation to his battered body,

161

his professional theatrical status became enhanced with this role, which won acclaim not only for the 66 live performances at the National Theatre between 5 February and 2 May 2011 but worldwide in cinemas when both the original casting (Cumberbatch as the Creature) and the reverse casting (Cumberbatch as Victor Frankenstein) became a hit for National Theatre Live, first in spring 2011 and through encore broadcasts the following year.

However, *Frankenstein* was a milestone in the actor's professional development for a more controversial reason as well. Although both he and Miller were "swaddled" for the recorded NT Live broadcasts, the actors played a prolonged "birth" scene in the nude. Cumberbatch had been seen nude on stage and screen before—as screen captures on fan websites gleefully illustrate—but this role proved how his comfort with his body and the requirements of a role had changed over the years. He once recalled being asked to audition for director Andrew Birkin, casting *The Cement Garden* during Cumberbatch's time at Harrow. The film dealt with incest between teenaged siblings (a theme Cumberbatch would eventually revisit with his role in *Wreckers*) and required nudity. "I was really prudish at that age" and "didn't want to take my clothes off. I was terrified. I didn't want anyone seeing what I looked like."[265] *Frankenstein* not only showed *Sherlock* fans exactly what the actor looked like, but it also proved how thoroughly Cumberbatch would transform himself in the most physically challenging theatrical role of his career.

Playing the Creature in the nude also made for humorous moments in a Q&A session after one performance. While seriously answering a question about

162

collaborating with Miller, Cumberbatch got as far as saying "I love working with his [Miller's] Creature"[266] before the audience collectively giggled, causing the actor to replay what he had just said. Cumberbatch blushed but forged ahead. He is not naïve or prudish, but when he becomes caught up in explaining his work, he may not realise unintentional innuendo. It is a surprisingly endearing trait in a man in his mid-thirties.

In this adaptation of Mary Shelley's now-classic story, playwright Nick Dear emphasises the again-modern debates between science and religion/philosophy and inspires audiences to consider how far may be too far in humanity's scientific quest for knowledge. The play also explores larger social issues such as parental responsibilities toward children and, in a larger sense, society's responsibilities for its experimental "creations" and precedents, which may not turn out as anticipated. NT promotional materials summarised the play's themes as "[u]rgent concerns of scientific responsibility, parental neglect, cognitive development and the nature of good and evil [which] are embedded within this thrilling and deeply disturbing classic gothic tale."[267]

The leads' performances were praised and, come awards season, *Frankenstein* brought nominations for theatrical excellence to director Boyle but, even more frequently, to Cumberbatch and Miller. They began awards season by sharing the Evening Standard Theatre Award for best actor and capped the theatre year by winning the coveted Olivier award for best actor. Along the way, Cumberbatch also was named best actor at the Critics Circle Theatre Awards, and fans voted him as their choice for best actor at the Whatsonstage.com

163

Awards, the only theatre awards selected by audience vote.

Despite the thematic need for the Creature and Victor to develop a symbiotic relationship and the actors to mesh aspects of their performance so that Creator and Created increasingly mirror each other's mannerisms, each actor approached the role of the Creature quite differently, from research to physical movement on stage. Audiences fortunate enough to see both actors play both roles gained a greater understanding of the complexity of the lead characters and the ways that two complementary interpretations of the Creature, in particular, add depth to Dear's script. In one interview during the play's rehearsals, Boyle explained that, despite the alternate casting, audiences need not see the actors in both roles in order to understand his and Dear's adaptation of the *Frankenstein* story.[268] However, the actors' individual interpretations highlighted different aspects of the themes Boyle and Dear thought most important to modern audiences, such as parental responsibility for children or the need for scientists (or Science) to consider the ramifications of what they create.

Cumberbatch approached the role scientifically, learning from the dead as well as the living. He attended autopsies, which undoubtedly helped him gain a greater understanding of Victor's research processes and his work to reanimate bodies. The living provided him with insights into body movement, and early research helped inform his performance as the Creature and engender empathy for him:

What's fascinating is seeing something come alive that's in a 30-year-old form and have to re-educate itself. I looked at stroke victims in recovery. I looked at people who'd had severe injuries, both in wars and car crashes, trying to re-educate their limbs and their bodies, and when you see that happening, the amount of vulnerability—it's a very endearing thing to watch evolve. You really care for [the Creature].[269]

The actor's research was apparent throughout the play, especially in its early scenes. Cumberbatch played the Creature as a fully formed man, no matter that he has been (re)born recently. The movements are often grotesque, as if the Creature truly is made from spare parts. The performance matches the actor's research into adult movement directed by a brain that does not function as well as it once did, almost as if the Creature "remembers" how to move but cannot get his current body to respond to his commands. Cumberbatch's performance in the "birth" scene also seems less joyful than Miller's and requires the Creature's greater concentration as he explores his physical abilities.

Miller, on the other hand, turned to an information source much closer to home when he prepared for the role of the Creature. "There's a lot of my two-year-old in him . . . . It's a blank canvas as a body, but the brain works extremely fast as it's a fully grown brain. All the learning comes super quickly."[270] Miller's interpretation emphasised the "blank canvas," and the Creature, once he learns how to walk, runs around the stage very much like

165

an excited baby, vocalising his pleasure in learning to manoeuvre his legs. He is inquisitive and can get lost in exploring his toes—before he tries to taste them. Miller's body language, loud babbling, and surprised responses to his environment perfectly mimicked the reactions of a baby or toddler. This sweet innocence allowed the actor to develop a much more stark contrast with the embittered, cruel Creature later in the play.

Cumberbatch's interpretation of the Creature as a reanimated being relearning how to be a man is apparent throughout the opening scene. The NT Live recording shows Cumberbatch "awakening" in the womb. The camera provides a close-up of his silhouette, and the actor's hand strokes backward down the side of the enclosure; a single finger pushes against the membrane to test its strength. The Creature's body pulses in time with a heartbeat sound effect reverberating throughout the theatre. After lightning flashes to the accompanying sizzle of the stage's hundreds of light bulbs, the Creature begins to emerge from the confining structure, falling outward and landing on a mat on stage. The actor's hands and toes flutter, and his legs twitch, the left more pronounced in its bending, flopping motions. These flailing movements indicate that Cumberbatch's research paid off; the Creature is unable to control the electrical impulses surging from his brain that cause his limbs to move spasmodically. Unlike in Miller's performance, which shows the Creature's entire body being electrified during birth and shuddering as a single unit, Cumberbatch's limbs do not all react the same way; one leg, in particular, always seems to have more difficulty with movement until the Creature learns to walk.

The Creature soon gains greater mobility, pushing his body across the stage, his hands bent backward at the wrists, as if Victor attached them incorrectly. The Creature's body position mimics the first of many yoga stances seen throughout the play. (Cumberbatch sometimes practices yoga in order to prepare for a role,[271] and whether consciously or not, audience members familiar with the discipline may recognise the Creature's use of modified yoga positions as he gains control of his body.) The cobra position, in which the torso is pushed upward while the legs and hips remain on the floor, is appropriate for the Creature's first attempt to raise himself from the floor and to gain forward momentum, but it is not a typical "baby" pose.

Learning to stand is a slow process as the Creature eventually becomes balanced on his feet. Again, Cumberbatch performs a yoga position—downward dog—in which the body's weight is distributed on the floor between the hands and feet until body weight is shifted backward onto the legs, in this case allowing the Creature gradually to stand. The next step in his development involves walking, and the Creature, as he will continue to do in later scenes after he has gained strength and grace, often walks on his toes, as if his feet do not quite work the same way as those of a normal man. The Creature slaps his feet against the stage as he awkwardly circles the womb. He laughs—the first vocalisation in this performance. When the womb catches his attention, he stops to stare at it, finally attempting to walk into the opening from which he emerged. He fails, bouncing against the membrane and falling backward. (Unlike Miller's Creature, Cumberbatch's tries to return to the safety of the womb, as if he already knows that the outside world will be cruel to him.)[272]

From the beginning, Cumberbatch's interpretation makes the Creature seem older and more analytical than he is in Miller's portrayal. The fully formed, educated Creature's later cruelty and violence thus seem far more premeditated than the actions of Miller's Creature. If this *Frankenstein* can be reduced to a discussion of "nature versus nurture" regarding the Creature's development, Cumberbatch's Creature, although certainly influenced by those who interact with him, makes more of a claim for nature. The inherent nature of Man, as illustrated by this performance, is dark and manipulative, and the Creature not so much learns for the first time about humanity but relearns how men can be cowed by fear or manipulated into doing one's bidding. Cumberbatch-as-Creature dislikes being at the mercy of others not so much to avenge his "childhood" treatment but because he increasingly enjoys being the one in power. He longs to be a king, like the men in history he has studied. He wants to gain more knowledge, not, like Victor, simply for its own sake, but to use it in order to control a situation. Once angered or betrayed, the Creature knows exactly how to punish humanity—Victor, in particular. He ultimately controls Victor's life or death, just as Victor once controlled him.

In the alternate casting, from the moment when Cumberbatch makes his entrance as Victor, he embodies an inwardly directed scientist. Coming into the laboratory to check his experiment, he discovers that the Creature is no longer where he was left—the body is on the floor. Victor holds a cloth to his nose, gagging, as he carefully approaches. When he touches the sleeping Creature, thinking him stillborn, the "baby" comes to life and begins to crawl toward him. Horrified, the scientist collapses and then crawls backward to escape the Creature, a reverse but parallel action. The audience thus receives the first indication that Victor and the Creature are inextricably connected and co-dependent. Whereas the Creature takes steps forward in his intellectual and physical development, Victor moves backward as a result of his experiment, becoming more paranoid, secretive, and isolated from other humans as the play progresses. The scientist's response—to back away in horror—to the forward progression of his experiment symbolises both characters' development in this adaptation. By the end of the play, Victor is far weaker in will and body than the Creature he abandons at the end of the birth scene; their roles have been reversed, and the Creature decides if or how Victor will live.

Especially in Cumberbatch's interpretation, Victor Frankenstein is far more scientist than parent and harbours no regrets at abandoning or destroying an experiment gone wrong. During the first confrontation between created and creator, the Creature asks "Why did you make me?" Victor's response—"Because I could"— is delivered more harshly when Cumberbatch voices this line, underscoring Frankenstein's lack of humanity and his inability to nurture a child. Similarly, in a much later scene, when Victor, talking to a hallucinated vision of his deceased little brother, discusses his educational preparation and reasons for wanting to understand the spark of life, Cumberbatch becomes impassioned and quickly rattles off scientific conclusions as quickly as

Sherlock Holmes spouts deductions. In a recorded technical rehearsal, Cumberbatch fluffed a line or two during this scene, but he remained in character as an agitated Victor so immersed in recalling details of his scientific methods that the mistake seems more a product of Victor's exuberance rather than an actor's momentary memory lapse.[273] The actor gestures animatedly as he describes the scientist's quest for knowledge and seems completely in his element.

This scene is a distinct contrast with one earlier in the play, when Victor's fiancée Elizabeth questions his preference for spending hours locked away with his work instead of spending time with her. She tells him that he should talk with her, and he is genuinely puzzled by her request, wondering what she would want him to say. This lack of understanding, not only of humanity but of women in particular, becomes the basis of humour when Victor is confronted by the Creature, who wants the scientist to make a female companion for him. Victor soon considers the scientific challenge of making not only an intelligent, functional being, but one who has the beauty and grace of a woman. He understands the physiological differences between men and women but becomes perplexed when determining how else women differ from men. "What are they good at?" Victor asks the Creature, and both are confused. Although the Creature's plaintive "I don't know" is amusing, the truth behind the scene is that neither Victor nor the Creature truly can relate to humanity in general, much less females in particular. They only are fully alive and experience emotion as a result of one another's actions, and, unfortunately, usually those actions are destructive and have tragic consequences. Cumberbatch-as-Victor takes on a harsher edge and a self-directed focus to the exclusion of everything else.

Behind the Scenes: The Evolution of a Production

When the actor's preparation for one, much less two, roles is considered, fans may more easily understand Cumberbatch's comment that plays take an inordinate amount of time and energy. If the payoff of a job is measured by the number of people internationally who see a performance and the expenditure of time, then theatre work is more often a heart than a head decision. As his fame increases and Cumberbatch is thought of primarily as a celebrity or star, as well as a fine actor, he is more likely to appear in films than on stage, a move that not only makes his work more accessible to a larger audience, but also makes a performance "permanent" in a recording. Film, as opposed to stage, work would necessarily limit his interaction with fans, many who stood outside the National Theatre's stage door night after night to greet the actor or get an autograph. Most film sets are closed and the majority of productions secret away their actors. In contrast, British theatre in particular seems more welcoming to fans willing to wait at the stage door for a glimpse of if not encounter with their favourite actors. Although Cumberbatch often wondered aloud (to fans or interviewers) why people would spend so much money to see multiple performances or travel so far to see the play, fan blogs, stage-door video, and anecdotes repeat stories of the actor taking time after a performance to meet with fans, or to send a theatre representative to let the waiting crowd know he was unavailable. Despite

171

being tired, and sometimes still sporting dabs of Creature make-up, the actor was often friendly and patiently posed or signed, although he chose what he wanted to sign. *Frankenstein* materials usually received preference, because he was doing the play at the time; paraphernalia from older roles frequently remained unsigned.

As discussed in Chapter 7, Cumberbatch truly does not seem to understand fandom, and at times he does not suffer fools—or those whose actions seems foolish to him. Several second-hand reports from fans tell similar stories about the actor's reaction to those who returned to the theatre, night after night, often sitting near the front. These anecdotes similarly report that Cumberbatch, when confronted by fans eager to explain how many times they saw the play or how they bought all the tickets they could, was not impressed or pleased, suggesting that people waiting long hours for the possibility of a day ticket or return might have used some of those tickets instead of the same fans watching the show again and again. He noticed which fans frequently approached him to sign autographs or take photos as well as those who ensured they were first at the expense of others. *Frankenstein,* following on his then-recent fame as *Sherlock,* seems to mark the actor's first awareness of fan obsession, and he could not then—nor even by 2013, when *Sherlock* fans more than ever approached him on film or television shooting locations—completely understand the need for someone to have proof of meeting or seeing him. Nevertheless, he appreciates his fans' support and sometimes applauds what he observes as positive fan behaviours.

172

One fan recounted to me a favourite memory of a Cumberbatch encounter. Because she had previously met the actor, she stood back to let those who had not yet talked with Cumberbatch after *Frankenstein* have their opportunity. The actor noticed not only what she had done but recognised her from an earlier positive meeting. He whispered to her, "You're a true fan."

Perhaps Cumberbatch's willingness to meet fans at the stage door, or to sign autographs after public events, is one reason why they hope he returns to the theatre, generally the most accessible medium for fans to meet actors. However, this type of interaction seems less likely as his fan base grows and safety concerns, for Cumberbatch and his fans, turns stage-door sightings into chaos reminiscent, several observers have claimed, of fan reaction to the Beatles.

Beyond anecdotes and fan-produced videos, a look at the *Frankenstein* stage bible provides a wealth of detail about the rehearsals and initial conception of the actors' roles, as well as the nitty gritty of behind-the-scenes activities during and after performances. It highlights the many unpublicised responsibilities that are important to an actor's life in the theatre.

Brief comments in the rehearsal notes dated 8 December 2010 indicate duties that go beyond learning a role and physically blocking movements for scenes. "If anybody wishes to schedule time with Mr. Cumberbatch or Mr. Miller—the afternoon of Wednesday 15th December is a possible time to look at. Please let David [Marsland, stage manager] know if you want to plan anything—i.e., Fittings, Make-up tests, etc."[274] Notes from the following day reminded cast and crew that, on

Friday, 10 December, Underworld would "record some Victor dialogue with Mr. Cumberbatch and Mr. Miller when they visit the rehearsal room . . . [This recording] may be used in the soundscape for the opening Incubator section. (Sound studio booked.)"[275] The recorded dialogue became part of the soundtrack played prior to the Creature's birth, at the very beginning of the play, when Victor Frankenstein explains his calculations and establishes his scientific methods. Although audience members finding their seats and checking out the womb-like incubator may not have given this background audio as much attention as it deserved, it nevertheless initially establishes Victor's perspective. Because the character has only a few minutes of stage time in the opening scene, the recorded voiceover gave the audience additional information about the scientist, and the actor's tone and pace indicate his approach to playing this role.

In addition to alerting cast and crew to such tasks beyond the expected rehearsals, the bible also documents the rehearsal process and the script's evolution in the months before previews. According to 16 December production comments, "There will be a Meet and greet in Rehearsal Room 1 on Monday at 10 am, which will be followed by a Model Showing. . . . Costume Designs [also will be] available. This will be followed by a Read Through. We will have new copies of the script available on Monday morning which will include changes made to rehearsal so far."[276] The actors were also involved in a "30-minute Meeting planned for 2.30 on Tuesday in the Olivier (after the lunchtime production meeting) to get all interested parties together to look at the use of radio mics in the space to offer vocal support if necessary alongside the soundscape."[277]

Costume design and fittings also progressed alongside stagecraft and the actors' rehearsals. First full-length photos of Cumberbatch facing front and at left profile show him with curly long Sherlock hair in late 2010. His smile is not quite a grin, but he looks far happier than Victor Frankenstein or his Creature ever would be. In his everyday clothes (an artfully designed long-sleeved brown pullover, dark trousers, and dark brown leather shoes), the casually dressed Cumberbatch looks much younger than his 34 years. Later photographs of costume fittings show Cumberbatch-as-Victor in a variety of moods. Wearing the crumpled linen shirt, dark trousers, and leather apron needed during Victor's first scene (Scene 3), Cumberbatch brandishes a water bottle and stands in a "ninja attack" pose in one photograph—his expression humorously mimics "horror" but mostly looks playfully "pouty/frowny" faced, an expression far removed from what he showed on stage when Victor encounters his creation. The actor is more serious, although pleasantly almost-smiling, in the photo of Victor in the coat and finer clothing needed in Scene 24 when he talks with wife-to-be Elizabeth. By the time these costume fittings took place, Cumberbatch's hair was a more natural ginger and far shorter, and his long sideburns marked him as an actor in a period piece. A third photo shows him in the final scene's furs; Cumberbatch's smile illustrates comfort with the clothes and his role. Whereas some actors ham it up during fittings while others remain in character, Cumberbatch seems somewhere in between—attentive but never

175

completely in character. The photographs show the actor, not the character, during rehearsals.

As Victor, Cumberbatch wore a few main costumes, with articles that could be added or used in more than one scene to create a new "look." The most striking costume involved a black t-shirt, leather trousers, tunic, padded lining, sheepskin mittens, and fur-trimmed felt books. He shared the grey-black wool circular caped cloak, dark charcoal oilskin coat, and leather apron with Miller, but all other identical items of Victor's or the Creature's wardrobe were customised for him. Costume notes indicate several QCs (Quick Changes) for Victor, especially in later scenes. For example, in Scene 25, Victor enters stage right, adding a clock, boots, and gloves before he steps on stage. By Scene 28, he has a QC to put on the leather apron, but the QC into Victor's wedding clothes is trickier. At the end of Scene 30, Victor exits via the revolving drum that lowers part of the stage. He changes into the fur costume while in the drum, before making his final entrance by ascending to the stage.

The Creature wears nothing in the first three scenes before donning a cloak for the next several. He puts on a set of ragged clothes under his cloak; these are set in the beggar's bag in the scene before the Creature meets his mentor, De Lacey. The Creature leaves the cloak on stage, revealing the raggedy outfit to be worn during the next several scenes. Unlike Victor, the Creature is on stage in far more scenes and makes fewer costume changes, the only QC into "smart clothes" consisting of a waistcoat, short jacket, and better trousers, before the wedding night scene late in the play.

These costume fittings were just another part of the actor's rehearsal period, but the NT Live filming required yet a further fitting. Two costume designs were considered for the Creature to keep him from being nude in the play's early scenes: a more revealing dance belt or a loin-cloth front/diaper-back style. The "diaper" won and was worn over low-fitting briefs covered by a bandage-like loin cloth.[278]

While rehearsals progressed, plans were made for the preview performances, which involved a great deal more technical specificity and planning. Although previews were still about six weeks away, the 23 December entry explains that "Danny [Boyle] is planning to tech Jonny as the Creature first, meaning that he would do the first 4 previews. Benedict would be teched in as the Creature on Thursday 10th February before playing this combination for the next 4 previews . . . . Benedict would probably play first Press Night as Creature and Jonny the second—this is still to be confirmed. If we could adjust schedules to reflect this. All of the above subject to alteration, and hasn't been discussed with the actors yet. Also awaiting confirmation from the planning office for this alteration to their draft schedule."[279] By 19 January, the casting for previews had been finalised: "The first Technical Rehearsal will be Benedict as Creature— Jonny as Victor. Thursday 10th Feb we Tech the alternate casting—Jonny as Creature—Benedict as Victor. . . . Beyond this, previews alternate (except on Matinee days where the Creature stays the same for both shows [a must for the lengthy make-up process required for the Creature, but playing him twice in one day was especially physically demanding for the actor]). Press Night on

177

Tuesday 22nd February will be Jonny as Creature-Benedict as Victor. Press Night on Wednesday 23rd February will be Benedict as Creature-Jonny as Victor."[280]

In January 2011, publicity increased, and multimedia became part of the marketing package. Stage notes on 11 January describe the upcoming "Trailer Filming and Marketing Photos. We will aim to do the first version (Jonny as Creature, Benedict as Victor) on Thursday 20th January—filmed early evening. (Friday not possible as an alternative as one of the guys is booked for a TV Chat show [Cumberbatch's visit on Alan Carr's *Chatty Man* program].) The second alternate version will need to be filmed at a later date. Currently looking at the logistics of Monday 24th January."[281] As a result of Miller being filmed as the Creature for the trailer and still photos, he had to go into make-up in the late afternoon in order to be ready for the evening recording session. While Miller was in make-up, Cumberbatch was having a rehearsal session which would end when it was time for him to go into make-up to have his hair styled as Victor, his role for the trailer and photo shoot that night.[282]

Out of the rehearsal room and on stage, the actors' interpretations of the roles and different bits of "business" they incorporated into scenes sometimes raised questions or, at least, further indicated that, although they were playing the same characters, the actors had unique concerns and feedback. One production note explains that the "Creature [as played by Miller] was playing in the snow and holding his tongue for [s]nowflakes. Is this a problem?"[283] Apparently the material used to make "snowflakes" was not deemed harmful to actors, because both characters, but especially Miller, ended up tasting and touching the snow as it fell on stage. The rehearsal cloaks also were designed to meet each actor's needs, because, as a note to the costume department explains, "Mr. Cumberbatch and Mr. Miller will have different requirements from the Cloak that is thrown over and then worn by the Creature. We should allow for having two rehearsal cloaks so that both gentlemen are able to [provide] feedback."[284] Other costuming and set notes in mid-January confirm that the Creature "will spend the majority of the show barefoot," but, because the Creature "is on the floor for the first few minutes of the show," director Boyle "is not averse to having the Creature in the Incubator with bandages protecting knees and elbows, should it become necessary for the actors."[285]

Additional safety notes for crew working with the set soon reflect concerns about the way the Creature slides from a "mountain ledge" down a pole onto the stage where he confronts Victor and, for the first time, the scientist talks with his creation. "Although the planned slide keeps the actor with his feet heading downwards, there is a possibility of them swinging under the bar. We should therefore look at whether there needs to be protection on the top facing the edge of the Jaw Wall. Also, we should keep the area below the Slide clear of Lighting and Sound equipment." The pole down which the actors slide onto stage "should not be textured. The bare [pole] that we have works well. Speed is controlled by the [actor's] hands. Clammy hands don't slip easily— so there should be a towel set in the Ashtray for the actor to dry his hands. (Talc we think will make the hands too slippery, and therefore take away control. Rosin we think would stop the slip. Happy to take advice.) We also need to bear in mind that the Creature climbs back up the structure at the end using more poles than just the Slide one."[286] Whatever conclusion the actors and production crew eventually reached, the audience was impressed with the Creature's dexterity and strength, which illustrate just how much he has matured physically by this point in the play and why Victor could be proud of the flexibility and durability of his creation. Although both actors nimbly descended (at the beginning of the scene) and ascended (at the end of the scene) by sliding or climbing the poles representing part of the mountain setting where the Creature's confrontation with Victor takes place, Cumberbatch moved more quickly (at least in the NT Live recorded version), especially in sliding to the stage. Such grace of movement underscores the Creature's success in retraining his brain to direct movement.

By the time of a complete "run of the play on Tuesday afternoon [25 January 2011] with Benedict as the Creature," followed by another run two afternoons later with Miller as the Creature, the actors had spent at least two months collaborating not only with each other, the other cast members, and the director, but with crew members responsible for safety in working with props and sets, costumes, wigs, make-up, soundtrack, and publicity. In the days before the official previews, crew were invited to attend "[f]urther runs from Saturday next week [29 January]—times tbc. Please let us know if you wish to attend, as space in the room is very limited"[287] for what would become a sell-out in London and an internationally in-demand NT Live event.

In the days leading to preview performances, the cast adhered to a rigorous schedule. The hourly breakdown of the pre-show rehearsal schedule for Saturday, 5 February 2011, shows the variety of activities required of crew and cast before a preview performance:[288]

8-10 am	Workshops notes on stage
10-12	Technical work on stage
12-1	Reset for dress rehearsals
1-2	Lunch
1:55	Half hour call
2:30-4:30	Dress rehearsal 2 (version A)
	(BC as Creature, JLM as Victor)
	Production photographer
4:30-6:50	Reset/strike production desks
7:30-9:30	Frankenstein Preview 1 (version A)
9:30-11	Technical notes in auditorium
11 pm	End of Call

The schedule through Wednesday, 9 February, was similar, except for a break on Sunday. On Thursday, 10 February, the reverse casting, listed as "Version B (JLM Creature, BC Victor)" began for the next five days, excepting Sunday. On Tuesday, 15 February, Cumberbatch as Creature faced a press photocall from 2:00 to 5:00 p.m.[289] These typical schedules, especially for such a high-profile production at the National Theatre, illustrate how much of an actor's time is required not only on stage for rehearsals or performances but to promote the play to the press, which, in turn, entices the public with images and interviews. That such activities take up so many hours may be a surprise to fans who think

181

primarily of an actor's work on stage or in preparation for a role, rather than the complete package of promoting a play or making adjustments as the play moves from rehearsals to previews to performances and, in the case of *Frankenstein*, to the added technical rehearsals and costume and camera additions necessary for NT Live broadcasts.

Even though the play had evolved considerably to this point, it would be additionally tweaked as a result of previews' live-audience response and critics' reviews. The actors' portrayals would morph as they worked closely with each other, day after day, and further grew into their roles. Nevertheless, the crew's instructions illustrate a carefully documented routine that offers insights into the nature of a typical night in the theatre once a production is up and running. *Frankenstein*'s stage management bible lists procedures to be followed for each of the two castings and highlights some aspects of Cumberbatch's life backstage.

For example, a crew member is instructed to "Take Benedict's dressing gown to the Make up room where he will be getting his 'Creature' make up done. Check that he has his ankle supports."[290] Given the very physical nature of the role and the actor's occasional bumps and sprains, the ankle support note is hardly surprising but is yet another reminder of Cumberbatch's commitment to the performance and the many contortions he underwent each performance as the Creature.

Other production notes further explain the rituals of preparing for the role and the brief off-stage respites needed to keep the actors going strong for the non-stop play:

Check that there is a full bottle of water for Benedict [with directions where the water bottles should be set at four locations stage left or right before a performance].

Check that Benedict's skipping rope is in [a specific cubicle], as well as a boot jack.

At 7 o'clock Benedict will come up to stage to warm up. Wait in the wings ready to take his slippers, dressing gown and skipping rope when he's done with them.

At 7.15 Benedict will start the preshow. Put his dressing gown, slippers and skipping rope in [another cubicle].[291]

Rapid costume changes are nothing new in the theatre, and a dresser helps the actor un- and re-dress within a few seconds. However, what the audience may not realise is the specificity of the instructions that must be followed if a character is going to be able to exit wearing one costume and return moments later wearing something else. The following example includes just a few of the many instructions required for just one smooth costume change:

Set the trousers on a chair ready to pick up. Have the shirt over one arm ready to put over Benedict's head and hold the boxers ready to hand to him as soon as he comes off [stage].

Benedict will come off after the Beggar's attack and take his cloak off, which [crew member] will take, as well as the prop trousers.

Hand him his boxers.

Put the shirt over his head.

Grab the trousers and hand them to him—he will put on himself.

As soon as Benedict is dressed and Sound and Wigs are finished, help him on with the cloak and put the hood up.[292]

"How to get dressed" instructions may seem unnecessary to those of us who do not work in the theatre, but the precise routine, to be completed night after night, is crucial to establish a logical order for donning the costume quickly and easily, as well as ensuring that all items are on hand and ready for the actor to wear.

Post-show activities are also referenced in the bible's notes, and laundry is an inevitable part of theatre life. One comment reminds crew to "[p]ut Benedict's dressing gown in the wash" after a performance and is followed by the more humorous and emphatic reminder to "Check the pockets first!." That kind of comment leads to all kinds of questions about what might have once been left in a pocket, and by whom.

Although Cumberbatch's hard work is often obliquely mentioned in press reports or interviews, fans may not realise exactly how many months of long days and many specialized tasks go into the making of such stellar performances as those of Cumberbatch and Miller in *Frankenstein*. Behind the exhilaration of performance or red carpet awards events are the ordinary and often repetitive tasks that are far more common occurrences in a working actor's life.

Tinker Tailor Soldier Spy (2011)

Cumberbatch's television and theatre stardom was assured after *Sherlock* and *Frankenstein.* Although Cumberbatch, in 2011, was not a film star, he assayed a role that indicated a change in status. He became a member of the high-powered ensemble of a major movie, one that would earn him another award nomination and ensure plenty of publicity. From autumn 2011 through early 2012, *Tinker Tailor Soldier Spy* reached mainstream audiences around the world and garnered plenty of awards and nominations in the U.S. and U.K. The film received three Academy Award nominations, including one for best adapted screenplay; in 2012, it was named Best British Film by the British Academy of Film and Television Arts (BAFTAs), who also chose it as best adapted screenplay. In *Tinker Tailor,* Cumberbatch is Peter Guillam, who supervises MI6's "scalphunters," those spies who do the agency's dirty work. Guillam is loyal first to the Circus, Britain's elite espionage force, but also to George Smiley (Gary Oldman), one of the agency's leaders and a parental figure to Guillam. One of the many secrets Guillam keeps is his sexual orientation; he has an established relationship with an older man, and the two share a home. Throughout the film, Guillam struggles with loyalty and betrayal, at work and at home, and ultimately must decide to whom he will give his loyalty and how he will deal with the consequences of betrayal.

Within the Circus, Peter Guillam has been brought up in the shadow of his five bosses: George Smiley, Percy Alleline (Toby Jones), Bill Haydon (Colin Firth), Toby Esterhase (David Dencik), and Roy Bland (Ciaran Hinds), who work for the all-powerful leader called Control (John Hurt). After Control is forced out in a power struggle, Smiley—Control's right-hand man—also is sent into retirement. When a mole within the Circus needs to be found, Smiley is brought out of retirement to determine which of his former colleagues is a Soviet double agent. Because Smiley can trust Guillam, he secretly enlists the younger man's help in a dangerous undercover assignment. Guillam is asked to go against all he believes in order to spy on "his own" and help destroy the mole.

The idea that someone subversive can hide in plain sight and fool even his closest companions takes on two meanings in Guillam's story. He believes in the organization for which he works and is sickened by the idea that someone who has mentored him may be a traitor. Similarly, in the macho world of 1970s-era real-life 007-styled spies, Guillam might be perceived as a traitor to the organization because he is gay. After all, the film takes place only a few years after the decrim-inalisation of homosexuality in Britain, and the macho world of the Circus is hardly likely to embrace an openly gay man.

In one of the few personal scenes in this spy thriller, Smiley warns Guillam that he is being carefully watched by his bosses and might want to "tidy up" or do some "housekeeping"—taking care of any secret relationships that might stand in the way of the job. The film cuts to Guillam arriving home, where his partner awaits. Although Guillam has no dialogue in this scene showing his lover packing and dropping off his key, the silence is telling. Guillam has effectively silenced his sexuality. He twists his "wedding" ring before removing it and breaking into tears once his partner is out the door.

Cumberbatch has few typical "mannerisms" across roles, but, in this scene as well as in *Frankenstein,* he bounces his leg to show anxiety. His characters sometimes have a moment when they have no overt outlet for their anxiety. They cannot scream, lash out, or even move beyond where they are sitting. Their pent-up emotion is released through the nervous tic of a rapid leg movement that is so subtle as to be barely noticeable. Guillam does that in this scene, perhaps because he is so used to being emotionally controlled in public that he also feels constrained at home, even when his heart is breaking. Perhaps, after Smiley's warning, Guillam realises that he likely is being observed and hopes not to break down "on camera." Although he does cry at the conclusion of this scene, in the moments preceding his tears, that too-tense leg is the only indicator of his emotional breakdown. (Similarly, in *Frankenstein,* the Creature also bounces his leg as he eagerly awaits the bride that Victor promises him if he will only wait quietly while the scientist completes his creation.)

In *Tinker Tailor,* Smiley becomes the focal point for Guillam's loyalty, no matter what emotional or physical peril results. Cumberbatch explained that "Guillam sacrifices a lot for Smiley, a man he respects enormously and regards almost as a parental figure. Guillam sees Smiley as a man who is trustworthy in an increasingly opaque and slippery moral landscape."[293] If Smiley tells Peter to get rid of his lover, for example, he trusts this advice and does so, and no mention is ever made of Guillam's sexuality in the rest of the film.

Some of the actor's choices reflect his character's deep-seated fear of discovery—likely, in part, because of his profession as much as his sexuality—and his ever-careful demeanour. He can never be sure who is watching or what conclusions they may draw, so his actions conform to the expected behaviour of a heterosexual man. Oldman noted during the *Tinker Tailor* DVD commentary that Cumberbatch has Guillam turn his head to look at a mini-skirted young woman passing by but not pay attention to any other passerby on his way to the Circus. Oldman praised Cumberbatch for his attention to detail to show that Guillam is always aware of the way others perceive him, "even when no one is [apparently] looking."[294] Guillam has to seem interested in pretty young women, even if he does nothing more than look.

Guillam's reactions to stress, however, nearly give him away several times. His hands shake nervously when he is afraid of being caught with papers pilfered from the Circus' archives. His eyes widen slightly when he is surprised and unsure how to react. His breathing rate changes when he is being subtly interrogated by one of his bosses at lunch (as shown in a scene deleted from the film but available on disc). Cumberbatch reveals the cracks in Guillam's carefully constructed façade and his fear of being discovered to be something he is not. In this role more than other major movie roles, Cumberbatch "shows" as much as "thinks" on screen. Guillam's inner life is carefully hidden in most scenes, but when it is revealed, Cumberbatch does so with subtle but important physical actions—shaking hands, a bouncing knee, widened eyes, or rapid breathing.

Tinker Tailor was better received in the U.K. than in the U.S., where audiences often complained of its slow pace (compared with spy thrillers like a Bond or Bourne film). At home, however, the best British film of the year earned Cumberbatch a British Independent Film Award nomination as best supporting actor. Perhaps more important to the actor, it was his first "grown up" role,[295] and the shoot was "absolutely extraordinary." The "making of" video was shot after a particularly memorable day's filming. "I'm framing my call sheet from yesterday," Cumberbatch enthused, "because it was Colin Firth, Kathy Burke, Tom Hardy, Steven Graham, Gary Oldman, Mark Strong, Toby Jones, Ciaran Hinds, John Hurt. I mean, it was an extraordinary day at work."[296]

Parade's End (2012)

Because Cumberbatch is in transition to becoming an international "product," to use a crass term, whose performances are sold to audiences outside the U.K., his star turn in Tom Stoppard's *Parade's End* is an interesting choice of role. The miniseries became a co-production of three companies, but the press most often emphasised the BBC-HBO partnership. *Parade's End* aired in the U.K. in autumn 2012, about a year after filming was completed in England and Belgium, and the miniseries was in post-production while Cumberbatch began receiving numerous nominations or awards for his work on stage, in film, and on television.

At the time the drama was cast, however, Tom Stoppard needed to help convince HBO executives that this actor would be perfect for the lead. The writer called the greatest living British playwright visited Cumberbatch on the set of Steven Spielberg's *War Horse* and, although he could not offer the role yet, knew he had found his Christopher Tietjens. Cumberbatch even was wearing his World War I officer's uniform, which allowed Stoppard to see how the actor might look in his own World War I drama.[297] In contrast, HBO—and, in large part, the U.S. audience in general—was unfamiliar with Cumberbatch's work. Director Susanna White recalled "a famous breakfast at The Ivy when HBO said, 'Who is this Benedict Cumberbatch?' And we said, 'Trust us, he's a truly great actor and by the time *Parade's End* has come out everyone will have heard of him'."[298] In truth, by the time the project was broadcast in the U.S. in 2013, the actor had become a much more familiar face because of *Sherlock* but also for the vast amount of speculation surrounding his role in *Star Trek*, much of which had been filmed in Los Angeles at Paramount Studios during the first half of 2012.

Perhaps it is ironic that an actor moving toward international appeal and selecting a variety of roles, either as a member of an international cast (e.g., *The Hobbit* trilogy, *Star Trek*) or as part of an U.S. film focusing on very regional American families (e.g., *Twelve Years a Slave, August: Osage County*), would be so clearly identified with Britain in his first starring role in what was touted as a high-profile HBO drama. Christopher Tietjens is a man out of time, even during his own era in the early 1900s; his moral compass and conservative pride harken to an Empire more than a century previous. He could not be more British, and U.S. audiences are not accustomed to their protagonists having quite such a stiff upper lip or, as the emotionally controlled Tietjens was fond of doing in many scenes, frowning, his downturned mouth a primary facial feature. As well, even among the trend of British series such as *Downton Abbey*, which U.S. audiences watched faithfully on PBS, *Parade's End* is concerned more than most miniseries with class manners, Anglican-Catholic differences, a determinedly British perspective on the Great War (including one character's condescension and derision of Canadian enlisted troops), and suffragettes. Cumberbatch summarised the miniseries as "an elegy to the death throes of the Edwardian upper classes seen through the paradigm of a love triangle between Christopher, Sylvia Satterthwaite, his wife, and a young suffragette, Valentine Wannop"[299]—not typically the stuff of HBO blockbusters. In another interview, Cumberbatch commented that *Parade's End* is far from "some crappy, easily digestible milk-chocolate" but is "hard work, but it will pay dividends if you stick with it."[300]

Nevertheless, the well-made, finely acted drama shows that Cumberbatch can carry a leading role in an extended movie/miniseries marketed to global audiences. (*Sherlock* is far more of an acting partnership that pairs Cumberbatch and Freeman in a majority of scenes. *Parade's End* separates its three leads in many scenes, so that Tietjens works "alone" in much of the miniseries.) Perhaps unfortunately for Cumberbatch's efforts to establish himself in Hollywood as well as London, his two television roles (2011-2013) with the potential to reach a mainstream American audience far more than can a single U.S. film or a high-profile science fiction/fantasy genre film are inherently British: Sherlock Holmes and Christopher Tietjens. Although he *is* British, he needs to avoid being typecast in Hollywood as a member of a specific class or national "type."

When HBO announced the broadcast dates for *Parade's End* (26-28 February 2013), critics questioned whether HBO knew what to do with the miniseries. The cable network's promotion was decidedly lower key than its usual media saturation for something like *Game of Thrones*. HBO ran two episodes of *Parade's End* on Tuesday and Wednesday nights, with the one-hour conclusion on Thursday. To some critics, the miniseries seemed buried in the middle of the week instead of being a centrepiece of weekend programming. *Variety* wrote that Cumberbatch's "emotionally stunted character and uncomfortable circumstances make this stiffest-of-upper-lipped love stories a muddy slog."[301] U.S. reviews, such as this one, lacked U.K. reviewers' fondness for Cumberbatch or the miniseries, which led nominations for the Broadcasting Press Guild Award in early February 2013 and led to Cumberbatch's best actor award.

Whatever its ultimate role in Cumberbatch's evolving career, *Parade's End* gave the actor a chance to play a character for whom he felt great affection. Initially, however, he had to overcome a few obstacles in order to "become" the character. In Ford Madox Ford's novel, Tietjens is overweight and bears no physical resemblance to Cumberbatch. The actor not only gained weight by "force-feeding" himself doughnuts, but he insisted on wearing a fat suit and facial bumpers in order to attain the character's appropriate introductory look.[302] As with any character, getting to his heart and understanding him required a lot more than window dressing. Cumberbatch explained that he visualised London's Mayor as an entry point to the character: "I saw him as Boris Johnson to start off with . . . [a] very intelligent but rather oafish buffoon."[303] Because Christopher Tietjens is not a typical protagonist, Cumberbatch initially feared that his character would not be able to compete with the drama's more emotionally revealing and extroverted characters. While filming battle scenes for the miniseries, he explained that "[t]he colours and variations of all the other characters are going to sort of mask [Tietjens'] very quiet journey, but then I thought that the real challenge is to bring that across, and that's a filmic skill, to do internal thought. Internal life with the camera is a great thing to be asked to do." The actor praised Stoppard's script, which allowed him "to play subtext with lines where you're mining something far deeper than the superficial wit . . . . Tom's fantastic script is . . . gold for that."[304]

"I sympathise with his care, sense of duty and virtue, his intelligence in the face of hypocritical, self-serving mediocrity, his appreciation of quality and his love for his country. He mourns a way of life that is being eroded by money, schemers and politicians, ineffectual military boobies and the carelessness of man's industrialised progress."[305] This type of quotation aligns Cumberbatch the actor with the weightiness and perceived intellectualism of a classic BBC production. The miniseries is not typical family viewing, and even the many critics who praised *Parade's End* noted that it was sometimes hard to understand. After the first two episodes that more faithfully follow Ford Madox Ford's first book in a much longer series, later episodes seemed rushed in order to complete the story within its allotted five. *Parade's End* is designed for thinking audiences who want to engage with the issues of this time period as much as enjoy an attractive, entertaining cast. In short, *Parade's End* seems to be created for an audience very much like Cumberbatch—intelligent, thoughtful, and well versed in history.

Audiences who tuned into *Parade's End* could understand why Cumberbatch is so highly prized in the acting community: his finely nuanced performance illustrates degrees of emotional conflict within a man his wife calls a "great lump of wood." Cumberbatch captured Tietjens' stiff bearing—in one scene, the uniformed Tietjens walks down a London street as if he is "at attention" with straight spine and excellent posture, his arms held stiffly a few inches from his sides as he marches purposefully forth. However, the actor also revealed that Christopher does have emotions but keeps them to himself, often to his wife's frustration and displeasure. When, in the second episode, she gently tells him that his mother has died, Cumberbatch's eyes and fleeting facial expressions are all he needs to eloquently convey Christopher's rapidly changing emotions and his return to ironclad control.

Cumberbatch's face is open and merely curious as he waits to hear what Sylvia says. When she tells him his mother has died, Cumberbatch looks down, but the audience understands that he really is looking inward, his eyes suddenly glimmering with tears he does not allow to fall. His open expression becomes deadened as he deals with this great loss. He nods slightly to pull himself together and swallows twice. He then adds the briefest hesitation to the line, "I did not expect it quite yet."[306] His body has not moved; there have been no grand gestures or actorly emoting to indicate the man's profound loss and heartrending sorrow. Cumberbatch has kept true to Tietjens' belief in keeping his emotions private with no outward outburst, but he allows the character to reveal his vulnerability and deepest feelings in a single moment of "weakness" when he is caught off guard by his wife's announcement.

For Christopher, this is an emotional outburst, and Cumberbatch shows Tietjens' deep love for his mother and the immediate sorrow at the realisation of what he has lost. He also is emotionally vulnerable in front of the wife who abandoned him for another lover and, more in this scene than most, expresses his emotions. He shows greater restraint in scenes audiences might expect to be highly emotive: his sexual romp with Sylvia on a train, bewilderment on the front lines, or reluctant courtship of Valentine. The only scene that similarly invites audiences to see Christopher's gentleness and understanding of tender emotion is one early in the miniseries when he comforts his baby son after a nightmare. Cumberbatch is very good at portraying Tietjens before, during, and immediately after World War I, but his internal battles are the ones most crucial to his and the audience's understanding of this character.

Director White explained why Cumberbatch is "one of only a handful of actors" who could convincingly portray Tietjens: "Benedict has a tremendous inner life as an actor. So even if he's not speaking in a whole scene, you read so much into what he's feeling. And that's a very special quality."[307] Cumberbatch makes the character's thoughts clear without dialogue or overt action. He knows how much—or how little—to show at a given time, but he obviously thoroughly understands and inhabits the character. This facet of Cumberbatch's acting is a skill well worth bringing to audiences' (if not directors') attention, but the ability to express what the actor terms "internal life" is a technical skill that not every viewer might appreciate.

Perhaps it is not surprising that Cumberbatch feels so at ease in portraying British characters living through the social upheavals wrought by the First World War. Not only did he conduct specific research for his roles in *War Horse* and *Parade's End*, but he is familiar with literature of the early 1900s. In a Cheltenham Music Festival interview, he referenced, for example, James Joyce's *Ulysses*. His readings during that event further illustrate his comfort with the art associated with such a nation-defining time. In fact, he wanted to participate in the 2012 festival because of his fascination with this era: "I've become a bit obsessed with [World War I] and the music of the period," not only through his involvement with *War Horse* and *Parade's End*, but from school. "It's something that's really got under my skin. I went to a school with a massive war memorial and [was] made very aware, very conscious of the sacrifices of generations of men our age, in the first and second world wars, as well as all the wars since then. . . . The First World War has always fascinated me. I met the last three survivors when I read at the Scimitar in 2009."[308] During filming of

Parade's End, he visited the area that once was the Western Front.[309]

Additionally, his familiarity with post-war artists who captured the fragmentation of society and provided a new way to look at art—and at oneself—resonate with his work in *Parade's End*. At the Cheltenham Music Festival, he commented upon Picasso, Cubism,[310] and the shift between romanticism and modernism, noting that "[c]ulturally we couldn't look at ourselves the same way [after the war]."[311] Certainly the characters of *Parade's End* also are equally fragmented as the elements of a Picasso; they put together the pieces of their lives in surprising new forms by the end of the story. The miniseries' title credits present images of the lead characters as mirror shards that create a kaleidoscope, an effect not only appropriate for the story's structure (e.g., scenes presented out of chronological order or referenced in flashback; intercut scenes showing the separated lead characters' wartime lives) but to the shattering of lives and social norms during this period of history. Cumberbatch not only understands these connections between the current adaptation and its associations with art and literature of the previous century, but his explanations help audiences develop a more thorough appreciation of *Parade's End*.

Turning Points and Transition

Each of these roles provided a turning point in the way the entertainment industry and audiences perceived the talent of Benedict Cumberbatch. *Hawking* introduced Cumberbatch to British television audiences in a dramatic role unlike anything he had previously played on screen.

197

As the title character, he delivered a believable but not maudlin performance, one that started a long progression of awards for his television work. Even today, *Hawking* remains one of Cumberbatch's most memorable performances and one frequently cited as a high point in his television career. *Sherlock* challenged Cumberbatch in a different way—as a lead and iconic title character in a television series, one so popular that it propelled him to international fame and made him a household name in Britain. *Sherlock* led to dozens of other roles and a wider global profile as an actor, one increasingly courted by high-powered directors. However, Cumberbatch's roots in the theatre also showcased his talent to a different audience worldwide. With the popularity of NT Live's broadcasts of *Frankenstein* and critical acclaim resulting in best actor awards, the *Sherlock* success story fed into *Frankenstein*'s popularity and proved that Cumberbatch can carry a production and achieve amazing dramatic heights (often requiring great physical sacrifice) in multiple media. Although HBO executives may not have been familiar with Cumberbatch when *Parade's End* was being cast, they and a growing American audience had been introduced to the actor by the time the miniseries was broadcast in the U.S. in 2013. By then, *Parade's End* and its cast were gathering awards for excellence. *Sherlock* and, to a lesser extent, *Frankenstein* fuelled Cumberbatch's recent film career, which began to include more big-budget films, including British best picture *Tinker Tailor Soldier Spy*. His success in *Parade's End* reminded casting agents and directors that Cumberbatch could be a lead in a major motion picture as well as a valued member of an all-star ensemble. Although

Cumberbatch's roles and successes began to market him more specifically to audiences beyond U.K. borders, he still was most closely associated with British characters and productions instead of commercial Hollywood films.

Chapter 6 Hollywood Knocking

"Maybe after *Star Trek*, then I'll become one . . . . I don't know, I mean, start calling me it, why not? I can be Benedict Cumberbatch, movie star."[312]
Benedict Cumberbatch, 2012

When Cumberbatch talked about his first extended foray into Hollywood to film *Star Trek: Into Darkness*, he both embraced the town and disavowed becoming a stereotypical Hollywood actor. He told the *Radio Times* that LA "is all about extremes . . . , so you get the worst excesses of everything—the health-kick thing, over-indulgence, recreational drug use, everything. It's paradise!"[313] In January 2012 he had decried becoming the Hollywood stereotype ("a huge blogging response to me selling out to Hollywood and dating a model and become a walking cliché. That was nice."[314]), after being linked with Lydia Hearst during the Academy Awards parties and being faulted for apparently dating a decade-younger, beautiful, rich, blonde lingerie model.[315] By August that year he had become so stressed from being "castigated as a moaning, rich, public-school b-----d, complaining about only getting posh roles" that he admitted that he might "want to go to America."[316] His growing celebrity and introduction to U.S. audiences via *Sherlock* made some fans (mostly in the U.K.) lament that Cumberbatch has "gone Hollywood," especially in light of an *Independent* interview that quoted him as saying "I'm playing a really big game now . . . . I'm going into studios to meet executives and heads of production . . . . I'm interested in just playing the game a little bit, because it gives you a lot more choice. It gives you power and if you become indispensable to that machine it gives you a greater variety, which is what I always wanted. My career is about longevity." As far as his role models, Cumberbatch cited Brad Pitt and George Clooney, two film stars "who get film screen net . . . . They're great people to emulate as a business model."[317]

Although choosing to work on a series of films back to back seems very much a cerebral decision in a head vs. heart debate, the truth is that, while Cumberbatch is still in transition to movie stardom, he often chooses the type of project with the greatest appeal, and possibly greatest long-term payoff, instead of going for the biggest cheque. Fans may be surprised to learn that movie work often does not pay as much as they might expect, especially when Cumberbatch is *this* close but not quite to the point of being a name that ensures big box office. *Star Trek,* for example, "was hard work, but you're paid to scale. The money with films is what directors get to play with, that's what you really notice. [As an actor] you can get paid more for doing TV work than you can for films. . . . I could have made much more money if I'd stuck around doing plays than if I was in *Star Trek*. But you just get to play with bigger toys that no other schedule or budget would allow in a TV structure."[318]

Star Trek also paid dividends with its big advertising budget; the actor became known to millions of American television viewers through the film's Super Bowl trailer, which was rated by fans and critics among the top trailers shown during the game. Super Bowl XLVII scored the third highest ratings in U.S. television history and was watched by 108.4 million viewers (71 percent of television households).[319] Of course, not everyone watches Super Bowl commercials and movie trailers, but they are so well done—and cost so much for that coveted advertising time—that the non-game time was as almost as closely watched at the football game itself.

Furthermore, Cumberbatch was singled out in several commentaries on the Monday after the Super Bowl. The Bleacher Report listed *Star Trek*'s as the best among a crowded field of summer blockbuster trailers and noted that "[m]uch of the *Star Trek Into Darkness* trailer focused on Benedict Cumberbatch's character, who's the main villain in the movie. . . . Those who have seen Cumberbatch in *Sherlock* and *Tinker Tailor Soldier Spy* will be able to attest to the skill of the British actor. He'll be a tremendous foil to Chris Pine."[320] Those who could not or did not watch the Super Bowl still could view the *Star Trek* trailer online, and sites like Sherlockology hyped the trailer; therefore, the resulting total number of people worldwide who watched Cumberbatch as Captain Kirk's nemesis likely greatly exceeds the Super Bowl audience.

Such anticipation for Cumberbatch's forthcoming films is new. Although he has worked in Hollywood-backed films before and had LA premieres, beginning with *Starter for 10* in February 2007, he has seldom been part of a film with such buzz. Not even the second film in *The Hobbit* trilogy has created quite so much interest as Cumberbatch's role, and although *War Horse* and *Tinker Tailor Soldier Spy* won award nominations, they still did not receive the amount of critical acclaim or the box office totals that might have been expected. *Atonement* also generated interest in Cumberbatch as the lecherous character who contributes to star James McAvoy's character's downfall and demise. This film, too, brought Cumberbatch to Hollywood and peripherally promoted him, but he was not the leading actor, and this "bad guy" character was hardly the legendary villain of a sci-fi blockbuster. Although Hollywood has come knocking numerous times previously, Cumberbatch has certainly opened the door to media blitz and global attention with his choice of film roles in 2012-13.

Atonement (2007)

Cumberbatch's role in *Atonement* got him noticed as an actor, but perhaps not in the way that ultimately would bode well for a long-lived Hollywood career. "Bite it. You have to bite it," Paul Marshall commandingly enunciates as he too-intently watches an underage girl slide a chocolate bar past her lips. The confectionary magnate at first seems to be magnanimously sharing his company's sweets with a friend's children, but Marshall's laser gaze and tense fixation on the girl quickly turn the scene ominous. Although Cumberbatch plays what *The Guardian* later called one of the actor's "small parts in big films,"[321] his moments are screen are suavely menacing. Marshall is a pivotal role in this tale of pre-World War II loss of innocence and the sequence of events that condemns one young man (played by James McAvoy) for the crime committed by another.

The film was hyped to win several Academy Awards, but, of its six nominations, including best picture, it took home only the Oscar for best original score. *Atonement* received the coveted best picture honour at home at the British Academy Film Awards. It won a great deal of Hollywood attention, especially for stars Keira Knightley, James McAvoy, and newcomer Saoirse Ronan, after being feted at film festivals from Venice to Vancouver. *Variety* praised the film's lead performers and heralded *Atonement* as "both a ravishing period romancer and sophisticated narrative puzzle."[322]

Cumberbatch frequently strode the red carpet and, especially at the London premiere, received more time with the media, which helped create a higher industry profile from his association with a major film receiving accolades around the world. Nevertheless, *Atonement* did less than might be expected to propel Cumberbatch toward film stardom. It more importantly brought the actor to the attention of future *Sherlock* producer and creator, Sue Vertue and Steven Moffat, who, after seeing *Atonement,* only thought of Cumberbatch when they were casting their Sherlock Holmes.[323] With hindsight, critics can trace Cumberbatch's later film success back to the breakthrough performance in *Sherlock,* which can be attributed to a well-received role in *Atonement.*

War Horse (2011)

As the author of *War Horse,* the book upon which Steven Spielberg's film is based, Michael Morpurgo received special on-set treatment. A *New Statesman* article reported the author "watching a scene and the actors Benedict Cumberbatch and Tom Hiddleston playing army officers, poring over a battle plan. Spielberg filmed take after take, altering an arm here, an expression there, the actors responding to his every direction," then turning to Morpurgo "after the tenth attempt to whisper:

'They're just like Ferraris.'"[324] Successful actors are able to "adapt [their] choices and training to suit the demands of different narrative, cinematic, and shooting styles . . . . Many actors see their ability to adapt to narrative and directorial demands as the special expertise for which they are hired."[325] In other words, effective actors are able to give directors what they want, and Cumberbatch and Hiddleston fit that description. Their training allows them to adjust their physical and vocal choices to the director's method of storytelling and vision for a film.

The scene being filmed near Dartmouth that day is a pivotal one in the film and Cumberbatch's role as Major Jamie Stewart. Because of Major Stewart's interpretation of the intelligence he receives, he develops a battle plan that quickly sours and leads to the death or capture of the soldier in his regiment. Cumberbatch is appropriately commanding in this scene, and as the cavalry mounts for battle, he delivers a stirring speech that was included in both the U.K. and U.S. movie trailers. The actor plays a confident officer assured of his command—and vain enough to think his powerful steed Topthorne can outrace any other horse—whose sudden realisation that those in his command are about to be slaughtered is yet another silent character-defining moment in Cumberbatch's film resume. The dawning horror of seeing German cannons and technology beyond swords and horses flashes across Stewart's face as he understands the depth of his mistake in underestimating his enemy. Even as the crane-mounted camera pulls back, Stewart can be seen at the corner of the ever-widening shot; he refuses to surrender and only dismounts, stabbing his sword into the ground, when he is surrounded by Germans and has nowhere else to ride.

Even at a distance, Cumberbatch's body language telegraphs the Major's pride and resistance to defeat.[326]

Cumberbatch earned more than the director's praise for his work on the film, but the casting got off to a rocky start. His agent relayed the exciting news that "Steven Spielberg has rung and he is a fan of Benedict Cumberbatch."[327] However, the actor was running late and could not find a parking space when he was scheduled to meet the director.[328] Fortunately, the script reading and chat with Spielberg went well, and a little more than a week later Cumberbatch learned he had the role. Achieving higher profile roles in major films has twice (for *War Horse* and *Tinker Tailor*) prompted the actor to say such news was a "grown up" moment. It also was a major step forward in his film career.

A skill necessary for the film, one requiring intensive lessons in preparation for filming, was horseback riding. Although "outward bound and gregarious" young Cumberbatch had long ago taken lessons as "just another activity that could stop me from getting into trouble,"[329] he needed to apply himself more diligently this time around. Not all went smoothly. At one point, the actor's horse spooked, sending him on a terrifyingly unplanned gallop; during another, he miscommunicated with his horse, which reared and nearly fell over backward.

Spielberg insisted on filming the pivotal cavalry scene with real actors and horses, not a few doubles and a CGI army. The result is a visually stunning cinematic triumph (perhaps even more so because the director also insisted on using 35mm film one more time in an industry committed to digital). Cumberbatch's riding lessons paid off in the exultation of filming the cavalry charge: "I cannot describe the feeling of riding that day. . . . [T]here is no other place on Earth for you to ride with 80 men and 80 horses. It was a real privilege to have been trained up to that level."[330] The actor became emotional after the first take. "I was so breathless with excitement I nearly fell off the horse. I actually saw stars in front of my eyes and thought I was going to faint. The second time I had a bit more control but was still giddy with excitement. And the third time I was an emotional wreck. I had to really try hard not to cry."[331]

The actor well recognised the cachet of being in a Spielberg film and being able to collaborate with the great director. "He can cast unknowns and have box office draw because it's his film. The point is this," Cumberbatch reiterated, "he is utterly human, approachable, avuncular, and inclusive."[332] Having such a positive working relationship with Spielberg, who has been free in his praise of Cumberbatch, moved the actor into greater prominence during Hollywood awards season. Cumberbatch may not have made a red carpet appearance at the Oscars in 2011, but he was highly visible at the many parties surrounding the ceremony. He sat at the director's table at the Golden Globes and was shown on camera a few times on U.S. television. *War Horse* may not have been Cumberbatch's star vehicle, but it was a leap forward in Hollywood and established a precedent in American media of being praised by a high-profile director discussing a long-awaited film project.

Star Trek: Into Darkness (2013)

"Enjoy your last moments of peace, for I have returned and shall have my vengeance. . . . So, shall we begin?"[333] Noting that Cumberbatch's "creepy voiceover and broody presence is the clear highlight of the short clip" released in December 2012 and complimenting the actor on "doing a great job of establishing menace," one critic immediately asked if the next stop for Cumberbatch might be the Oscars.[334] The actor's rich, dark voice neatly balanced the mayhem director J. J. Abrams promised would be revealed to excited fans already awaiting the May 2013 premiere. Interestingly enough, Cumberbatch's voice is heard in the trailer long before his face appears on screen, emphasising what many critics and fans say is the actor's strong point and most marketable feature: his voice.

In many ways, this snippet of dialogue from the first teaser also signals a major shift in the way the film industry perceives Cumberbatch and tips the scale toward his being recognised globally as a true movie star. At the end of 2012, Cumberbatch may have been enjoying his last moments of peace before his already-escalating career pace and popularity enter a whole new dimension. The actor may not be seeking vengeance on those who doubted his talent or ability to gain star status, but *Star Trek: Into Darkness* is a definitive beginning for Cumberbatch's star phase as an internationally recognised celebrity and a potential Hollywood A-lister. The release of this trailer in December 2012 was carefully timed to coincide with a peak movie-going time of year. The film's first official publicity included a teaser poster, a media PR event in Tokyo, and a nine-minute trailer distributed to select IMAX cinemas, many in the U.S. showing *The Hobbit* and thus providing a welcome bit of cross-promotion for the actor.

In Japan in early December to promote the movie with Captain Kirk himself (Chris Pine), Cumberbatch looked pleased to be accosted by so many ardent female fans. This encounter meant more than just another international gathering of Cumberbatch's faithful being overwhelmed and awed by his visit. Paramount paired Cumberbatch—the lead villain generating most of the buzz about the next instalment of the *Star Trek* franchise—with the film's and franchise's de facto hero Kirk. The good guy-bad guy dichotomy made for intriguing speculation about the film and Cumberbatch's obviously impressive role in it, but it also marked the first time that Cumberbatch significantly stood out from the rest of the cast in publicity for a forthcoming film. The trailer received an enormous amount of positive press and, if such a thing possible, seemed to generate additional fan frenzy. Cumberbatch was placed firmly in the spotlight as a Hollywood blockbuster star with this first *Star Trek* promotional junket.

Another interesting development occurred in December 2012. For the first time since becoming popular as Sherlock, Cumberbatch was identified in the media as "*Star Trek*'s Cumberbatch" instead of the previously common "*Sherlock*'s Cumberbatch." The shift was not lost on the actor's management, who, according to Cumberbatch, "was just wetting themselves" when the early teaser trailer received such immediate acclaim. On his way home from Japan, Cumberbatch stopped in Los Angeles and attended the Children's Defense Fund Beat the Odds gala at the Beverly Hilton Hotel. He told one reporter that his talent agency "were ringing me up and sending me emails. It's really exciting."[335]

That *Star Trek* marked another big shift in his career was duly noted about a year earlier, when Cumberbatch enlisted the help of two friends during the holiday season to submit an audition recording filmed on an iPhone. Abrams was reportedly highly impressed, and Cumberbatch was "pleased when I got the offer. But I know the second [Abrams' *Star Trek* film] will become far-bigger scale, so I felt terror instantly."[336] A year later, the actor began enjoying the results of his stellar performance and its appeal not only to audiences, which will gain him fans within another genre (science fiction) and a broader international fan base, but to Hollywood insiders who can see him as a bankable actor for much higher-profile films. Cumberbatch may have invested his heart in getting the role under some difficult time constraints and with limited technology to assist him in presenting the best audition possible, but his head not only recognised the potential of this acting challenge in December 2011 but, in late 2012, began to realise just how far this film might take him.

Prominent media magazines such as U.K. film specialist *Empire* and U.S. pop culture favourite *Entertainment Weekly* featured Cumberbatch in his *Star Trek* role on the covers of February 2013 issues, months before the film's release. The film's premiere date was scheduled earlier—with the U.K. receiving the film a week before U.S. audiences would see it—indicating not only intense interest in what was expected to become *the* summer blockbuster but giving Cumberbatch's home turf the film release advantage.

During the first press interviews for this film, the actor described his as-yet-unrevealed character as "very ruthless . . . not a clearly good or evil character. He is a villain but the actions he takes [have] intent and reason. He is a complicated character not to be judged by white-or-black, or good-or-evil. But this is the appeal of JJ's works and I felt challenged as an actor."[337]

Even in the brief glimpse provided by the trailer, Cumberbatch's character is commanding and confident. His focus is intense, and he clearly has the intelligence and determination to carry out a well-planned attack. According to the teaser's dialogue, he also is deeply emotional, if highly controlled, choosing to destroy the world to protect his family and to exact vengeance for what had been done to them. As the actor noted in the Tokyo promotional event, his character may be ruthless and his destruction worthy of the label of a villain, but he also may be, to a lesser extent, sympathetic because of the reasons behind his destructive acts. Perhaps more than most actors, Cumberbatch excels at again revealing the "inner life" of a character and making him multidimensional beyond the limitations of dialogue or, in the case of *Star Trek*, big-budget action sequences.

The Fifth Estate and *The Imitation Game*

In early October 2012, Cumberbatch began talks with Dreamworks about a new film detailing the early days of Wikileaks and its founder, Julian Assange.[338] By November, Cumberbatch had signed on, and the rest of the cast was assembled by December. At that time the film had the working title *The Man Who Sold the World*.[339] When it went into production a few weeks later, it had been retitled *The Fifth Estate*. Whereas Peter Jackson's *Hobbit* trilogy rescheduled star Martin Freeman's scenes so that he could film the second series of *Sherlock,* the third series of *Sherlock* was bumped back from its original January start date to accommodate the actors' schedules. Cumberbatch began filming *The Fifth Estate* around the time that he originally planned to return to playing Sherlock. The Assange project went quickly into development from initial discussions to casting to filming, perhaps in part because other films with similar subject matter also had been announced to be filmed in 2013. It is interesting that *Sherlock's* producers and the BBC could accommodate Cumberbatch's increasingly crowded schedule, and fortunate for the actor that he could play both intriguing roles guaranteed to bring him to greater attention in the entertainment industry.

When *Star Trek: Into Darkness* began filming in January 2012 in Los Angeles, a few fans managed to send autograph requests to Cumberbatch via Paramount studios. At that time, the actor was well known for *Sherlock* but not yet a hot property in the U.S. Within a few weeks, not only Trekkers/Trekkies clamoured for any insider information (or leaked photographs, some showing Cumberbatch in a deadly battle with Zachary Quinto's Spock), but Cumberbatch fans also were scouring websites and studio locations for a glimpse of the latest *Star Trek* villain. After the famous photo leak, Abrams had a huge wall constructed around the set to pre-empt paparazzi or ardent fans from getting too close a look at filming.

How much difference a year makes, especially once Hollywood and global media begin following the actor whom several critics have declared a star to watch in 2013. When *The Fifth Estate* began filming in mid-January 2013, Dreamworks released a still only days into production. That this studio began shooting earlier than two other announced films about Wikileaks' Julian Assange was a coup; later films would naturally have to compete with the first and be compared with it. The lone photograph showed Cumberbatch with long white-blond locks, seriously tweezed eye brows (especially in comparison with red carpet photographs from the Golden Globes earlier in January), and a differently shaped face, which fan tweets attributed to false teeth to make Cumberbatch look much more like Assange. Within a few hours of the photograph's release, it had appeared on news, entertainment, and fan sites and generated plenty of buzz. Sites like CBS News and CNN in the U.S., which previously had not carried Cumberbatch news, ran articles with the just-released photograph. These U.S. mainstream news outlets carry entertainment news but do not promote it exclusively like the E! entertainment network or online/print magazine *Entertainment Weekly,* but the choice of controversial subject matter (both Assange and Wikileaks) undoubtedly made the start of filming more newsworthy to them. It also provided Cumberbatch with wider coverage in the U.S. of his role in a forthcoming, and now more likely audience-anticipated, film.

Dreamworks also announced the film's release date as 15 November,[340] a quick turnaround for a mainstream film, but it would allow *The Fifth Estate* to be considered for Academy Award nominations and, with Cumberbatch as the film's lead, suggests that Dreamworks will put him forward for best actor consideration. If that speculation becomes fact, Cumberbatch's status in Hollywood would be considered the proverbial "meteoric rise" in the two years since *War Horse* was nominated for Oscars and Golden Globes and the actor merely sat with other cast members at the director's table.

As further testament to fan interest in Cumberbatch, the studio carefully guarded filming locations, only noting that they were "abroad" from the actor's London home base. On Twitter, however, fans shared grainy candid photos of Cumberbatch on set in Iceland and debated when shooting moved to Germany.[341] Further tweets about the casting of extras and the film's current shooting location illustrate how closely fans follow Cumberbatch and effectively establish their own network. Unlike in 2012, when a few lucky fans received autographs and replies to mail addressed to Paramount, by 2013 the actor and studios more closely guarded production schedules and the actor's whereabouts because he was being more methodically sought by a greater number of fans.

Films like *The Fifth Estate* are far more likely to appeal to a wider adult audience and to make Cumberbatch a more recognisable, and thus bankable, name as a film lead. With Dreamworks behind the film, it is practically guaranteed a good deal of publicity and could be the next big stepping stone toward Cumberbatch's Hollywood film career. Although *Star Trek* and *The Hobbit*, for example, have provided Cumberbatch with more press and generated more general audience interest in his career, these films are still part of niche genres that, although highly appealing to science fiction or fantasy fans, often do not reach a wide middle-of-the-road audience and are not as often singled out for critical praise for its actors. At least, if *The Fifth Estate* proves to be a critical and box office success, it could ensure that Cumberbatch could have his pick of future film roles and determine the direction his film career will take internationally.

Although *Sherlock* instigated the recent spate of film opportunities, Cumberbatch's careful choice and variety of roles (including blockbuster *Star Trek* and high-profile roles in *The Fifth Estate, Twelve Years a Slave,* and *August: Osage County,* among other projects released globally in 2013-14 and prepped to debut in time for U.K. and U.S. awards seasons) is the culmination of more than a decade of heart-head decisions nudging him toward prominence in film while, incongruously among most actors, keeping him busy with roles in a variety of often less lucrative and lower-profile roles in other media.

Just when fans wondered what the actor might be doing in 2014, because announcements of new projects had slowed for a few weeks, *Variety* announced yet another film role: the lead in director Guillermo Del Toro's *Crimson Peak* for Legendary Pictures. Probably because, at the time, Del Toro was reworking the script, the film could only be described as a "haunted house thriller" or ghost story.[342] Such a film would add horror/supernatural to the many genres Cumberbatch has embraced in his career, but, like sci-fi and fantasy, it appeals mostly to a niche or cult audience. Nevertheless,

Del Toro is a well-known and –respected director whose films get a great deal of industry and public attention. Association with Legendary Pictures also could add more fans to Cumberbatch's legions; this studio prides itself in "owning, producing and delivering content to mainstream audiences with a targeted focus on the powerful fandom demographic."[343] In addition to combining Legendary Comics with its film studio, the company acquired pop culture media giant Nerdist industries. It also is the studio home of blockbusters *Man of Steel* (2013) and *The Dark Knight Rises* (2012), which, along with Del Toro's reputation for intriguingly different films (e.g., *Hellboy, Pan's Labyrinth*) should help boost critical and fan interest in Cumberbatch's role.

By the time filming began on the third series of *Sherlock*, Cumberbatch quite obviously had become a man firmly in control of his career options and smartly making the most of his fame. Some choices would broaden his fan base, especially within genres well known for their dedicated fans (e.g., science fiction, fantasy, horror), especially within the U.S., where studios like Paramount, Dreamworks, and Legendary are based. Hollywood keeps knocking, and Cumberbatch has opened the door on a film career that will draw him to the U.S. for future projects. Although in December 2012 Cumberbatch was discussing publicity for *Star Trek*, the actor also unconsciously prophetically proclaimed about his film career, "We're only at the beginnings of it." For Cumberbatch, his management, and his ever-broadening, increasingly vocal fan base interested in seeing the actor in cineplexes worldwide, this is very good news indeed.

Chapter 7 The Shift from Actor to Celebrity or Star

"I read profile pieces—or I used to, before now. [Acting as if he reads a tabloid.] Oh, I learned something about that actor; oh, he sounds a bit pompous; he sounds a bit petty; he sounds funny; he sounds lovely; she sounds great; she's gorgeous; she's not so pretty; she's not who I thought she was.' Awful, judgmental s--- which, now that I'm going through it, I wish I could eat it all back."[344]
Benedict Cumberbatch, 2012

In *Star Studies: A Critical Guide,* Martin Shingler defines an actor's traditional path to stardom: "Many film actors become stars following a 'breakthrough' role in which their performance attracts the attention of film critics, receives rave reviews and is subsequently nominated for a major film award. On the back of this, they often gain a higher public profile, attain star status (with leading roles, top billing, and star vehicles) and sometimes acquire a recognizable and distinctive (often imitable) signature style."[345] Benedict Cumberbatch only somewhat has followed this pattern. Unlike most Hollywood stars, who may move from stage to film, film to television, or television to film, and primarily con-centrate on one medium, Cumberbatch is developing a film career primarily based on his international breakout role in *Sherlock,* but his parallel career in the theatre also provided him with an international breakthrough via dual roles in *Frankenstein.* Although Cumberbatch's *Sherlock* fans helped make *Frankenstein* a sell-out hit for the National Theatre, *Frankenstein*'s publicity and awards elevated Cumberbatch's profile as a leading man in the theatre. Because the recorded performances were shown globally through the NT Live program, they brought Cumberbatch-the-stage-actor to the attention of a much wider audience than did his star turn in the pre-*Sherlock* *After the Dance*. If Cumberbatch's "breakthrough" performances can be categorised by medium and degree of international attention, then *Sherlock* deserves that distinction for television but, at roughly the same time, *Frankenstein* must equally be considered the break-through role for the theatre.

However, going back a decade, *Hawking* must certainly be deemed a more traditional breakthrough performance, garnering Cumberbatch a great deal of attention and respect, plus awards. Nevertheless, this performance was not the big break that might have been expected if this actor's trajectory to stardom were going to follow a traditional order of star-making events. When so many of Cumberbatch's television, film, or theatre performances are award nominated and critically praised, "breakthrough" has less meaning than it might in a "traditional" star career. Unlike most actors who attain star status after one primary breakthrough role in one medium, Cumberbatch has mastered roles in multiple media and often had complementary star trajectories in several media at once, especially in television and theatre.

Cumberbatch's film career requires that one "breakthrough" role to make him a bona fide international film star. *Star Trek: Into Darkness* seems an appropriate vehicle for maximum attention by summer blockbuster movie crowds who may never have seen *Sherlock*, much less watched Cumberbatch's well-acted roles in films like *Tinker Tailor Soldier Spy* or *War Horse*. However, using

Star Trek for a star-making role is an interesting choice, if only because science fiction or fantasy films seldom earn much respect from the voting bodies who determine who wins major awards—including BAFTA and the Academy of Motion Picture Arts and Sciences. Playing a high-profile *Star Trek* villain and winning rave reviews from critics and fans can gain Cumberbatch a lot more media attention and the opportunity for new roles and a wider fan base, but it likely will do less for his reputation as a "serious actor" in Hollywood, where sci-fi blockbusters are better known for their box office receipts than Oscar recognition.

Similarly, no matter how fantastic a performance Cumberbatch gives as Smaug the dragon in Peter Jackson's *Hobbit* trilogy or is heavily featured in the second film, *The Desolation of Smaug,* the actor's voice is the "star" of this performance. Ask Andy Serkis, who received critical praise for his work as Gollum in *The Lord of the Rings* and *The Hobbit,* King Kong in Jackson's *King Kong* remake, and Caesar in *Rise of the Planet of the Apes*, how thoughtfully the Academy considers his work as an actor when he dons a motion-capture suit. Although for years fans and film critics have argued that an actor's performance, not whether that performance requires CGI, needs to be evaluated when determining best actor nominations, so far roles that involve CGI and motion capture have not received the same level of professional recognition as more traditional roles in which the actor can be clearly seen as him/herself, even in heavy make-up or prosthetics. Thus, Cumberbatch's much-anticipated roles in *Star Trek* or *The Hobbit* are unlikely to become his big breakthrough film roles—no matter how much money the movies make, how many new fans they bring him, or whether as a result he becomes a more familiar name around the world.

Which role may become his breakthrough international film role, one to rival the number of awards, amount of media attention, and enhanced professional reputation resulting from *Sherlock* or *Frankenstein*? *The Fifth Estate* is one possibility (as of the time of this book's publication in 2013). The role of Julian Assange is controversial. (Assange himself has decried the film in the press as propaganda but then reports surfaced that he and Cumberbatch are email buddies.)[346] The film gives Cumberbatch top billing as the title character. The film is being promoted by Dreamworks and scheduled for a late-2013 release so that it can be considered for major awards. In many respects, it seems like the dream role to make Cumberbatch a breakout film star. Nevertheless, to play Assange, Cumberbatch wears a white wig, and his chiselled cheekbones are less obvious when his face is rounded to look more like Assange's. As is typical of his performances, he should receive praise for his acting and his chameleon ability to portray characters far from his "look" or personality, but that tendency may not help him become as easily identifiable as a "typical" Hollywood leading man. Audiences unfamiliar with Cumberbatch before they enter the cinema may respect his acting talent, but they may not be able to easily recognise him outside this role.

The same is true for another role in a film to which Cumberbatch was attached in early 2013, *The Imitation Game.* After a flurry of announcements that Cumberbatch was considering the role of Alan Turing, a part once considered by Leonardo DiCaprio when the project was under development with another director, *Screen Daily* reported that FilmNation head "Glen Basner and his sales team will introduce *The Imitation Game* to buyers at the EFM [European Film Market]. Benedict Cumberbatch is attached to star in the drama, which CAA represents for US rights."[347] The Berlin film sales event has become a key place to find backers or distributors for proposed films. Using Cumberbatch's name to help sell the proposed film further indicates his growing significance in the film industry. *Variety* noted that "[o]n the three pics FilmNation introduced—the untitled Hugh Grant-Marisa Tomei romantic comedy, *Solace* and *The Imitation Game*—most territories will be pre-sold at Berlin." Further, the industry newspaper explained that EFM "underlined the indie biz's march towards the mainstream" and "underscored new indie sector film financing and sales energy in the U.S."[348] Although cinemas in 2013-14 showcase Cumberbatch in a number of interesting roles, from characters in ensemble pieces to dramatic leads to blockbuster villains, the biggest budgeted films made by the studios with greatest name recognition among fans may not provide Cumberbatch with an appropriate dramatic breakthrough film role. A "smaller" film, like *The Imitation Game,* may be a more appropriate, if far less traditional, vehicle to gain a major lead actor award for film. In the U.S., he may get more respect as an actor on the indie circuit of film festivals and be able to establish a firm footing in Hollywood because of a breakthrough role in an indie.

The final part of Shingler's description of a classic rise to stardom involves the actor having a recognisable style, such as gestures, mannerisms, vocal quality or inflection, or even a recognisable look from film to film. Again, Cumberbatch fails to fit the typical mould. Although, as mentioned in a previous discussion of *Tinker Tailor Soldier Spy* and *Frankenstein*, the actor often bounces his leg in some roles as a way of showing barely restrained physical tension, he does not truly have a "style" or mannerisms that identify him from role to role. His deep voice is prized for its velvety sexiness, but not all roles are appropriate for such a voice. Sherlock's voice, for example, is much deeper than Martin Crieff's, and the actor appropriately varies his inflection and accent to match a character's regional origins or emotional state. Given the number of times make-up specialists dye and style Cumberbatch's hair (e.g., very dark with extensions for *Star Trek,* less dark but longer and curlier for *Sherlock,* natural ginger for Victor Frankenstein, white and very straight for Julian Assange), the actor looks very different in the roles he plays, especially noticeable now that he has taken on many film roles within a very short time. Whether by style or appearance, Cumberbatch defies easy categorisation.

Cumberbatch's stardom has been accomplished in an atypical way from most Hollywood stars. He must be considered either as a star at different stages of development given the medium, or as a British star on his way to international stardom, or as a star of a specific genre of film. In some of these areas, Cumberbatch is recognised as a star more than in others. As films prepare to saturate the market with his performances in 2013-14, this actor is more likely to be perceived as a new A-list star because of one or two breakthrough performances, but in truth he has been a star of British television, then international television, then theatre, for far longer than his level of international film recognition indicates.

How an Actor or a Star Behaves:
Lessons from *Cabin Pressure* and *Sherlock*

Strangely enough, two of Cumberbatch's series have dealt with stardom or celebrity and played on public perceptions of the differences between stars and everyone else. In *Cabin Pressure*'s episode "Cremona,"[349] MJN ferries a famous actress—a dream job for Martin Crieff but especially for Arthur Shappey, who thinks of himself as her greatest fan because he knows everything about her role in a fantasy movie he adores. The reality of working with the famous is not quite as lovely as the crew expected, however. The actress is friendly on the surface; her public persona is carefully in place as she flirts with the crew. However, when Arthur is about to gush that he is such a fan, he overhears her disgustedly discuss the type of people who claim that title. They only know her for her fantasy role and have not bothered to see the rest of her films, and she despises the fact that she is best known for a less-than-stellar movie. Her arrogance and disdain when she does not find her travel arrangements up to her standards put Martin in the awkward position of trying to keep up appearances that the airline is affluent enough for someone like her and to keep his meagre budget balanced. Only MJN's owner, Carolyn Knapp Shappey, decides exactly how to put the actress "in her place" as a civil human being—not a celebrity or star who

223

"deserves" better treatment than anyone else because of her popularity or her money. "Cremona" jovially suggests that not all stars are personally worth the amount of adulation automatically given them because they portray a favourite character or are a media celebrity. This episode tweaks how a star "typically" behaves, places Cumberbatch's Martin Crieff in the role of a fan, depicts die-hard fans who cosplay and lovingly stalk their favourite but know an actor only one role (such as Sherlock), and, by extension, humorously considers the nature of fanaticism.

"Cremona" was first broadcast prior to the post-*Sherlock* years when Cumberbatch might be expected to "go Hollywood." It gave Cumberbatch-as-Crieff the opportunity to see fandom and stardom from an opposite perspective, but, when replayed after the actor's *Sherlock* fame, also can be interpreted as poking a bit of fun at those who criticise the actor for his comments or activities since he became more famous.

Whereas *Cabin Pressure* pokes fun of stars, *Sherlock* explores the darker side of celebrity in "The Reichenbach Fall." At the height of his London popularity, Sherlock Holmes is praised for the many highly publicised cases he solves. His photo appears regularly in the newspapers, and he is publicly presented gifts from the grateful victims he saves. John Watson cautions the detective to take low-profile cases for a while and to stay out of the news, because the media tend to build up celebrities only to enjoy tearing them down. Sherlock fails to heed this advice, especially when his nemesis Jim Moriarty returns. Through Moriarty's manipulation of the media, a carefully placed tabloid reporter intent on getting a "scoop" any way possible, and the public's fickle nature toward celebrities, Sherlock is effectively convicted in the media of being a fraud.[350] Although Cumberbatch's less-than-pleasant run-ins with reporters have been far less damaging than Sherlock's, the actor nonetheless has suffered some backlash as a result of the way he has been quoted in interviews and has had to request retractions or needed to clarify his comments. When everything Cumberbatch says is subject to public commentary, he has become increasingly aware that he is as likely to be faulted as praised for what he says.

How Cumberbatch "Acts" at Work

Before *Sherlock,* when Cumberbatch was well known but still considered a "working actor" instead of a media star, those who observed him on the job, as noted throughout this book, praised his devotion to research, performance quality, and affability in the workplace. When he performed in an independent film or a lower-budget project, he often carried equipment onto the filming site and enjoyed (or suffered) the same conditions as everyone else, without anything approaching "star treatment." *Third Star* scriptwriter Vaughan Sivell, for example, once commented about Cumberbatch "carrying his kit up the steps from Barafundle Bay,"[351] even though he was tired from the day's filming; he, like everyone else, pitched in to make the film.

The accommodations nowadays may be better, and Cumberbatch may have more on-set perks, but his work ethic remains the same. Even the glimpses of Cumberbatch busy with filming *The Fifth Estate* in Berlin early in 2013 support the same types of comments and reports provided on numerous other sets practically as long as the actor has been working. An extra on the film's last shooting day in Berlin had the opportunity to watch Cumberbatch in preparation and during filming; her report, like many posted online by extras or fans who had the opportunity to watch the actor on or near set, was retweeted dozens of times among fans. It illustrates some now-commonly observed Cumberbatch behaviours during a typical day's filming.

The fan described Cumberbatch pacing the stage used in the scene, going over lines out loud. Ear buds in place and iPhone in hand, he also checked lines while sitting on the floor during a particularly long set-up. When he spilled a drink on the floor, a crew member hurried over to take care of it, but Cumberbatch cleaned up the mess himself. As expected, he thanked the hair/make-up specialist who frequently adjusted his white-blond Assange hair or crew who brought him something. While a lighting technician crawled along the floor during a scene, the actors cracked up, to the point that Cumberbatch, while standing, mimicked crawling and occasionally poking his head up to look around, leading the extra to write that she now knew what Cumberbatch as a child must have been like.

When it came time for a take, Cumberbatch sometimes fluffed a line; during one scene he had so much trouble that he tried to correct himself while the camera kept rolling, only to swear and have to start again. At the end of the difficult scene, he mock-punched the camera on his way off set.[352] In short, Cumberbatch is still doing what he has always done—getting along with cast and crew, sometimes being irreverent or funny even when onlookers may "report" him, and being as well prepared as possible to shoot a scene but, quite humanly, not always getting it right the first time.

In addition to having new respect for the "hurry up and wait" atmosphere of a set and the long breaks between scenes, this extra also gained a better appreciation for the times that Cumberbatch has apologised to fans who have waited for him and want his autograph or a photo with him; after a long day in the theatre or on set, and sometimes at the close of an event after a work day, he has said that he is so tired that he cannot stay longer, or he does not want photographs of him, tired or partially in make-up, to be placed online. If nothing else, fan or actor reports from a set underscore Cumberbatch's attempts to be as accommodating as possible, but sometimes he simply cannot do more.

When *Sherlock* is filming new episodes, especially once it gained rampant popularity, fans flock to outdoor shooting locations and immediately share video, photographs, and set reports. Such was the case only a week into filming in 2013, when Cumberbatch and the *Sherlock* crew had a night shoot around Bristol, filming in Portland Square 25 March. Although some videos (such as one showing Cumberbatch and Amanda Abbington preparing to film a scene) disappeared shortly after they were posted, spoilers based on one night's filming of a single scene soon became fan fodder. In photographs in which Cumberbatch is aware that he is being captured (such as by local newspaper reporters), he smiles for the camera and looks very relaxed. Photos captured by fans standing on the sidelines, often when the actor was preparing for a scene, show a much more serious Cumberbatch, checking his phone, talking with crew, or, in a video, standing ready to run toward a bonfire. Abbington prepared for the dash by rocking forward and backward on her feet. Cumberbatch stood motionless in concentration until seconds before he had to run on cue; then he bounced on his toes and tore off the moment "action" was called.[353] What is most interesting about the candid shots is the difference between the working actor and the television star who knows his face will grace dozens of websites as soon as the photo is taken. The actor, through interviews and set photos, seems happy to be working on his hit television series, but he is ever more careful of his demeanour around the press.

Only a few weeks before, Cumberbatch was reported to have said that he had agreed to a fourth series of *Sherlock,* and the breaking news gained a great deal of attention among fans and the media. A few days later, however, the actor publicly recanted that statement, saying that he was tired after finishing filming *The Fifth Estate* and had just arrived back in London in time for the Broadcasting Press Guild awards; he noted that he was pressured to say something about *Sherlock.* He added that, as soon as the news broke, he had received a text from Mark Gatiss that a fourth series was news to him. Whether Cumberbatch was hopeful about a fourth series because he would like the programme to continue, he was attempting to add some pressure so that a fourth series could be commissioned, or he simply spoke too soon, his on-camera retraction days later indicates that his wrists were soundly slapped. Although Cumberbatch is clearly learning how to react in public whenever *Sherlock* is mentioned, sometimes he still seems to slip up and say what he thinks, without considering consequences of his tone or the way he phrases a line. His public persona is much more obviously in place in 2013 than it was in 2010, but he has not yet become isolated from talking openly instead of through a publicist, meeting or being seen by fans, or working in public spaces (the latter which is more likely in U.K. than U.S. television). At times, especially when caught off guard on a work site, the actor still has trouble separating his private, public, and professional personas.

Private, Public, and Professional Personas

During a 2011 interview with *Entertainment Weekly,* Neil Patrick Harris aptly defined the differences among an actor's professional, personal, and private lives.[354] The professional life is most obvious: the actor's roles, interviews, and appearances in relation to his career. Personal and private are often confused by the media and fans, but actors successful at navigating celebrity and the media clearly differentiate the two. Personal information may be shared with fans or the media; it has nothing to do with the actor's current projects or career but is simply "nice to know" details about the actor. The private persona is known only to those closest to the actor and is the "real" person away from work or media scrutiny.

Cumberbatch's growing celebrity—or attention paid to him because he is a higher-profile actor, not specifically because of one of his roles or association with a project—also means that he has gained the

229

attention of paparazzi following him in order to sell their work to tabloids or entertainment outlets. His public and private lives, not always kept so neatly separate as he might like, are now the stuff for tabloids. After his photograph on a California beach was published on tabloid and fan sites around the world, Cumberbatch commented to *InStyle* that he thought at the time "'Wow, I'm becoming the person in the magazine I used to beg Olivia [Poulet, his former long-time partner] not to read.' It was one of those moments where you stop and think, 'Oh God—this is really happening to me now.'"[355]

An actor's personal life may be shared through brief, vague insights into non-work life. Cumberbatch does that when, for example, he shared that, on his last night in LA after *Star Trek* wrapped, he "strolled down the beach and ate a sarnie on the sand dune."[356] It is an insight into the actor's life away from work and establishes him as a certain type of person. It also seems to reveal more than it actually does. None but Cumberbatch and those closest to him know the details of his private life—what goes on at home with friends and family—but a few personal titbits dropped into interviews here and there give readers the impression that the actor is forthcoming about his non-work life.

Sometimes the public persona overlaps with the private for a moment, as occurs sometimes during Cumberbatch's transition from "well known" into "highly tracked and sought." When he and Poulet ended their relationship in March 2011, tabloids first broke the "news," which was then picked up by entertainment media; his publicist issued a statement. Cumberbatch, however, seemed surprised that paparazzi knew where he lived and were waiting when he left home the day the story went public. Perhaps this was an important lesson about the media's growing interest in his private life, which would demand some kind of response from the actor publicly. Later interviews with newspapers, in which he was asked about his relationship, included public-persona quotations like "Naturally, I miss the proximity of a partnership with someone I know and love—and I still love Olivia to bits—but being single's fun."[357]

The most daring information that Cumberbatch has publicly provided about a relationship occurred during an interview for *Parade's End* when he was discussing an eerie occurrence that took place during location filming in Belgium. The *Huffington Post* version of the story quotes Cumberbatch this way: "I was asleep and my then-girlfriend woke up . . . . I woke up to her saying 'Are you all right' and she screamed. She told me, 'You were sitting on the end of the bed, and then I turned to where your voice was and you were lying down. You turned round where you were sitting and half your face was missing, you seemed to be in some sort of uniform, and just sort of vanished . . . and I looked back to you, and it looked like the image had vanished into you.'"[358] The implication is that he and his girlfriend were sleeping together, nothing terribly shocking but far more revealing than previous comments about his relationships. (Of course, they could have been sleeping separately and only talking together after the nightmare. The implication, however, is more salacious.)

What is perhaps more interesting is the way that the BBC Media Centre had published a more ambiguous

231

account in its long interview with Cumberbatch about *Parade's End*: "I was next to someone, they woke up and asked me a question and when I answered they screamed and said they had seen me sat up on edge of my bed but when I spoke they saw I was lying down next to them. They looked back and the figure turned round and half its face was missing and it was in a First World War uniform. It was a clear image then dissolved into light. I believe in energy and carrying things around but I'm not sure."[359] The shift in pronoun from *she* to *they* is important in that it makes the person gender neutral (although it also is grammatically incorrect to pair *they* with the singular *someone*). The "someone" is never identified; neither is the context. At times, when the actor may "slip up" and inadvertently reveal more than he intended about his private life, those invested in his professional life may alter the timbre of an interview to better separate the private, public, and professional personas. Especially in a long BBC interview, which will be archived and more easily referenced by future researchers or fans, and in which Cumberbatch is more importantly descriptive about his role, the emphasis *should* be on his professional persona.

Cumberbatch, his agent or publicist, or the production companies or networks for whom he works are less able to control paparazzi photographs. With the public's continuing interest in Cumberbatch, he has become a more profitable target for paparazzi, and even the most innocuous events become fodder for public consumption and commentary. When the actor, meeting with friend and fellow actor Tom Hiddleston at a café, learned that his car was about to receive a parking ticket, he approached the officer to discuss the matter. Cumberbatch appeared to be friendly but concerned in the many paparazzi shots but still received the parking citation.[360] The comments attached to the series of photos, however, attempt to read more into the actor's body language. Because the actors seemed to have a script with them, speculation circulated that Cumberbatch was showing Hiddleston the top-secret *Star Trek* script. Others not so kindly scrutinised Cumberbatch's clothing and his personal taste, or ability to wear clothes well, away from photo shoots. Then there were the complaints that an actor making far more money than most "commoners" should not try to talk his way out of a ticket. All of these comments were pure speculation, not even Sherlockian deductions, based on a series of photographs taken while the actor went about his daily life. Far more often of late, the actor's private life sometimes becomes very public just because he leaves the workplace or his home. Cumberbatch has admitted that "[y]our privacy becomes something you have to protect and that puts you into an odd place as a human being, . . . especially someone who's always been very open and not worried about what they say or where they go or what they do."[361]

Perhaps one of the most invasive and potentially dangerous public paparazzi "sightings" occurred in December 2012, a few days after *The Hobbit: An Unexpected Journey* arrived in London cinemas. Paparazzi spotted Cumberbatch and an attractive blonde leaving Notting Hill's Electric theatre. Overly enthusiastic photographers even climbed onto the car in order to take an exclusive shot through the windscreen.

233

The actor later admitted that he was worried because he could not see to drive because of so many flashbulbs. The *Daily Mail* soon published an article about Cumberbatch's "date night,"[362] and speculation began whether the woman was romantically linked to the actor. One photo shows him smiling from the driver's seat, as if trying to be accommodating, only later to become worried about driving away as the paparazzi would not quit. The woman with Cumberbatch was his niece, who works as his personal assistant, not a "date," but the incident further exemplifies the rise of Cumberbatch as a media celebrity, the flow of speculative tabloid stories built around even ordinary activities, and the potential perils of so much interest in his private life being forced into public view.

There also is a matter of trust among those he may know casually or who see him regularly. In March 2013, the actor was reportedly cyberstalked by a neighbour who documented Cumberbatch's at-home life on Twitter. "I had someone live tweeting my movements while I was in my own house. It was such a strange and a direct thing to see these tweets saying what I was doing as I was doing them. I found it really worrying, and, yes, of course, very hard to deal with. I worked out after a while who it was who was doing it, so, when it came to it, I didn't actually call in the police, but I was prepared to do so."[363] In an age of instant information and near-constant electronic access, even people who are unlikely to monetarily benefit from news about Cumberbatch may like to claim "status" on Twitter through "insider" knowledge of the actor's private life. The fact that many people feel it is not only all right but their duty to report sightings—in this case, even at the actor's home—takes "fandom" to a potentially dangerous level and certainly goes beyond the bounds of privacy or decency. In response, several of the actor's fans tweeted that they would no longer retweet personal messages about sightings because they could be deemed a gross infringement of the actor's right to privacy.

Celebrity, Separate from Stardom

By 2012-13, Cumberbatch had become a barometer of British popularity to the extent that, even in entertainment news only peripherally related to the actor or *Sherlock,* his name is included in article titles simply because they will garner more interest, greater periodical sales, or more website hits. Two example headlines refer to the Cumberbatch-*Sherlock* connection's success and controversy.

A *Radio Times* interview to promote new detective series *Father Brown* was entitled "Father Brown's Mark Williams on Following in Benedict Cumberbatch's Footsteps"; in the article Williams was asked if he might become a sex symbol like Cumberbatch, who earlier had brought an iconic sleuth to television popularity.[364] (For the record, Williams was not worrying about becoming a sex symbol.) When Lara Pulver (Irene Adler) was cast as Ian Fleming's wife in a forthcoming film, headlines such as "Sherlock Star Who Stripped Nude for Benedict Cumberbatch to Play 'Bond Girl'"[365] were common, as were comments that Pulver had been linked romantically to Cumberbatch. Any connection to Cumberbatch seems guaranteed to gain attention, which is another mark of Cumberbatch's transition from actor to star or celebrity.

As long as Cumberbatch's work is mentioned, the link is more "professional" and equated to his stardom; comments about his love life, however, are merely celebrity bait.

Whatever Cumberbatch says in interviews is reported, cut into short quotations (sometimes losing their original context), and reported for months afterward. His personal life is sensationalised, whether he goes to the beach or cinema with friends or family, shows up other than alone at a party or an event, or goes to the market. When he travels abroad to make movies, tweets keep the public alerted to shooting locations, and fans arrive in hopes of seeing him. In these encounters, Cumberbatch has been polite, although he sometimes reveals his stress or distress in being followed or "captured" by paparazzi. Only when a situation becomes potentially problematic for his career, however, has he, through his publicist or agent, stepped in to correct the public's impression of what he has done or said.

Cumberbatch often does not "act" like a star or a celebrity might be expected to act: publicly demanding special treatment or throwing a tantrum when he does not immediately get his way. Many fans (and I as well) have observed him thanking his interviewers or crew members; he is well mannered and respectful of those around him. When an actor like Cumberbatch receives so many awards, so much publicity, and so much fan love, it seems inevitable that he will "change"—or at least public perception of him will—as he learns to cope with constant scrutiny and loss of privacy.

You May Be a Celebrity If . . .

Although being a celebrity is a big business, as well as a complete profession for some, the nature of celebrity is separate from being a star. Some stars are also celebrities, but *star* designates a recognised level of achievement within the acting profession. *Entertainment Weekly* columnist Mark Harris defined a movie star as "someone whose past work enriches your experience of, and deepens your pleasure in, his or her present work."[366]*Celebrities,* on the other hand, are defined as people who are well known for being well known; their popularity is often the creation of self-publicity. Author, film critic, and cultural historian Neal Gabler identified celebrities as people who "are living out narratives that capture our interest and the interest of the media—narratives that have entertainment value. Or put another way, what stars are to traditional movies, celebrities are to . . . the 'life movie'—a movie written in the medium of life."[367] In some cases, celebrity may involve more luck than training; it may be limited to one nation (e.g., the celebrities of a reality show popular only within a country); it may require one to play an exaggerated version of him/herself instead of formally playing a fictitious character. However, a celebrity may also be an actor who becomes well known for a reason other than or in addition to acting. An actor who becomes famous as a philanthropist is a celebrity, for example. *Celebrity* requires the public to be interested in someone's personal story and to want to know more about that person. In the popular vernacular, "you may be a celebrity if . . . ."

- People are interested in everything you do or say; they analyse your every word or move; they may deliberately or inadvertently misquote you to create controversy.

- Professional photo ops are carefully orchestrated so you look and sound your best on the red carpet, at philanthropic events, as a fashion spokesperson, etc.

- Paparazzi and fans follow (or possibly stalk) you to get autographs or candid photos.

- Your name is used to promote products and projects with which you are not in any way associated.

- You have become a cultural icon, and your image in popular culture has taken on a life of its own.

- Your fan base numbers thousands, if not millions, who vote for you in polls or for awards and keep Twitter, Tumblr, Facebook, and other social media hot with discussions about you.

Benedict Cumberbatch has become a celebrity.

What Did You Say?
***Parade's End* as a Tipping Point between Being an Actor and a Celebrity "Commodity"**

Cumberbatch received a great deal of criticism for comments he made during the promotion of *Parade's End* in the U.K. in late summer 2012. Although he later said his remarks about *Downton Abbey* were taken out of context (he was speaking facetiously but what was printed made his words seem hypercritical), his comments about his miniseries' superiority to the wildly popular *Downton* did not win him a lot of fans in the days before *Parade's End* debuted on the BBC. Similarly, his statements about the American Sherlock Holmes series, *Elementary*, starring Jonny Lee Miller, also were misquoted, according to the actor, who contacted the *Hollywood Reporter* to clarify what had been reported.[368]

Around the time of *Parade's End*, Cumberbatch faced the kind of backlash common to actors who seem to gain "overnight" success and become celebrities whose every word is reported and analysed. Although his comments concerning the London riots of 2011 were carefully stated in the press, some in the U.K. felt that he really could not understand the situation because he is a "posh" actor not of the same social strata as the rioters. Some *Sherlock* cast and crew—but not Cumberbatch— had been evacuated from a filming location when rioters approached. The actor unsympathetically doubted these rioters' "socio-political reasons" for destruction, adding, "I came from an incredibly privileged bubble so the minute I open my mouth I can sense the comeback of, 'What the f--- do you know?' And that's fair. [Indeed, that is exactly the type of reply he later received in some forums.] But my sympathy is with the people who do know what they're talking about, who have been brought up on estates and live morally decent, contributing lives and who have seen opportunists destroying all their work."[369]

In 2012 his comments about being typecast as "posh" led to a series of articles, including those questioning whether—if Cumberbatch was bringing it up—U.K. society might need to address class issues more seriously. Headlines published in U.K. media during a few days in mid-August show the progression of the "posh" controversy: "'Posh Baiting' May Drive Benedict Cumberbatch to the US,"[370] "Posh-bashing: It's Enough to Make You Want to Leave the Bullingdon Club,"[371] and "Is Benedict Cumberbatch Right That Posh-bashing Has Gone Too Far?"[372] The actor was reported as saying that he is tired of being portrayed as "posh" when he was not born into titles or land and feels that posh-bashing is so prevalent in the U.K. that he is thinking of relocating to the U.S. Ironically, in the *Radio Times* interview that resulted in fan or critical backlash, the interviewer also wrote that "Cumberbatch is so engagingly unguarded, and cheerfully forthcoming, it would be easy to forget just how big a star he is, for there is none of the bland wariness of a Hollywood commodity in his manner."[373]

After this interview made the rounds of fan sites, tweets bemoaned Cumberbatch "going Hollywood" and despaired of comments reporting that he "couldn't afford another five months in the theatre or a major TV gig." The backlash continued across media. A BBC Wales radio talk show guest reminded Cumberbatch that he probably would not be considered posh in the U.S. but thought of as merely an Englishman, and typically Englishmen are relegated to film roles as villains.[374] Articles further reprimanded the actor for having a chip on his shoulder; they stated that all actors play to class distinctions (much as distinctions by age or height) and mentioned previous media reprimands of other actors (e.g., Helena Bonham Carter) who also whined about being rich. Another critic said that she, among other fans, did not like this side of their favourite and might not be as much of a fan in the future.[375]

Public furore had hardly died down over Poshgate when *Parade's End* interviews highlighted and repeated across multiple magazines and newspapers that Cumberbatch was afraid of his obsessed fans, although he had said he fears *for* fans who become so obsessed with a series or a performer.[376] Furthermore, he reportedly was so full of himself that he publicly berated the beloved *Downton Abbey* not once but twice and felt his project intellectually far superior to that of ITV's period piece. The *Sunday Times' Culture* magazine quoted Cumberbatch as saying *Parade's End* is a rare production "about this class of people that is this accurate, this funny, pointed but also three-dimensional. We're not serving purposes to make some clichéd comment" about "this upstairs-downstairs divide. It's a little bit more sophisticated." The writer emphasised the "whiff of disdain" in the actor's comments about *Downton* vs. *Parade's End*.[377] In two interviews Cumberbatch was quoted as saying that the second series of *Downton Abbey* is "[expletive] atrocious"; *Parade's End* is far more sophisticated than *Downton Abbey*.[378]

After the backlash came the "saviours," including *Downton Abbey*'s producer, Julian Fellowes, who stated that he has "known Ben since he was a little boy" and thought his comments must have been misquoted or taken out of context.[379] A few days later, the *Guardian* published an analysis of interviews to clarify what the actor actually said and in what context.[380]

The actor had said in January 2012 that he was "mortified" by the PR nightmare after first joking about *Downton Abbey*,[381] but the bad press in August required even more of a public response from the actor (as did a published negative September comment about Jonny Lee Miller's Sherlock Holmes series, *Elementary*[382]). The August series of *Parade's End* interviews—as published—seem far more mean spirited and self-serving than previous interviews about *Sherlock* or film projects. They also seem to fly in the face of Cumberbatch's friendly, often self-deprecating persona on the red carpet and in fan encounters or at public events, as well as quotes from interviews as recent as June and July 2012. Perhaps the "backlash" escalated because of personal interpretations of what the actor said or what critics or fans thought he had said or meant. Whatever the case, Cumberbatch was in the press every day, and more than 150 articles repeating variations of the originally published quotations were running rampant across the Internet prior to *Parade's End*. They kept the actor's name in the news, but they detracted from the miniseries' publicity and made the press "all about Ben."

The media attention, perhaps more than the miniseries itself, signals the transition between Cumberbatch remaining a well-known actor who answers questions candidly within the context of an interview and a media sensation who must carefully consider each word and its possible impact on the project he is promoting, his public persona, and media usage of his words as sound bites that sell magazines or boost the number of website hits. The media brouhaha illustrates a man who is willing to clarify his thoughts—indicating that he cares about what others write or how they perceive him—but pragmatically must protect his public image. The very fact that Cumberbatch's words were given such gravitas as to suggest the U.K. might want to now seriously consider the perils of "posh-baiting" or to be given so much press indicates this actor's stature in British pop culture. The backlash—a natural tearing down of celebrities once they get too big for their egos or the public perceives them that way—was quickly brought under control by a series of high-profile "we like Ben" articles from people within the entertainment industry. Kind, humble Cumberbatch is clearly the persona the BBC wants to cultivate, not only for *Sherlock* but because the actor has, in many ways, become the face of BBC—as evidenced through his bookending narration of the London Olympics broadcasts and even off-hand comments like "I owe a lot to the BBC . . . . I actually thought about changing my initials to BBC. They've given me some fantastic breaks."[383] His higher profile on BBC projects and success as a British export may depend on Cumberbatch continuing to be seen as a good guy, rather than an opinionated actor who suddenly displays a less-than-genial attitude during interviews (what one critic called having a tanty) and threatens to abandon his homeland for the U.S.

One of the most interesting, and in some ways most painful to watch, interviews during this time took place on *The One Show* in late August. Dressed in jeans and plaid shirt with the top buttons undone, sitting on one leg during the first part of the interview, Cumberbatch looked the definition of casual and far from "posh." Soon after introducing the actor, the hosts launched into a game of "Cumber Fact or Cumber Fiction," which was again played toward the end of the programme; the BBC talk show gave the actor a friendly (if contrived) forum in which to explain his side of the controversial interviews. The actor squinched his eyes closed when asked about his *Reader's Digest* comment that *Downton Abbey* was not very good and firmly said "Cumber Fiction." He explained the context of the comparison he had been making between *Parade's End* and *Downton Abbey*: "There was one question about comparing the use of war, and I was talking about that, and I used language I shouldn't have used, but I would never say [anything derogatory] about it. I have friends and family who are in it. My dad was in the Christmas special." He next praised the series and said it well deserved the accolades given it in the U.K. and U.S. Cumberbatch next was asked with mock incredulity "Were you taken out of context?" The actor smiled, "It could've happened."

With the initial damage-control segment out of the way, the show continued with a Paralympics segment before Cumberbatch was finally asked about *Parade's End*. Although the actor, as always, eloquently discussed the miniseries and his role, he seemed a bit ill at ease, and, as he often does during televised interviews or acceptance speeches that put him on the spot, displayed some nervous mannerisms like scratching a shoulder or rubbing his face, as if he has too much energy to be contained. Uncharacteristically, he forgot a character's name, thanking the host for supplying it a moment later.

After the *Parade's End* segment, the "game" continued with a question about being posh. Again stating that the statement attributed to him was "Cumber Fiction," Cumberbatch provided a carefully worded

244

explanation of how lucky he feels to have had so many opportunities to work. Unlike the rest of the interview, the actor did not hesitate, interject an "uh" or "um" as he gathered thoughts, or fidget—it seemed as if he were delivering a scripted response. That is not to say that the actor seemed insincere—on the contrary, he seemed honestly concerned that he had been taken out of context, not because of potential career damage (although a publicist probably had impressed the need for damage control upon him), but because he truly did not intend for his words to have been interpreted in such a controversial way. Cumberbatch concluded that "It's very easy to say something and have it blow up into a national debate, especially about class," adding a final comment that such a discussion is important, but instigating a debate about being posh was not his intent.[384]

The One Show interview gave the actor another opportunity to discuss *Parade's End* slightly more than an hour before the first episode debuted in the U.K., but it also afforded him the chance to make a good impression on audiences who might not have appreciated his reported comments about *Downton Abbey* or socioeconomic class and, if they only planned to watch *Parade's End* because it stars Cumberbatch, might have changed their minds about viewing it. The *One Show* interview segments also shed light on Cumberbatch as an actor in transition— suffering the ignominy of celebrity by having his every word scrutinised and sensationalised and having to address another PR nightmare—all because he continues to interact with interviewers as he always has, by being forthright and talkative and having a conversation rather than mouthing innocuous answers. The media depictions of Cumberbatch in August 2012 may signal a turning point in the way the actor decides he must relate to the press or to his fans, which is what many fans, who treasure the actor's candour and accessibility, fear may change as Cumberbatch becomes not only a film star but a celebrity commodity.

Coming to America

Whether Cumberbatch ever moves to the U.S. or simply spends more time working there, he is being featured more often in American entertainment media when he visits the States to make a film, promote a project, or attend a Hollywood event. The amount of attention paid him at the Golden Globes in 2012 was vastly different from that received a year later. In 2012, Cumberbatch attended the Golden Globes as part of the *War Horse* contingent. He was photographed at parties, but the amount of press was minimal and the resulting photos mostly the stuff of fan pages or the U.K. press, which has always paid far more attention to the actor's on- and off-screen activities. *War Horse* did not win as best film, and the camera only passed by the director's and cast's table a few times. Although *Sherlock* also failed to be a winning production for Cumberbatch at the 2013 Golden Globes—as with the U.S. Emmy awards, Kevin Costner instead won the best actor statue for his role in *Hatfields & McCoys*—Cumberbatch received far more attention. Ironically, it was not expressly for playing Sherlock. The E! "Fresh Faces to Watch" promo shown during the Golden Globes red carpet broadcast emphasised Cumberbatch's upcoming role in *Star Trek: Into Darkness*.[385]

The actor also was featured on the entertainment network's fashion cam and, much to fans' delight, he was interviewed on camera. That interview, however, further illustrates differences between what the *Guardian* described as the "very British" actor and his gushing American interviewer, Giuliana Rancic, who received immediate criticism via Twitter for her lack of knowledge about Cumberbatch. He provided the usual just-happy-to-be-nominated comment, which, in Cumberbatch's case, does seem to be sincere. He joked that he was pleased that people knew his name and added that Rancic got it right (whereas Jessica Alba stumbled a bit on his name when announcing the best actor nominees). Nevertheless, Rancic did ask the actor if he had met the "U.S. Sherlock, Robert Downey, Jr.," and then seemed at a loss of what else to say.[386] The *Guardian* live blog during the Golden Globes red carpet coverage advised the actor simply to keep talking; it mentioned that Cumberbatch "makes the mistake of being far too British for the red carpet, and actually stopped talking when he didn't have anything else to say. 'So thrilled to be here,' he says, . . . before going quiet in the absence of an actual question."[387]

At the BAFTA 2013 tea party in Los Angeles, held the evening before the Golden Globes, Cumberbatch admitted to a BBC reporter that he still became "starstruck" at such events, and meeting actors he has always admired is a "surreal experience." After discussing the variety of roles and projects covered by his category's nominations, he asked, "If I win tomorrow, or if I don't, how do people judge?"[388] He seemed content to be nominated and pleased that his work was being recognised in the U.S.

Cumberbatch's body language, on the other hand, indicated his discomfort with being photographed at the event and facing the gauntlet of reporters. Although, as usual, charming and willing to give variations on answers to the same questions so that each reporter had a bit of something different to write or broadcast, the actor made little eye contact with his interviewers and responded to shouted commands from photographers (e.g., "Ben! Ben! To the right! Turn a little bit more to the right! Big smile, Ben!") with a rather tight smile. He seemed to accept the attention as part of his job, not court or demand it.

Contrast these "Hollywood"-style interviews and photo ops with a less publicised MTV interview on the Golden Globes red carpet. In it, Cumberbatch seemed more "himself"—or at least the public persona that hints at the actor's enthusiasm and genuine enjoyment of the celebrity aspects of his career. Cumberbatch's previous MTV interviews have been interesting for fans to read or watch and seem to be more relaxed for the actor. This MTV interview was more substantive and allowed Cumberbatch to comment on the activity going on around him (and even to offer a highly prized titbit about *Star Trek*). The interviewer described Cumberbatch as "distracted by Robert Pattinson" as he walked by. Cumberbatch next gushed about his *War Horse* director, Steven Spielberg: "He's such a wonderful man. He's been incredibly supportive of my career and said incredibly lovely things about me . . . . I've only got light compliments to return to him. He's incredible." To Adele, who arrived near the actor during the interview, Cumberbatch enthused, "oh my God, Adele . . . . We're in the same choir, and we do our nails at the same salon."

248

The reporter noted that the *Star Trek* revelation (a line of dialogue) took place once the actor was "reined in."[389] Cumberbatch's smiles are much wider and freer, his language much more fluid and energetic, his gestures more frequent when he discusses roles or talks about projects. Unlike some actors who play up to interviews and relish their celebrity, Cumberbatch in 2013 still remains low-key and starstruck in his press interviews at high-profile events.

During the short interview with Rancic, he seldom made direct eye contact, prompting one fan to post the comment that he seemed nervous ("but he's gorgeous, so who cares"),[390] a fact that endeared the actor to his fans even more than if he had been glib and seeking attention like some of his peers at the event. Not only fans made the "gorgeous" comment on websites or through tweets throughout the broadcast. A *Wall Street Journal* live blog included Cumberbatch as one of the men's fashion standouts at the Globes, "though he's not wearing a bow tie but rather a straight-tie."[391] Whether walking the red carpet, smiling humbly (and not applauding himself) as his name was announced as a nominee, or talking with reporters, Cumberbatch continued to exude charm, self-effacing good humour, and good fashion sense. The difference at the 2013 Golden Globes is that he stepped out from being part of the *War Horse* ensemble to being recognised in a leading role (in *Sherlock*) and that he was being formally introduced to millions of Americans, as well as Golden Globe watchers internationally—a much wider mainstream audience.

Cultural Icon *The Simpsons*

Long-running television series *The Simpsons* is more than animated entertainment; it has been a barometer of Western popular culture for decades. Cumberbatch's roles in the Valentine's weekend 2013 episode became a step into further pulling him into the mainstream public's awareness of his work as well as making him more of a pop culture icon. A clip released the Friday before the broadcast—something done far less often in the series' later years—allowed fans worldwide to hear Cumberbatch. To promote the *Simpsons* episode, *Entertainment Weekly* provided the clip, accompanied by this description: "Benedict Cumberbatch–that coldly dashing *Sherlock* star who is playing the villain in *Star Trek Into Darkness*—pulls brilliant double duty by voicing both a Hugh Grant-like British Prime Minister and Severus Snape from *Harry Potter*. Let the British invasion of your heart begin now by watching his scene now."[392]

Additionally, the issue of *Entertainment Weekly* going on sale that Friday featured Cumberbatch on the cover, and the magazine ran a multi-page feature about *Star Trek: Into Darkness.* Cumberbatch thus received a great deal of online and print media attention for very different roles being marketed specifically to U.S. audiences in mid-February but also reaching a far wider global audience. (U.K.-based Sherlockology, for example, directed fans to both the *Simpsons* clip and the *Entertainment Weekly* cover.) The clip and episode introduced more people to Cumberbatch's popular impersonation of Alan Rickman (who plays Severus Snape in the *Harry Potter* movies). Long-time

250

Cumberbatch fans have heard the impression before—on a British cooking show and, in response to the popularity of that impromptu impersonation, on talk shows.

The Simpsons' roles were brief—three lines as the Prime Minister, one as Rickman/Snape. As appropriate for the roles, Cumberbatch voiced the characters to reflect the British movie icons referenced in the scene. *The Simpsons'* introduction of Cumberbatch-the-voice linked him with all that is British in an episode that lampooned U.K. film culture. *Love, Indubitably* (a *Love, Actually* parody) is the film that Homer and other romance-challenged men watch in order to learn how to be sensitive. As a Grant-type "Prime Minister" confesses his undying love for his Eliza Doolittle-sounding, Bridget Jones-looking secretary, Parliament cheers. Images representing the U.K. include Beefeaters, the Union Jack, the TARDIS, characters from *The Full Monty* and *Harry Potter* movies, and the Beatles. Not only are these iconic images that Americans associate with the U.K. Like *Sherlock* and *Parade's End*, *The Simpsons* helped introduce Benedict Cumberbatch to American audiences, but their context emphasise him as a British actor and not the typical Hollywood type.

More important, however, is the way this episode of *The Simpsons* plays a key role in Cumberbatch's transition to international star. Famous names lend their voices to the animated series—it is a mark of being cool or recognisable in popular culture to be either parodied as a character or to voice a character. By playing two roles on America's culturally iconic series, Cumberbatch has achieved another level of international celebrity. Because Fox and entertainment media, including *Entertainment*

251

Weekly, heavily promoted Cumberbatch's *Simpsons* roles, the episode was perceived as more important than most of this series' *Simpsons* episodes. Finally, because *The Simpsons* and *Entertainment Weekly* are U.S. productions—although they have a strong international presence—they marketed the actor to a very wide general television or movie audience, many who might not have been familiar with Cumberbatch.

Ben-Addicted Cumberbitches:
The Perks and Perils of Fandom

As a result of so many multimedia projects in a short time, the publicity generated by them, and a concerted global marketing effort to introduce international audiences to Benedict Cumberbatch, the actor's fan base continues to expand. Whereas his female fans initially identified themselves as Cumberbitches, the actor suggested the softer term Cumberbabes, which many fans adopted. Others simply admit they have Ben-Addicted for quite some time. In addition to many websites devoted to specific projects, such as *Sherlock,* fan sites devoted to the man himself are visited by hundreds, if not thousands, daily. When rumours about Cumberbatch (such as a vaguely written late March 2013 article reporting he had just been married), Twitter and Tumblr explode with fan comments. As news about filming in public locations is leaked online, fans brave cold temperatures and endure long waits just in the hope of seeing Cumberbatch for a moment. Whereas these types of activities are common in fandom, Cumberbatch for a long time has seemed bewildered by this behaviour.

252

"I see people at the stage door who are obsessed with me, sometimes more than I do my own mother, which is a bit weird," Cumberbatch once said in an interview.[393] Indications are that he has never been a fanboy. His interests are diverse and far from shallow, but he never has become immersed solely in one interest for a long period of time. He has trouble understanding just why anyone would be obsessed with him or a role he plays.

Uncharacteristically (and given the possibility that his words may have been misstated in the media), Cumberbatch's discussion of *Star Trek* fandom was not as fluid or as easy to follow as his usual analyses of roles or projects: "I'm doing all these things that are fanboy fodder and I never, ever had that amazing, tribal and really wonderful thing of really knowing everything about something or being obsessed about watching something . . . . I'm playing catch-up is what I'm trying to say."[394]

Such public comments mesh with secondhand anecdotal stories about Cumberbatch's fan encounters. At times he can seem harsh with fans who persistently approach him for multiple autographs or photographs. He was quoted as saying "There is some obsessive behavior, which is quite worrying. I worry for them, not for me."[395]

A fan encounter with Cumberbatch in New Orleans in summer 2012, when he was filming *Twelve Years a Slave* in Louisiana, sheds a more positive light on an impromptu "sighting." Cumberbatch likely did not expect to be recognised when he and a friend bought ice cream in the French Quarter one afternoon, but a young woman spotted him and shyly approached as he was leaving the shop. Cumberbatch graciously agreed to pose for a photograph; his friend even snapped it.[396] The photo, published and then circulated among fans online, shows a casual Cumberbatch in t-shirt and baseball cap grinning into the camera. It is not a posed shot, and the actor looks like an average guy, not a carefully coiffed and dressed performer. Such fan encounters, like others previously mentioned in this book, are highly likely to be shared online; they illustrate how quickly the actor's private life can shift into public-persona mode. In a 2012 interview he reflected that "I'm quite sensitive to people noticing me. There are times when I'm relaxed, then others when it does make me self-conscious [the term used in the Twitter message asking fans not to post images from *Sherlock*'s Portland Square shoot in Bristol]. I'm not complaining . . . it's all come from good things."[397]

When *Sherlock* had a night shoot in Bristol in late March 2013, fan reports blazed onto Twitter and Tumblr almost as fast as the bonfire at the centre of the scene being filmed. Several fans reported that Cumberbatch asked that no photos or videos be placed on the Internet, leading to two camps within fandom—those begging for news and those angry when spoilers were posted. Understandably, cast and crew want to keep episodes as much a surprise as possible, and online spoilers are difficult to contain. Because Cumberbatch does not have a Twitter account, a friend tweeted a message from the actor: 1) "Guys, I have a message from Benedict and he would appreciate it if it could be RTd and redirected to all those following tonight's filming." 2) "Could those following Sherlock #setlock please NOT post photos. The cast and crew have a long, cold and dangerous night ahead and ..." 3) "need to be able to concentrate. Benedict is feeling v self-conscious right now and they're only rehearsing! He says thanks and sends love. xx."[398]

Dozens of fans watching the production were brought into the scene as impromptu extras to react, take after take, to what the actors or their stunt doubles were doing. As time permitted, Cumberbatch signed autographs for the fan-extras or chatted with them. [399] They were, in essence, helping the production and playing fair about photographs/videos because they were busy on set. In this situation in particular, Cumberbatch won greater fan loyalty from his friendly interaction with the extras, although Twitter continued the debate about whether his request for no spoilers was reasonable. In the name of the production's safety (especially during a night in which a fire stunt was key to the scene), the actor's request is reasonable, as it is regarding his ability to do his job well without distraction. It also is reasonable considering the fact that so many people associated with the production want the stories to be surprising—and *Sherlock* is particularly appealing because of its twists of canon and reinvention of the Holmes' legend. However, such a message also reflects a lack of understanding of many fans' ardent desire for spoilers, the way that fandom shares information immediately online, and difficulty discerning why it may be all right for local news media to cover a city event but not similarly all right for fans to post their own interpretation (often marked with spoiler alerts) of the night's filming. If *Sherlock* films in a public place, many fans reason, then they should be permitted to take photos or video, as long as they do not disrupt the company at work.

Since that first location shoot in Bristol, Sherlock cast and crew were followed around England and Wales on successive days, their movements tracked by fans posting updates, photos, and video via Twitter (#setlock). Whereas some fans observing Cumberbatch on series two public filming locations have recounted times when the actor only reluctantly approached fans, the most recent reports indicate that he is making more of an effort. Cumberbatch, although accommodating of fans who are respectful and with whom he can interact without jeopardising his work, will always prioritise acting first.

At least one fan encounter was documented by a Cheltenham news outlet and the story distributed by other entertainment media and fans. Cumberbatch seems to relate to fans much better one on one, and a 16-year-old and her father talked with the actor as he left a night shoot. The article provides a he said-she said report of the conversation, which not only shows the type of fan devotion the actor commonly receives but also describes him as a kind man who understands a teenager's anxiety upon meeting her idol. According to *This is Gloucestershire,* the encounter went something like this. The fan

> asked him if he had any time because I absolutely love him. He said 'Aw, thank you, it means a lot'. I told him I wrote him a letter, but gave it to someone else to hand to him . . . . 'Yeah, I got it, thank you so much. I wrote you a letter back on the back of the envelope and

got my friend to bring it out to you but he couldn't find you, you'd already gone, and I'm going to get a picture signed and sent to you. Thank you[;] it really means a lot.' . . . He asked me if I was on Twitter, and for me to give everyone a message from him who was there today that he's sorry he didn't come out and see them, but he's got so much work to do that he just couldn't. He also thinks that the Sherlock fan base are a very intelligent bunch, and he's very proud and appreciative of us.[400]

When the fan asked to have a photo taken with him, Cumberbatch complied and made certain she was happy with it, then signed her book. Such official reports in local media help promote Cumberbatch's public persona as fan friendly and to offset other fans' shared stories of the actor being more direct in asking why they have approached him or seem intent on seeing his every performance or visiting every filming location.

Another point in the Cheltenham article illustrates Cumberbatch's widespread fame and British fans' expectation (or resignation) that the actor will not be content to be based in London much longer. Cumberbatch is named "the Hollywood heartthrob," a title that even his most ardent U.K. fans would not have given him a year earlier, and more of his film projects are backed by U.S. studios. The fan mood surrounding the third series' filming seemed to be one of bittersweet appreciation— those who love *Sherlock* are thrilled to still have some access to the cast on location shoots, but they also are far more aware that these encounters are unlikely to occur much longer.

The Polls

Unscientifically designed polls to determine the most influential, best looking, most popular, and so on are integral fluff in newspapers, magazines, and tabloids. As a measure of fandom and the ability to rally fans to vote, however, they are useful in determining an actor's place within current popular culture. Whether identified as Cumberbitches, Cumberbabes, or simply Cumberbatch fans, they get out the vote very well.

After being highly ranked, sometimes Number One, on a variety of polls in 2012 ranging from *Time*'s most influential people (where Cumberbatch came in eighth, with President Barack Obama twenty-first)[401] to the *Sun*'s sexiest man, which Cumberbatch easily won, besting second-ranked David Beckham, One Direction's Harry Styles (sixth), and other actors such as Ryan Gosling, Zac Efron, Johnny Depp, and Bradley Cooper.[402] Such had been his recent popularity that when a January 2013 *Tattler* poll to name Britain's "most fascinating" person listed Cumberbatch only in fifth place—right behind the Queen—the *Radio Times* set up its own poll to see how readers felt about the ranking. It listed the *Tattler*'s top five (Clare Balding, Pippa Middleton, Roman Abramovich, the Queen, and Cumberbatch) and again asked voters to select the most fascinating. After the first two hours of voting, Cumberbatch had 92.6% of the votes, far ahead of the next two candidates, the Queen (3.54%) and Balding (2.91%).[403]

In July 2011 I conducted an online, English-language fan survey of *Sherlock* fans and received 563 responses from around the world (49.2 percent from North America, 44.9 percent Europe, 5.7 percent Australia/Oceana, and 4.6 percent Asia). The majority (91.3 percent) are female, and although fans from 10 to 80 years old took the survey, the two age groups with the highest percentage of respondents are 20- to 29-year-olds (32.6 percent) and 15- to 19-year-olds (21.2 percent). They answered many questions about their reasons for watching *Sherlock*, their favourite/least favourite actors or aspects of the series, and their participation in fan activities.

These fans' opinions of *Sherlock* also revealed a great deal of love and respect for Cumberbatch, the man and the actor. Although he was chosen most often (by 65.6 percent) as fans' favourite actor in *Sherlock*, write-in responses about questions, used to clarify multiple-choice answers, most often were complaints that only one "favourite" could be chosen from the list of *Sherlock* actors. Many fans explained that they could not truly choose between Cumberbatch and Freeman, or, in a later "favourite character" question, Sherlock and John, because they work so well together and their on-screen partnership is what makes the series special. However, in later responses, these fans also detailed why Cumberbatch the actor is so desirable and, secondarily, assessed him as a person, based on anecdotal or personal stories of meeting him.

The most frequently used words or phrases to describe Cumberbatch's acting were "versatile" and "real," and he was praised for the "quality of his skills" and "believable physicality." Fans wrote that he is "by far one of the most talented actors" and he "brings a unique energy to Sherlock." Cumberbatch's physical appearance generated the most comments, and fans most often described him as "gorgeous," "cute," "beautiful," "pretty," "hot," "sexy," or "distinguished." His "mesmerising deep baritone" or "voice like melted dark chocolate" was his best feature, according to these fans, but at least a few responses praised his cheekbones, eyes, lips, and original ginger hair colour. His personality attracted many fans, who wrote of his "ability to relate to fans" and labelled him as "eloquent," "intelligent," "polite," "thoughtful," "extremely caring," "kind," "humble," and "modest" and called him "a class act," "excellent human being," or "gentleman." They "love his name" and "always admired him." Regarding his work, three specifically mentioned knowing the actor from *Hawking* or promotional materials for *Star Trek.* As a group, they identified themselves as "Cumberbatched" or "Cumberbatch addicts" who "quite fancy him," "love him," or have "a huge crush" on him. The majority who wrote responses as to why they favour this actor simply noted "because I love Benedict Cumberbatch," "I love everything about him," "I love him so much," or "because he's Benedict."

Whether from the unscientific results of my poll or the instant-response polls used by magazines or news media to take the public's pulse, these polls at least indicate a high degree of current interest in Cumberbatch and a primarily young, female fan base eager to support him through voting him as the best or favourite in just about anything.

Fan Philanthropy

Cumberbatch's many projects encourage the development of separate fan bases by genre (e.g., sci-fi or fantasy fans), project (e.g., *Sherlock, Star Trek*), or medium (e.g., theatre, film), for example, but the actor also has a broader-based personal fandom who will follow him wherever he goes or whatever he does. Only recently has the actor, through the media (such as interviews or publicist's statements) or Twitter (via friends with accounts), begun to establish a few boundaries between himself and fans to allow him to do his work or live his life while not alienating his loyal followers. Even if he does not understand fandom personally, he increasingly has seen its power and begun to realise its perks as well as its perils.

Some fans do not respect boundaries and will attempt to do just about anything to get close to their idol or be able to post information (i.e., video, photos, spoilers, sightings) before anyone else. However, the majority of Cumberbatch fans are eager to meet the actor or gain his attention, but they often do so in unobtrusive or polite ways. "Fandom" as a group also bands together to support philanthropic events or fundraising activities as another way to show their support for the actor and, along the way, also gain his appreciation.

As Sherlockology and Cumberbatchweb wrote when Cumberbatch signed up for a 45-mile bicycle ride to raise funds for the Prince's Trust (which took place on 14 October 2012), "He'd be very grateful if you would consider sponsoring him—you're such a wonderfully generous fandom and Benedict is a patron of The Prince's

Trust so it's a cause very dear to his heart. Every penny counts!"[404] They then linked fans to Cumberbatch's fundraising page. Fan support kept Cumberbatch near or at the top of the sponsorship tally before the ride; his fans raised more than £23,000.[405] Similarly, to celebrate birthdays or holidays, fans often identify a charity and raise money in lieu of sending gifts to the actor. Fandom often gets a bad reputation, and, because of a few individuals, it can be deserved in some cases; however, the majority of Cumberbatch fans may be extremely enthusiastic but they often channel their fan love through philanthropy.

Cumberbatch is still learning how to navigate the murky waters of celebrity while becoming a multimedia star, and, if he may never completely understand fandom, at least he can see some personally rewarding perks of having such a devoted fan base to offset the annoying or occasionally frightening aspects of dealing with paparazzi or fans who do not recognise the tentative boundaries he has begun to set.

Chapter 8 The Transitional Phase

"I treat each job as a new experience. I'm not nervous of the work drying up. It's been great to have back-to-back, well-received work."[406]
Benedict Cumberbatch, 2012

"[Fans] know you from the trail you leave with your work,". . ., the slightest edge of frustration in his voice. "They assume things about you because of who you play and how you play them, and the other scraps floating around in the ether. People try to sew together a narrative out of scant fact."[407]
Benedict Cumberbatch, 2012

During *Rhinoceros'* run in 2007, shortly before *Atonement* opened in the U.S., Benedict Cumberbatch was asked about his career ambitions, especially in light of James McAvoy's success in films. Cumberbatch was quoted as saying "James is someone I respect immensely. I know I ought to say my ambition is to take over the world and be the lead in everything, but I'm really happy with the way it's going. One interviewer asked if I was worried about being trapped in the theatre. I said 'it's the best place to be. . . . I'm just ambitious for the work to be good. I don't strategise."[408] How times change. By 2013, Cumberbatch was appearing far less often in the theatre and instead taking on one lead film role after another, causing many British fans to speculate that, contrary to the actor's protests, he would soon abandon radio, theatre, and television in favour of a film career, preferably based in Hollywood. Cumberbatch certainly seems to be planning career moves wisely, guided by agents in the U.K. and U.S., and the emphasis—commitment to *Sherlock* aside—is to embrace a film career while so many people are offering him such interesting big screen roles.

During the January 2013 party celebrating *Radio Times* covers of the previous year, *Sherlock* co-creator Steven Moffat professed a wish to be able to keep Freeman and Cumberbatch, "two of the biggest film stars in the world playing the leads in our show. But they seem to like doing it and we hope we can hang on to them for a bit."[409] The fact that Moffat mentioned that at an event that spotlighted the people and series gracing *Radio Times'* covers—many which featured *Sherlock* or, independently, Cumberbatch—indicates some pressure on the BBC and the actors to continue their support for the award-winning series. The problem remains scheduling more than desire, it seems, and if Cumberbatch's 2013 schedule is any indication, future *Sherlock* adventures may be fewer or farther in between. As long as filming can be coordinated around the actors' many other projects, the BBC has a global audience clamouring for more episodes. If Cumberbatch remains based in Britain, as is Freeman, and chooses only to periodically visit instead of relocate to Hollywood, *Sherlock* is more likely to continue. Film, however, provides a potent allure, and Cumberbatch recently has been wooed by a number of production companies eager to have him join or head their casts.

When *Deadline* announced that, in the midst of filming *The Fifth Estate,* Cumberbatch was in deep discussions to play Alan Turing in *The Imitation Game,*

264

the actor's number of projects hit an all-time high for a single year; the productions ranged from films made in 2012 and scheduled for release a year or more later to three announced films starring Cumberbatch in a lead role, to three episodes of *Sherlock*, to the HBO broadcast of *Parade's End* in the U.S. and other markets, to radio dramas and his regular series *Cabin Pressure*—and these projects were the ones only in the books by February 2013. No wonder *Deadline* speculated that Cumberbatch "might be the hottest actor to cross the pond in recent memory."[410]

In the first chapter I suggested reasons why Cumberbatch's fans, as well as media reporters and critics, follow the actor. Here is one more, and perhaps the definitive reason why Benedict Cumberbatch will continue to be a successful actor for as long as he chooses, no matter how long his international celebrity as a "hot property" or sex symbol lasts: He intrigues and never bores his audience. He consistently pulls audiences into his performances—whether portraying historic or iconic literary figures, modern newsmakers, or the man next door, whether these characters are heroes, villains, or complex men somewhere between those extremes. Cumberbatch never fails to surprise audiences with glimpses into a character's thoughts or inner life; he chooses a glance, mannerism, line reading, pause, or pace that reveals new depths even to characters he has played before or those audiences know or think they know well.

Not everyone at the to-date height of his film career would choose to portray real-life controversial figures like Alan Turing, the genius mathematician who chose to be chemically castrated instead of going to

265

prison for being homosexual, or Julian Assange, of Wikileaks fame and infamy, who continues to fight against extradition to Sweden because of a sexual assault warrant. Not all would choose characters in the fantasy or science fiction genres that, although having blockbuster appeal to a very large audience, usually fail to lead to BAFTA or Academy Award acting nominations. Not all would choose lower-paying roles in films over bigger potential paychecks to star on Broadway or the West End or longer running starring roles on television. Yet, in collaboration with his U.S. reps at UTA or long-time U.K. agent John Grant at Conway Van Gelder Grant, Cumberbatch has chosen these roles as part of his recent career strategy.

Actors who gained clout through the years and have used their talent, fame, and celebrity to their advantage, whether to promote films or to advance humanitarian causes, equally intrigue Cumberbatch. He has professed interest in being like Brad Pitt or George Clooney when he "grows up" in the entertainment industry. Unlike these two actors, however, Cumberbatch has not built his career on sex appeal, as Pitt or Clooney did to get Hollywood's attention early in their careers. Cumberbatch is an attractive man, but his looks are more often described as unique instead of conventionally handsome, even by those who know and support him most. *Sherlock*'s Una Stubbs, for example, understands his sex appeal but adds that "he's just so unusual. He's *joli laid*. One minute, you think [she breaks off and does a little *moue* of distaste], but then the next minute you think, 'Oh, you're so *gorgeous*.'"[411] For all the fans who lust after Sherlock of the sharp cheekbones, dramatically

266

swirling coat, and smouldering stare, or share hot photos of the actor in various stages of formal dress or undress, there are those who just do not understand his physical appeal. Few, however, question or criticise his talent, which is another type of sexiness. What is most memorable about Cumberbatch is his ability to take characters that others might not find worthy of their interest, are far from sex gods, or seem controversial or socially difficult to portray and make these performances stand out in memory long after the film, television series, or play becomes part of entertainment history.

Yet Cumberbatch is not a character actor. Such actors are often perceived to look quirky or like a particular type and thus typecast. Cumberbatch more frequently plays leads, if not always leading men. He and his characters redefine *handsome* as well as *heroic;* they are provocative and thought provoking. When Cumberbatch is promoted as the hottest, best, or most watchable actor, the labels are not hyperbole. Cumberbatch delivers. He chooses the difficult or the unexpected, the underappreciated or the outcast, the infamous as well as the famous, in order to stretch himself as an actor. Perhaps it is superfluous to his career, but he also stretches the audience—by illustrating what is most human in a character and causing us to reflect on what his characters say about humanity.

His talent brought him fame as well as the opportunity for more work, but the fame also invited media to think of Cumberbatch for the first time as a celebrity in addition to being an actor. His comments about the British class system or another television drama earn him almost as much press as the official interviews designed to promote his projects. Every time he is in public view, intentionally or not, everything from his companions to his clothing to his attitude or actions is subject to immediate scrutiny and global awareness or speculation. As Twitter in particular proves, the actor's whereabouts are less of a closely guarded secret than he—or his employers—may wish, and a vast network of benevolent fans sharing such information with each other may attract far less welcome attention from paparazzi or detractors. As Cumberbatch stated in a *Radio Times* interview, no one can truly know him from a brief encounter at the stage door or on the street or a formal interview, much less by patching together secondhand information. Neither can his personality be reduced to that of the characters he plays. Cumberbatch's private life cannot be gleaned by analysis of his public or professional lives, no matter how much information is available because of his increased international celebrity profile or promotion of professional work. However, Cumberbatch's private life should not be the point—he should be able to enjoy his privacy beyond any media or fan expectations. What can be understood is that Cumberbatch is an extraordinarily talented actor who shares so many insights into the nature of acting and, inadvertently, into international obsession with celebrity, that his impressive and expansive body of work should be studied in order to greater appreciate it and the range of subjects it embraces.

Shortly before the March 2013 Cambridge Science Festival, for which Cumberbatch was guest director, he was briefly interviewed about his interest in science and his role with the festival. In great detail, and with great enthusiasm, he explained how he became engaged with ideas after hearing a Royal Society discussion of where science may be headed in the next few years. "It was so eye opening, so articulate, and the level of discussion was so invigorating that I just, I kind of went out on a high. I hadn't really heard such extraordinarily clear ideas, brilliant communicators, fantastically interesting subject matters discussed with such intelligence for a long, long time." His interest led to a lengthy conversation with Professor of Clinical Neuropsychology Barbara Sahakian. "I got talking and, of course, I started getting very excited thinking about the ethics of science [regarding] my work and *Frankenstein* and the little sort of shards of involvement or links to her incredible expertise that I had and an interest that I had in them," which, several months later, led to an invitation for the actor to serve as guest director, a position that intrigued him although he also recognised that he was far from a scientist. Nevertheless, "I sort of suggested a couple of things, and I wrote the introduction. I wish I could be there in person, but as I begged them to realise early on, because of my very fortunate position at the moment, I seem to be working nonstop."[412]

Such is the current life of Benedict Cumberbatch while he is still in transition. He is interested in many subjects that he would like to pursue more fully, but his participation often is limited because of his commitment to acting. In recent years, as Cumberbatch has moved toward stardom in multiple media, head-versus-heart decisions have become more common. His heart may have room for multiple loves, including, in addition to his art, science and such opportunities as participating in the

Cambridge Science Festival. However, his head (and likely his agent) remind him of the many job offers afforded him at this point in his career, including those that allow him to play, among many characters, a range of brilliant scientists. His work/life balance may seem to be out of kilter as he takes on one role after another with barely a breath between, but he tries to find a way to make time for as the most pressing projects that pique his curiosity. Being so much in artistic demand is "a very good thing in an actor's life, so I have to just keep on doing that until the offers dry up," he added in his apology for wanting to be at the festival, which would take place during early filming of the third series of *Sherlock*. Perhaps Benedict Cumberbatch just needs to realise that, with his level of talent; intelligent, research-oriented approach to character development; and dedication to his art, the offers are not likely to "dry up."

In a few years, Benedict Cumberbatch will no longer be "in transition" from respected, reliable, well-recognised actor in the U.K. to international film star and reluctant celebrity who has been learning how to more successfully keep his private life secretive. He will be an established "commodity" to the media or producers. The paparazzi will calm down when they see him on the street, and fewer young women may offer to have his babies. That is to be expected within a global entertainment culture that loves to love the new and the upcoming only to grow complacent or even bored after that star is born. However, also to be expected is audience expectation that Cumberbatch will remain part of our entertainment lives and popular culture and will enlighten fans with his insights into the human condition through his roles in a variety of media. Benedict Cumberbatch will soon no longer be in transition to, as one fan called it, "global domination," but he will always be an actor to watch and, more important, from whom to learn.

Endnotes
Introduction

[1] John, Emma. "Benedict Cumberbatch Interview: On the Couch with Mr. Cumberbatch." *The Guardian.* 3 September 2011.

[2] Dowell, Ben. "Parade's End Marches Away with Four Broadcasting Press Guild Awards." *The Guardian.* 14 March 2013. and Torin, Douglas. "Benedict Cumberbatch and Rebecca Hall Take Acting Honours as Parade's End Wins 4 Prizes." Broadcasting Press Guild. 14 March 2013.

[3] "Nicholas Hoult and Benedict Cumberbatch are Stars to Watch in 2013." *Forbes.* 7 January 2012.

[4] Lazarus, Susanna. "Sherlock Takes Home Two Prizes at the Royal Television Society Programme Awards." *Radio Times.* 19 March 2013.

[5] Mellow, Louisa. "Benedict Cumberbatch on the Future of Sherlock." Den of Geek. 19 December 2012.

[6] "Martin Freeman: 'Sherlock' is Best Written Thing." What's On TV. 27 December 2012.

[7] Rollings, Grant. "Ben Has Trouble With Girlfriends Because He's So Much Like Sherlock." *The Sun.* 14 January 2012.

[8] "Highlights from the PBS/Masterpiece Sherlock Series 2 Event in NYC." Storify. 2 May 2012.

[9] PBS/WNET. Livestream of the *Sherlock* Series 2 event.

[10] Johnson, Carrie, and Dockser, Ellen. "PBS' Masterpiece Mystery! 'Sherlock, Series 2' Uncovers Remarkable Ratings." PBS. 7 May 2012.

[11] Itzkoff, Dave. "Role to Role, From Sherlock to 'Star Trek.'" *New York Times.* 26 April 2012

[12] Wilson, Ben, and Elston, Charlotte. "Record Profits Driven by Rising International Creative Exports." BBC Worldwide. 12 July 2011.

[13] Although Cumberbatch most often discussed Sherlock in light of the way the character is written for the BBC series, in talks like Louise Brealey's Cheltenham Festival interview with him, he talked about Conan Doyle's canon. A partial transcript of the 6 October 2012 interview is available at fan site Cumberbatchweb.

[14] Lobb, Adrian. "The Lonely Detective." *The Big Issue* (Scotland). 20-26 August 2012, p. 25.

[15] Aitkenhead, Decca. "Welcome to the Pleasure Zone." *Radio Times.* 18-24 August 2012, p. 11.

[16] "Sherlock Speaks German: The Making of the German Version." *The Baker Street Chronicle.* Summer 2012, p. 15.

[17] Pedigree 4 a Day Official Ad (UK).YouTube. September 2012.

[18] McNary, Dave. "'Twelve Years a Slave' Dated for Dec. 27 by Fox Searchlight." *Variety.*28 March 2013.

[19] Rutter, Claire. "Sherlock's Benedict Cumberbatch Beats David Beckham & Harry Styles to 'Sexiest Man.'" Entertainmentwise.com. 7 May 2012.

[20] "The 2012 Time 100 Poll." *Time.* 18 April 2012.

[21] "Benedict Cumberbatch Talks about Sherlock and War Horse." *Mirror.* 31 December 2011.

[22] "Benedict Cumberbatch." *Short List.* August 2012.

[23] Ibid.

Chapter 1

[24] Seale, Jack. "Benedict Cumberbatch on Fame, Science and His New Radio 3 Play, Copenhagen." *Radio Times.* 11 January 2013.

[25] Shakespeare, William. *Romeo and Juliet.* Act II, Scene II, Lines 45-49.

[26] de Moraes, Lisa. "*Sherlock* Premiere Scores High Ratings." *The Washington Post.* 9 May 2012.

[27] JimmyKimmelLive. "What is a Cumberbatch?" YouTube. 18 September 2012.

[28] Ferguson, Liz. "Jimmy Kimmel Makes Fun of Actor Benedict Cumberbatch's Name—Not Polite, Not That Funny and Not Very Original, Either." *The Montreal Gazette.* 18 September 2012.

[29] *Alan Carr: Chatty Man.* YouTube. 24 January 2011 (original broadcast).

[30] Kelly, Laura. "'I've Been the Next Big Thing for about 10 Years." *The Big Issue* (Scotland ed.). 16-22 May 2011, p. 19.

[31] Lawson, Mark. "Under Their Skins." *The Guardian.* 28 April 2008.

[32] Dessau, Bruce. "Benedict Cumberbatch's Rising Star." *The Times.* 3 November 2007.

[33] Wilson, MacKenzie. "Benedict Cumberbatch and His Mom Chat with 'Saunders and French.'" BBC America. 3 January 2011.

[34] Lawson, Mark. "Under Their Skins." *The Guardian.* 28 April 2008.

[35] Rollings, Grant. "Ben Has Trouble with Girlfriends Because He's So Like Sherlock." *The Sun.* 14 January 2012.

[36] Ibid.

[37] Ibid.

[38] "Eee! It's Wanda's Little Wonder." *Daily Mirror.* 24 July 1976, p. 5.

[39] Bell, Jack. "The Solid Gold Girl Comes Back." *Daily Mirror.* 29 October 1977, p. 15.

[40] "Tips for Nervous Santas." *Daily Express.* 17 December 1979, p. 17.

[41] Stanford, Peter. "It's No Good, Benedict Cumberbatch Can't Stop Us Liking Him." *The Telegraph.* 18 August 2012.

[42] Knowles, Stewart. "Timothy, Wanda . . . and the Rose That Changed Her Mind About Marriage." *ITV Playhouse/TV Times.* 28 July 1979, pp. 9-10. The article has been discovered by fans and appears in transcripts or scans on several fan sites.

[43] Brealey, Louise. "Sherlock: Meet Lara Pulver, Louise Brealey and Una Stubbs—the Baker St Babes." *Radio Times*. 16 January 2012.

[44] Spencer, Kathryn (Ed.). "When Veteran Elaine Knew a Star Was Born." *The Express*. 14 September 2007. British Library Newspaper Index. Record No. 58644804.

[45] Kingsley, Hilary. "Is Wanda Laughing All the Way to Bed?" *Daily Mirror*. 6 December 1980, p. 15.

[46] BBC Press Office. "William Golding's 'To the Ends of the Earth.'" 19 May 2005.

[47] Sivell, Vaughan. "On Benedict Cumberbatch." Mug7. 9 September 2011.

[48] Wilson, MacKenzie. "Benedict Cumberbatch and His Mom Chat with 'Saunders and French.'" BBC America. 3 January 2011.

[49] Ibid.

[50] Ibid.

[51] Mitchison, Amanda. "Benedict Cumberbatch on Playing Sherlock Holmes." *The Guardian*. 16 July 2010.

[52] Secher, Benjamin. "Plummy Depths." *The Telegraph*. 11 August 2012, p. 39.

[53] Rochlin, Margy. "Holmes at Last." *New York Post*. 6 May 2012.

[54] Curtis, Nick. "Benedict Cumberbatch—Stepping into the Lead." *London Evening Standard*. 1 June 2010.

[55] Ibid.

[56] Jarvis, Alice-Azania. "Benedict Cumberbatch: Success? It's Elementary." *The Independent*. 29 January 2011.

[57] *The Rattigan Enigma*. BBC. Benedict Cumberbatch, writer. 28 July 2011 (original broadcast).

[58] "Extracts from the Introduction to Songs." *The Harrovian*. 1 December 2012. Vol. CXXVI, No. 11, p. 114.

[59] BBC Press Office. "William Golding's 'To the Ends of the Earth.'" 19 May 2005.

[60] Jarvis, Alice-Azania. "Benedict Cumberbatch: Success? It's Elementary." *The Independent.* 29 January 2011.

[61] LAMDA—The London Academy of Music and Dramatic Art. "Where Are They Now?"

[62] LAMDA. The Acting Courses.

[63] Comment to Unencumberbatched forum. February 2011. No longer available online.

[64] Secher, Benjamin, "Plummy Depths," *The Telegraph.* 11 August 2012. p. 39.

[65] Lawson, Mark. "Under Their Skins." *The Guardian.* 28 April 2008.

[66] Cole, Tom. "Benedict Cumberbatch Joins Stephen Hawking at the Premiere of His New Documentary Series." *Radio Times.* 6 September 2012.

[67] Cumberbatchweb. September 2012.

[68] BAFTA. Press Release. "Benedict Cumberbatch Announced as Juror for the 2013 EE Rising Star Award." December 2012.

[69] Rutter, Claire. "Sherlock's Benedict Cumberbatch Announced as Guest Director of Cambridge Science Festival." 22 January 2013.

[70] Barnes, Henry. "Benedict Cumberbatch Landed Star Trek Role with Pitch Filmed on iPhone." *The Guardian.* 27 April 2012.

[71] *The Rattigan Enigma.* BBC. Benedict Cumberbatch, writer. 28 July 2011 (original broadcast).

[72] Fox, Hilary. "From 'Sherlock' to 'Star Trek' for Cumberbatch." 14 December 2011.

[73] NPR. "Benedict Cumberbatch: 'Sherlock,' Smaug, and Spying." *Morning Edition.* 3 May 2012.

[74] Itzkoff, Dave. "Role to Role, from 'Sherlock' to Star Trek." *New York Times.* 26 April 2012.

[75] "Benedict Cumberbatch Talks About Sherlock and War Horse." *The Mirror.* 31 December 2011.

[76] BFI screening. *Sherlock*. "A Scandal in Belgravia." 7 December 2011. London.

[77] Kinnear, Lucy. "The 5-minute Interview: Benedict Cumberbatch, Actor." *The Independent*. 7 February 2008.

Chapter 2

[78] Kennedy, Hannah. "20 Questions with Benedict Cumberbatch." WhatsOnStage.com. 25 April 2005.

[79] Annand, Simon. "The Half." SimonAnnand.com.

[80] Annand, Simon. *The Half: Photographs of Actors Preparing for the Stage*. London: Faber & Fabre, 2008, pp. 218-219.

[81] Glanfield, Tim. "Benedict Cumberbatch As You've Never Seen Him Before." *Radio Times*. 21 February 2012.

[82] Kennedy, Hannah. "20 Questions with Benedict Cumberbatch." WhatsOnStage.com. 25 April 2005.

[83] Dalglish, Darren. "Benedict Cumberbatch." LondonTheatre.co.uk. 19 July 2010.

[84] Gross, John. Review of *As You Like It*. 16 June 2002.Reprinted in *Theatre Record*, 22(12), p. 768.

[85] Taylor, Paul. Review of *As You Like It*. *The Independent*. 17 June 2002. Reprinted in *Theatre Record*, 22(12), p. 768.

[86] Coveney, Michael. Review of *Love's Labour's Lost*. *Daily Mail*. 22 June 2001. Reprinted in *Theatre Record*, 21(12), p. 757.

[87] Coveney, Michael. Review of *The Lady from the Sea*. *Daily Mail*. 16 May 2003. Reprinted in *Theatre Record*, 23(10), p. 650.

[88] Gross, John. Review of *As You Like It*. 16 June 2002.Reprinted in *Theatre Record*, 22(12), p. 768.

[89] Willocks, Sarah. Review of *As You Like It*. *Time Out*. 19 June 2002. Reprinted in *Theatre Record*, 22(12), p. 768.

[90] Cook, Mark. Review of *Oh! What a Lovely War*. *Time Out*. 31 July 2002. Reprinted in *Theatre Record*, 22(15), p. 980.

[91] Marmion, Patrick. Review of *Oh! What a Lovely War. Mail on Sunday*. 28 July 2002. Reprinted in *Theatre Record*, 22(15), p. 980.

[92] "Almeida Brand Video." YouTube. 6 March 2011.

[93] Edwards, Jane. Review of *Hedda Gabler. Time Out*. 23 March 2005. Reprinted in *Theatre Record*, 25(6), p. 348.

[94] Macauley, Alistair. Review of *Hedda Gabler. Financial Times*. 21 March 2005. Reprinted in *Theatre Record*, 25(6), p. 348.

[95] Marmion, Patrick. Review of *Period of Adjustment. Daily Mail*. 17 March 2006. Reprinted in *Theatre Record*, 26(6), p. 304.

[96] Spencer, Charles. Review of *Period of Adjustment. Daily Telegraph*. March 18 2006. Reprinted in *Theatre Record*, 26(6), p. 305.

[97] Macauley, Alistair. Review of *Period of Adjustment. Financial Times*. 22 March 2006. Reprinted in *Theatre Record*, 26(6), p. 306.

[98] Evans, Lloyd. Review of *Period of Adjustment. Spectator*. 25 March 2006. Reprinted in *Theatre Record*, 26(6), p. 306.

[99] "Benedict Cumberbatch—Rhinoceros Stage Play—Casting the Lead." YouTube. 15 August 2010. This video is no longer available.

[100] Billington, Michael. "Rhinoceros, Royal Court, London." *The Guardian*. 27 September 2007.

[101] Fisher, Philip. "Rhinoceros." British Theatre Guide. 2007.

[102] Taylor, Paul. "First Night: Rhinoceros, Royal Court Theatre." *The Independent*. 28 September 2007.

[103] Ionesco, Eugene. *Rhinoceros*. Trans. Martin Crimp. London: Faber and Faber, 2007.

[104] *Rhinoceros*. Videorecording made at the Royal Court Theatre, matinee performance, 6 December 2007. Victoria and

Albert Museum, performance archives, Blythe House. Accessed 22 March 2013.

[105] Comey, Jeremiah. *The Art of Film Acting: A Guide for Actors and Directors.* Oxford: Focal Press, 2002, p. 29.

[106] *"Rhinoceros* Post-Show Talk." 20 September 2007. British Library Performance Archives, London. Accessed 14 March 2013.

[107] Ibid.

[108] Ibid.

[109] Ibid.

[110] Ibid.

[111] Frisch, Max. *The Arsonists.* London: Methuen Drama, 2007, p. 56.

[112] *The Arsonists* Post-Show Talk. Royal Court Theatre. Recording. 13 November 2007. Accessed 25 June 2012 at the British Library.

[113] Spencer, Charles. "The Arsonists: A Blast, and Then a Damp Squib." *The Telegraph.* 7 November 2007.

[114] Loveridge, Charlotte. *"The Arsonists." Curtain Up.* 13 November 2007.

[115] Thomas, Simon. *"The Arsonists." Music OMG.* 15 December 2007.

[116] Benedict, David. *"The Arsonists." Variety.* 14 November 2007.

[117] Frisch, Frisch, Max. "The English Stage Company at the Royal Court." *The Arsonists.* London: Methuen Drama, 2007.

[118] "Benedict Cumberbatch—*The City* (Royal Court Theatre) Cast and Creatives Podcast April 2008." YouTube. 14 January 2012.

[119] Crimp, Martin. *The City.* London: Faber and Faber, 2008, pp. 55-56.

[120] "Benedict Cumberbatch—*The City* (Royal Court Theatre) Cast and Creatives Podcast April 2008." YouTube. 14 January 2012.

[121] Crimp, Martin. *The City*. London: Faber and Faber, 2008, p. 35.

[122] *"City* Post-show Talk." Royal Court Theatre. Recording. 8 May 2008. Accessed 25 June 2012. British Library.

[123] Ibid.

[124] Kelly, Laura. "'I've Been the Next Big Thing for about 10 Years." *The Big Issue* (Scotland ed.). 16-22 May 2011, p. 16.

[124] Boucher, Geoff. "'Sherlock' and 'Star Trek': Benedict Cumberbatch Lights It Up." *Los Angeles Times*. 9 May 2012.

[124] "Benedict Cumberbatch—*The City* (Royal Court Theatre) Cast and Creatives Podcast April 2008." YouTube. 14 January 2012.

[125] *"City* Post-show Talk." Royal Court Theatre. Recording. 8 May 2008. Accessed 25 June 2012. British Library.

[126] "Benedict Cumberbatch—*The City* (Royal Court Theatre) Cast and Creatives Podcast April 2008." YouTube. 14 January 2012.

[127] Ibid.

[128] *"City* Post-show Talk." Royal Court Theatre. Recording. 8 May 2008. Accessed 25 June 2012. British Library.

[129] Frisch, Max. "The Company." *The Arsonists*. London: Methuen Drama, 2007. and Crimp, Martin. "The Company." *The City*. London: Faber and Faber, 2008.

[130] Kennedy, Hannah. "20 Questions with Benedict Cumberbatch." What's On. 25 April 2005.

[131] *Hedda Gabler*. Produced by Robert Fox at the Almeida Theatre. Recorded 13 July 2005 at a matinee performance for the National Video Archive of Performance. Accessed 22 March 2013 at the Victoria and Albert Museum's performance archives at Blythe House, London.

[132] Porter, Lynnette. "Celebrity and the Celebration of Art: The Transformation of Benedict Cumberbatch." PopMatters. 27 April 2011.

[133] Ibid.

[134] *After the Dance,* by Terence Rattigan, National Theatre. Programme.

[135] *After the Dance* Stage Management Bible. Rehearsal Notes, 23 April 2010. National Theatre. Accessed 5 December 2010, National Theatre archives, London.

[136] *After the Dance* Stage Management Bible. Rehearsal Notes, Number 13, 14 May 2010. Accessed 5 December 2010, National Theatre archives, London.

[137] *After the Dance* Stage Management Bible. Rehearsal Notes, Number 8, 6 May 2010. Accessed 5 December 2010, National Theatre archives, London.

[138] *After the Dance.* Recording. Accessed 5 December 2010, National Theatre archives, London.

[139] *After the Dance* Stage Management Bible. Rehearsal Notes, Number 2, 27 April 2010. Accessed 5 December 2010, National Theatre archives, London

[140] *After the Dance* Stage Management Bible. Rehearsal Notes, Number 16, 20 May 2010. Accessed 5 December 2010, National Theatre archives, London

[141] Sands, Sarah. "Many of Us are 'Fruitcakes' Now, Mr. Cameron." *London Evening Standard.* 22 November 2011.

[142] *Sherlock:* Season Two. DVD set. Commentary, Part 1. BBC Worldwide. 2012.

[143] *After the Dance* Stage Management Bible. Rehearsal Notes, Number 16, 20 May 2010. Accessed 5 December 2010, National Theatre archives, London

[144] *After the Dance* Stage Management Bible. Niks Cue Sheet. Act One Notes. Note 6. April 2010. Accessed 5 December 2010, National Theatre archives, London

[145] *After the Dance* Stage Management Bible. Rehearsal Notes, Number 2, 27 April 2010. Accessed 5 December 2010, National Theatre archives, London

[146] Hitchings, Henry. "After the Dance Shows the National Theatre At its Best." *The London Evening Standard.* 9 June 2010.

[147] Billington, Michael. "After the Dance." *The Guardian.* 8 June 2010.

[148] White, Lesley. "The Fabulous Baker Street Boy." *The Sunday Times.* 15 August 2010.

[149] Cumberbatch, Benedict. "Holiday Holmes: Benedict Cumberbatch in the Seychelles." *London Evening Standard.* 25 November 2011.

[150] Preston, John. "The Rattigan Enigma, BBC Four, The Camera That Changed the World, The Code, BBC Two, Review." *The Telegraph.* 30 July 2011.

[151] Sweeting, Adam. "The Rattigan Enigma, BBC Four." The Arts Desk. 29 July 2011.

[152] NT Live broadcasts of *Frankenstein* were, in some cases, not truly "live" but broadcast within hours or days of the performance. However, the original broadcasts were treated as live performances and were not edited before worldwide broadcast.

[153] "Behind the Scenes on *The Turning Point.*" *Sky Arts Live!* YouTube. 14 September 2010.

[154] Day, Elizabeth. "Benedict Cumberbatch: 'I Felt Like I Had Rabies or Was a King.'" *The Guardian.* 6 November 2010.

[155] Cumberbatchweb. "Review of The Children's Monologues." 2010.

[156] Sherlockology. "The Playwright's Playwrights: Look Back in Anger." 7 July 2012.

[157] Walker, Tim. "Sherlock Actor Benedict Cumberbatch Plans to Play Hamlet." *The Telegraph.* 20 June 2012.

[158] Wilson, Benji. "Benedict Cumberbatch." *Reader's Digest.* September 2012.

Chapter 3

[159] *Masterpiece. The Last Enemy.* PBS.

[160] *Silent Witness.* "Tell No Tales: Part 1." Dir. John Duthie. BBC. 19 October 2002 (original broadcast). "Tell No Tales: Part 2." Dir. John Duthie. BBC. 20 October 2002 (original broadcast).

[161] *Cambridge Spies.* Episode 2. Dir. Tim Fywell. BBC. 16 May 2003 (original broadcast).

[162] *Heartbeat.* "The Good Doctor." Dir. Paul Walker. ITV. 30 January 2000 (original broadcast).

[163] *Heartbeat.* "No Hard Feelings." Dir. Judith Dine. ITV. 11 April 2004 (original broadcast).

[164] *Tipping the Velvet.* Dir. Geoffrey Sax. BBC. 2 October 2002 (original broadcast).

[165] *Fortysomething.* ITV. Dir. Hugh Laurie. 2003. Episode 1.2. 6 July 2003 (original broadcast). The series was broadcast between 29 June and 9 August 2003.

[166] Cumberbatchweb. "The Times—New Benedict Cumberbatch Interview Promoting Third Star." 14 May 2011.

[167] Spero, Josh. "Josh Spero Talking about Benedict Cumberbatch on BBC Radio Wales Aug 2012." YouTube. 15 August 2012.

[168] Pahle, Rebecca. "Benedict Cumberbatch to Depress Audience Members with Alan Turing Biopic?" TheMarySue.com 2 February 2013.

[169] Cumberbatch, Benedict. *Inspired by Music: Personal Reflections of How Music Changed Our Lives.* London: Shoehorn Publishing, 2009.

[170] "Benedict Cumberbatch Used Sherlock Skills to Survive Armed Kidnapping Ordeal." *The Mirror.* 12 January 2012.

[171] Hutchison, Tom. "Sherlock Star's Gun Scare." 12 January 2012.

[172] BBC Press Office. "William Golding's *To the Ends of the Earth.*" Press release. 5 May 2005.

[173] Millar, Paul. "Benedict Cumberbatch's Van Gogh Docudrama Fetches 960k." Digital Spy. 6 April 2010.

[174] Deacon, Michael, Horsford, Simon, O'Donovan, Gerard. and Reynolds, Gillian. "The Daily Telegraph's TV Desk's Pick of 5 April's Television and Radio Available on the BBC's Catch-up Service, the iPlayer." *The Telegraph.* 5 April 2010.

[175] "What's New: Arts Channel Open Week." SkyWatch. December 2012, p. 7.

[176] Clifton, Jane. "Van Gogh Seen in Letters to His Brother." *The Dominion Post,* 12 December 2012, p. A13.

[177] Ibid.

[178] Drake, Philip. "Reconceptualizing Screen Performance." *Journal of Film and Video,* 58(1-2), p. 85. Cited in Shingler, Martin. *Star Studies: A Critical Guide.* London: Palgrave Macmillan/BFI, 2012, p. 45.

[179] The "fourth wall" is a film/television/theatrical term in which a character acknowledges being a character by talking directly to the audience or author. Some sources differentiate between the "third wall" (i.e., directly confronting the audience and bringing the audience into the story) and the "fourth wall" (i.e., directly confronting or interacting with the author).

[180] HD Warrior (Philip Johnston). "Van Gogh 'Painted with Words' BBC Docu-drama . . . Filmed During December 2009." 5 April 2010.

[181] Comey, Jeremiah. *The Art of Film Acting: A Guide for Actors and Directors.* Oxford: Focal Press, 2002, p. xii.

[182] Ibid., p. 14.

[183] *Inseparable.* Dir. Nick White. Area 17, 2007. Area17.com.

[184] Sherlockology. "Inseparable review." 2011.

[185] White, Nick. Email. 23 October 2012 and 9 April 2013.

[186] Ibid.

[187] Ibid.

[188] Porter, Lynnette. "DR Hood and the 'Dramatic Poetry' of Wreckers." PopMatters. Deep Focus. 6 January 2011.

[189] "Wreckers Q&A with Director D.R. Hood, Benedict Cumberbatch, and Shaun Evans." Curzon Cinemas Ltd. YouTube. 22 December 2011.

[190] Hood, D R. Email. 17 November 2012.

[191] Ibid.

[192] Ibid.

[193] Porter, Lynnette. "DR Hood and the 'Dramatic Poetry' of Wreckers." PopMatters. Deep Focus. 6 January 2011.

[194] Sivell, Vaughan. "On Benedict Cumberbatch." Mug7.com. 9 September 2011.

[195] "Benedict Cumberbatch." ShortList.com. August 2012.

[196] Sivell, Vaughan. "On Benedict Cumberbatch." Mug7.com. 9 September 2011.

[197] Porter, Lynnette. "'Third Star,' Making the Festival Rounds, Pits Benedict Cumberbatch Against a Taboo Topic." PopMatters. 1 June 2011.

[198] Sivell, Vaughan. "On Benedict Cumberbatch." Mug7.com. 9 September 2011.

[199] Muir, Kate. "Benedict Cumberbatch on Fame, Death, and a New Film." *The Times*. 14 May 2011.

[200] McDonald, Paul. "Why Study Film Acting? Some Opening Reflections." In Cynthia Baron, Diane Carson, and Frank P. Tomasulo (Eds.), *More Than a Method: Trends in Contemporary Film Performances* (pp. 23-41). Detroit: Wayne State University, 2004, p. 32.

Chapter 4

[201] "The Allure of Benedict." *Jaguar Magazine* #5. iPad. Or Microsites.jaguar.com, PDF p. 42.

[202] Anderson, Kyle. "Neil Gaiman's 'Neverwhere' Radio Play's All-Star Cast." Nerdist. 5 December 2012.

[203] Reynolds, Gillian. "Neverwhere is a Reminder that Radio is Already Innovative." *The Telegraph*. 26 March 2013.

[204] "Radio Plays." BBC 4 Radio Plays by Year. SuttonElms.org.uk.

205 Finnemore, John. "Two Things You Might Be Interested In." 2 May 2008. Johnfinnemore.blogspot.co.uk.

206 Grant-West, Charlotte. "Benedict Cumberbatch Not Too Big for Radio 4 Sitcom." 21 November 2012. Entertainmentwise. com.

207 Finnemore, John. "Cabin Pressure IV—Prepare for Boarding." 14 November 2012. Johnfinnemore.blogspot.co.uk.

208 Finnemore, John. "Stage Direction: [DING] Ding! [DING] Ding! [DING] Ding!" 9 July 2011. Johnfinnemore.blogspot. co.uk.

209 Finnemore, John. "Newcastle." 19 July 2011. Johnfinnemore.blogspot.co.uk.

210 Finnemore, John. "I Wish I Could Find the Setting for 'Jelly Babies to Automatic.'" 11 July 2011. Johnfinnemore. blogspot.co.uk.

211 Finnemore, John. "'Ours Blanc.' Or 'Ours Polaire.'" 1 July 2011. Johnfinnemore.blogspot.co.uk.

212 *Cabin Pressure.* "Wokingham." Dir. David Tyler. BBC Radio 4. 6 February 2013.

213 Child, Ben. "Benedict Cumberbatch and Gemma Arterton Up For Absolutely Anything Monty Python Film." *The Guardian.* 7 November 2012.

214 Finnemore, John. "Yverdon-Les-Bains." Forget What Did. 15 February 2013. Johnfinnemore.blogspot.co.uk.

215 Ibid.

216 Ferguson, Liz. "Cumberbabes: Listen to Benedict Cumberbatch Talk in a Brainy Way about Nuclear Physics, in the Play Copenhagen, on BBC Radio." *Montreal Gazette.* 17 January 2013.

217 Key, Graeme. "Copenhagen—The Director's Blog." BBC Radio. 10 January 2013. BBC.

218 Seale, Jack. "Benedict Cumberbatch on Fame, Science, and His New Radio 3 Play, Copenhagen." *Radio Times.* 11 January 2013.

[219] "Behind the Scenes of Copenhagen." BBC Radio. 2013.

[220] Seale, Jack. "Benedict Cumberbatch on Fame, Science, and His New Radio 3 Play, Copenhagen." *Radio Times.* 11 January 2013.

[221] *Copenhagen.* Dir. Emma Harding. BBC Radio 3. 13 January 2013 (original broadcast).

Chapter 5

[222] BBC Press Office. *Hawking.* Press release. 2 April 2004.

[223] Ray, Amber M. "Benedict Cumberbatch: The Uncensored 'Sherlock' Interview." *Metro.* 6 May 2012.

[224] BBC Science and Nature. *Hawking.* August 2006.

[225] BBC Press Office. *Hawking.* Press release. 2 April 2004.

[226] Christie, Nicola. "Bright Star." *The Times.* 10 April 2004. p. 29.

[227] Ibid.

[228] *Hawking.* BBC. Dir. Philip Martin. 13 April 2004 (original broadcast).

[229] Gilbert, Gerard. "A Series to Challenge *Downton.*" *The Independent, Radar* magazine. 11 August 2012, p. 7.

[230] "Benedict Cumberbatch: 'I Think Like Holmes.'" What's On TV. 9 December 2012.

[231] *Sherlock* screening. "A Scandal in Belgravia." British Film Institute. 7 December 2011. London.

[232] *Sherlock.* "A Study in Pink." BBC. Dir. Paul McGuigan. 25 July 2010 (original broadcast).

[233] Ray, Amber M. "Benedict Cumberbatch: The Uncensored 'Sherlock' Interview." *Metro.* 6 May 2012.

[234] PBS. *Masterpiece. Sherlock* Season 2. Co-Creator Live Chats: Mark Gatiss. 14 May 2012.

[235] "Co-Creator Live Chat: Mark Gatiss." PBS.org. 14 May 2012. Video.

[236] Mumford, Gwilym. "Sherlock Returns to the BBC: 'He's Definitely Devilish.'" *The Guardian.* 16 December 2011.

[237] *Sherlock.* "A Scandal in Belgravia." BBC. Dir. Paul McGuigan. 1 January 2012 (original broadcast).

[238] *Sherlock:* Season Two. DVD set. Commentary, Part 1. BBC Worldwide. 2012. Similar comments were made at the BFI screening, which took place the evening before the DVD commentary was recorded.

[239] Rosenberg, Alyssa. "Steven Moffat on 'Sherlock's Return, the Holmes-Watson Love Story, and Updating the First Supervillain." ThinkProgress. 7 May 2012.

[240] *Sherlock:* Season Two. DVD set. Commentary, Part 1. BBC Worldwide. 2012.

[241] *Sherlock* screening. "A Scandal in Belgravia." British Film Institute. 7 December 2011. London.

[242] Ibid.

[243] Conlan, Tara. "Sherlock is Cheeky Entertainment, Insists BBC after Nudity Complaints." *The Guardian.* 11 January 2012.

[244] Elbert, Lynn. "Benedict Cumberbatch Defends 'Sherlock' Nude Scene." *The Huffington Post.* 6 January 2012.

[245] *Sherlock:* Season Two. DVD set. Commentary, Part 1. BBC Worldwide. 2012.

[246] *Sherlock.* "The Hounds of Baskerville." BBC. Dir. Paul McGuigan. 8 January 2012 (original broadcast).

[247] *Sherlock:* Season Two. DVD set. Commentary, Part 1. BBC Worldwide. 2012.

[248] Chater, Eos. "How I Taught Sherlock Holmes to Play the Violin." *The Guardian.* 4 January 2012.

[249] Earth Observing System. "Sherlock on the Fiddle." Blog. 2 January 2012.

[250] *Sherlock:* Season Two. DVD set. Commentary, Part 1. BBC Worldwide. 2012.

[251] *Sherlock* 2 Fan Q&A in New York. PBS. 2 May 2012. http://video.pbs.org/video/2232626419

[252] "The Allure of Benedict." *Jaguar Magazine #5*. iPad. or Microsites.jaguar.com, PDF, pp. 40-43.

[253] *Sherlock:* Season Two. DVD set. Commentary, Part 1. BBC Worldwide. 2012.

[254] O'Hare, Kate. "'Star Trek 2': 'Sherlock' Star Benedict Cumberbatch Dyes Hair, Loves J.J. Abrams." Zap2It. 25 April 2012.

[255] Swashbuckled. "No Shit Sherlock." Blog. 16 May 2011.

[256] *Sherlock* screening. "A Scandal in Belgravia." PBS.org. 2 May 2012. New York. Streaming video.

[257] "Benedict Cumberbatch 'Desperate' for U.S. Success." NME. 27 April 2012.

[258] *Sherlock:* Season Two. DVD set. Commentary, Part 1. BBC Worldwide. 2012.

[259] Ibid.

[260] Seale, Jack. "Danny Boyle: Benedict Cumberbatch is 'One of the Leading Actors in the World.'" *Radio Times.* 9 April 2012.

[261] *Sherlock* screening. "A Scandal in Belgravia." PBS.org. 2 May 2012. New York. Streaming video.

[262] Kelly, Laura. "'I've Been the Next Big Thing for about 10 Years." *The Big Issue* (Scotland edition). 16-22 May 2011, p. 16.

[263] Boucher, Geoff. "'Sherlock' and 'Star Trek': Benedict Cumberbatch Lights It Up." *Los Angeles Times.* 9 May 2012.

[264] Kelly, Laura. "'I've Been the Next Big Thing for about 10 Years." *The Big Issue* (Scotland edition). 16-22 May 2011, p. 16.

[265] Secher, Benjamin. "Plummy Depths." *The Telegraph* magazine. 11 August 2012, p. 39.

[266] *Frankenstein* Q&A. National Theatre. 21 April 2011. London. A transcript is available at fan site Cumberbatchweb.

[267] Shelley, Mary. *Frankenstein.* New York: Norton, 2012, pp. 35-36.

[268] Costa, Maddy. "Frankenstein: Man or Monster?" *The Guardian.* 17 January 2011,

[269] *Frankenstein: A Modern Myth.* Dir. Adam Low. Lone Star Productions and National Theatre, 2012.

[270] Ibid.

[271] White, Lesley. "The Fabulous Baker Street Boy." *The Sunday Times.* 15 August 2010.

[272] *Frankenstein,* original casting. Dir. Danny Boyle. National Theatre, 2011.

[273] *Frankenstein,* alternate casting. Dir. Danny Boyle. Technical rehearsal recording. National Theatre Archives, London.

[274] *Frankenstein, Olivier Theatre 2011, Stage Management Bible.* Section 26—Rehearsal Notes, Wednesday, 8th December 2010 Frankenstein Issue 3. Accessed at the National Theatre Archives, London, 6 December 2011.

[275] *Frankenstein, Olivier Theatre 2011, Stage Management Bible.* Section 26—Rehearsal Notes, Thursday, 9th December 2010 Frankenstein Issue 4, p. 2. Accessed at the National Theatre Archives, London, 6 December 2011.

[276] *Frankenstein, Olivier Theatre 2011, Stage Management Bible.* Section 26—Rehearsal Notes, Thursday 16th December 2010 Issue 9. Accessed at the National Theatre Archives, London, 6 December 2011.

[277] Ibid.

[278] *Frankenstein Olivier Theatre 2011. Costume Bible.* Sections Benedict Cumberbatch, Jonny Lee Miller, and Misc. Accessed at the National Theatre Archives, London, 8 March 2013. The descriptions of costumes all come from this book.

[279] *Frankenstein, Olivier Theatre 2011, Stage Management Bible.* Section 26—Rehearsal Notes, Thursday 23rd December 2010 Issue 14, p. 1. Accessed at the National Theatre Archives, London, 6 December 2011.

[280] *Frankenstein, Olivier Theatre 2011, Stage Management Bible.* Section 26—Rehearsal Notes, Wednesday 19th January 2011 Issue 28. Accessed at the National Theatre Archives, London, 6 December 2011.

[281] *Frankenstein, Olivier Theatre 2011, Stage Management Bible.* Section 26—Rehearsal Notes, Thursday 23rd December 2010 Issue 14, p. 2. Accessed at the National Theatre Archives, London, 6 December 2011.

[282] *Frankenstein, Olivier Theatre 2011, Stage Management Bible.* Section 26—Rehearsal Notes, Tuesday 11th January 2011 Issue 21, p. 2. Accessed at the National Theatre Archives, London, 6 December 2011.

[283] *Frankenstein, Olivier Theatre 2011, Stage Management Bible.* Section 26—Rehearsal Notes, Friday 14th January 2011 Issue 24. Accessed at the National Theatre Archives, London, 6 December 2011.

[284] Ibid.

[285] *Frankenstein, Olivier Theatre 2011, Stage Management Bible.* Section 26—Rehearsal Notes, Saturday 15th January 2011 Issue 25. Accessed at the National Theatre Archives, London, 6 December 2011.

[286] *Frankenstein, Olivier Theatre 2011, Stage Management Bible.* Section 26—Rehearsal Notes, Friday 21st January 2011 Issue 30, p. 1. Accessed at the National Theatre Archives, London, 6 December 2011.

[287] *Frankenstein, Olivier Theatre 2011, Stage Management Bible.* Section 26—Rehearsal Notes, Saturday 22nd January 2011 Issue 31. Accessed at the National Theatre Archives, London, 6 December 2011.

[288] *Frankenstein, Olivier Theatre 2011, Stage Management Bible.* Section 20, Pre-show rehearsal schedule, Frankenstein Production Schedule 09-issued (p. 4), Saturday 5th February. Accessed at the National Theatre Archives, London, 6 December 2011.

[289] Ibid.

[290] *Frankenstein, Olivier Theatre 2011, Stage Management Bible.* Section 10, Frankenstein—Tash's Notes, Version A-Benedict –'Creature', Jonny-'Victor'. Accessed at the National Theatre Archives, London, 6 December 2011.

[291] Ibid.

[292] Ibid.

[293] Palmer, Martyn. "'I've Always Wanted to Play a Spy . . . You Are Never What You Seem': Benedict Cumberbatch on Fulfilling His Acting Dream." *Mail Online.* 13 July 2011.

[294] Oldman, Gary. Commentary. *Tinker Tailor Soldier Spy.* Universal. DVD. 2012.

[295] White, Lesley. "The Fabulous Baker Street Boy." *The Sunday Times.* 15 August 2010.

[296] *First Look: The Making of* Tinker Tailor Soldier Spy. Focus Features, 2011. HBO.

[297] BBC Media Centre. "Interview with Sir Tom Stoppard." 1 August 2012.

[298] Singh, Anita. "Parade's End—'Who is This Benedict Cumberbatch?'" *The Telegraph.* 27 July 2012.

[299] BBC Media Centre. "Interview with Benedict Cumberbatch." 1 August 2012.

[300] Gilbert, Gerard. "Parade's End: A Series to Challenge Downton." *The Independent.* 11 August 2012.

[301] Lowry, Brian. "Parade's End." *Variety.* 19 February 2013.

[302] Cole, Tom. "Benedict Cumberbatch 'Force-Fed' Himself Doughnuts for Parade's End Role." *Radio Times.* 24 August 2012.

[303] Gilbert, Gerard. "Parade's End: A Series to Challenge Downton." *The Independent.* 11 August 2012.

[304] BBC Media Centre. "Interview with Benedict Cumberbatch." 1 August 2012.

[305] Ibid.

[306] *Parade's End.* Mammoth Screen Ltd., 2012. DVD. Produced by BBC, HBO, Lookout Point, and Mammoth Screen. Dir. Susanna White. Episode Two.

[307] *Parade's End.* Mammoth Screen Ltd., 2012. DVD. Produced by BBC, HBO, Lookout Point, and Mammoth Screen. Dir. Susanna White. Disc 2. "Behind the Scenes." Interview with Susanna White.

[308] Cheltenham Music Festival. "Benedict Cumberbatch— Cheltenham Music Festival." 13 July 2012. YouTube.

[309] Frost, Caroline. "Sherlock Star Benedict Cumberbatch's Curious Incident In The Night-Time, During 'Parade's End' Filming." 12 September 2012.

[310] Cumberbatch also mentioned Cubism, as well as Vorticism, in relation to *Parade's End* during an *Independent* interview: Gilbert, Gerard. "Parade's End: A Series to Challenge Downton." *The Independent.* 11 August 2012.

[311] Ibid.

Chapter 6

[312] Lobb, Adrian. "The Lonely Detective." *The Big Issue* (Scotland). 20-26 August 2012, pp. 22-25.

[313] Aitkenhead, Decca. "Welcome to the Pleasure Zone." *Radio Times.* 18-24 August 2012, p. 11.

[314] Itzkoff, Dave. "Role to Role, From Sherlock to 'Star Trek.'" *The New York Times.* 26 April 2012.

[315] Nathan, Sara. "Sherlock Star Has Forged 'Very Special' Relationship with Blonde Daughter of Patty Hearst." *Mail Online.* 28 February 2012.

[316] Aitkenhead, Decca. "Welcome to the Pleasure Zone." *Radio Times.* 18-24 August 2012, p. 13.

[317] Gilbert, Gerard. "Parade's End: A Series to Challenge Downton." *The Independent.* 11 August 2012, p. 9.

[318] Jeffery, Morgan. "Benedict Cumberbatch on 'Parade's End': 'My Look Suits a Period Drama.' Digital Spy. 21 August 2012.

[319] Hinckley, David. "Super Bowl XLVII Scores 3rd Highest Ratings in U.S. Television History." *New York Daily News.* 4 February 2013.

[320] Zucker, Joseph. "Super Bowl Commercials 2013: Ranking Top Movie Trailers from Big Game." The Bleacher Report. 3 February 2013.

[321] Mitchison, Amanda. "Benedict Cumberbatch on Playing Sherlock Holmes." *The Guardian.* 16 July 2010.

[322] Kaufman, Anthony. "Atonement." *Variety.* 15 November 2007.

[323] *Sherlock* Master Class. Edinburgh International Television Festival. 24 August 2012. Several sites later published reports about the event (e.g., Young, Bill. "Sherlock Master Class Highlights." 25 August 2012).

[324] Elmhirst, Sophie. "The Man with the Child in His Eyes." *New Statesman.* 17 November 2011.

[325] Carnicke, Sharon Marie. "Screen Performance and Directors' Visions." In Cynthia Baron, Diane Carson, and Frank P. Tomasulo (Eds.), *More than a Method: Trends in Contemporary Film Performance* (pp. 42-67). Detroit: Wayne State University, 2004, p. 47.

[326] *War Horse.* Dir. Steven Spielberg. Dreamworks. 2011.

[327] Myall, Steve. "Benedict Cumberbatch Talks about Sherlock and War Horse." *Daily Mirror.* 31 December 2011.

[328] "Cumberbatch Late for Spielberg Meet." *Belfast Telegraph.* 11 January 2012.

[329] Roach, Vicky. "Benedict Cumberbatch, Movies' Man of 2012?" *The Herald.* 29 December 2011.

[330] Ibid.

[331] Spielberg, Steven. *War Horse: The Making of the Motion Picture.* New York: It Books/HarperCollins, 2011.

[332] "Benedict Cumberbatch: Dream Come True to Work with Steven Spielberg on War Horse." *The Telegraph.* ITV video. 9 January 2012.

[333] Cumberbatch, Benedict. *Star Trek: Into Darkness* teaser. December 2012. Paramount.

[334] "Next Stop the Oscars for Star Trek's Benedict Cumberbatch?" Contactmusic.com. 7 December 2012.

[335] Malkin, Marc. "Star Trek Sequel Trailer: Why Co-star Zoe Saldana Made Benedict Cumberbatch Blush Over It." E!online. 7 December 2012.

[336] Brew, Simon. "Benedict Cumberbatch on Star Trek: Into Darkness." Den of Geek. 5 December 2012.

[337] Brew, Simon. "Benedict Cumberbatch on Star Trek: Into Darkness." Den of Geek. 5 December 2012.

[338] Fleming, Jr., Mike. "DreamWorks Julian Assange Pic Talk Focusing on Benedict Cumberbatch and Joel Kinnaman?" Deadline New York. 2 October 2012.

[339] Moore, Ronnie. "Title Revealed for Benedict Cumberbatch-led WikiLeaks Film." The Film Stage. 20 December 2012.

[340] Child, Ben. "Benedict Cumberbatch as Julian Assange in the WikiLeaks Movie—First Picture." *The Guardian.* 23 January 2013.

[341] Tweets from several sources were retweeted. A Live From Iceland webcam (http://www.livefromiceland.is/webcams/austurvollur/) captured images of a long-distance night shoot on 18 January. Fans like @nandochick and @CindyC1000 retweeted news about filming and Cumberbatch's "fake teeth" for the role. Twitter. 22 January 2013.

[342] Kroll, Justin. "Benedict Cumberbatch to Star in Del Toro's 'Crimson Peak' (Exclusive)." *Variety.* 4 April 2013.

[343] Legendary Pictures.com.

Chapter 7

[344] Ray, Amber M. "Benedict Cumberbatch: The Uncensored 'Sherlock' Interview." *Metro.* 6 May 2012.

[345] Shingler, Martin. *Star Studies: A Critical Guide.* London: Palgrave Macmillan/British Film Institute, 2012, p. 37.

[346] Dibdin, Emma. "Benedict Cumberbatch 'Emailed Regularly by Julian Assange.'" Digital Spy. 25 March 2013.

[347] Kay, Jeremy. "FilmNation Acquires International Rights to 'The Imitation Game.'" *Screen Daily.* 7 February 2013.

[348] Hopewell, John, and McNary, Dave. "Berlin Fest's Big Bang Theory." *Variety.* 11 February 2013.

[349] *Cabin Pressure.* "Cremona." BBC Radio. 16 July 2008 (original broadcast).

[350] *Sherlock.* "The Reichenbach Fall." BBC. 15 January 2012 (original broadcast).

[351] Sivell, Vaughan. "On Benedict Cumberbatch." 9 September 2011. Mug7.com.

[352] "Cumberbatched in Berlin." 1 February 2013. Tumblr.

[353] Koch, Emily. "Sherlock Filming Causes Stir in Bristol." *The Post.* 26 March 2013.

[354] Harris, Neil Patrick. "My Hollywood Survival Guide." *Entertainment Weekly.* 22 September 2011.

[355] Pavia, Lucy. "Hollywood's Most Wanted." *InStyle* (UK). August 2012, p. 111.

[356] WENN.com. "Benedict Cumberbatch Snags The Simpsons Role." Hollywood.com. 5 July 2012.

[357] John, Emma. "Benedict Cumberbatch Interview: On the Couch with Mr. Cumberbatch." *The Guardian.* 4 September 2011.

[358] Frost, Caroline. "Sherlock Star Benedict Cumberbatch's Curious Incident in the Night-Time During Parade's End Filming." *The Huffington Post.* 12 September 2012.

[359] BBC Media Centre. "Interview with Benedict Cumberbatch." *Parade's End.* 1 August 2012.

[360] Tumblr devoted a site to the photos and comments, as did sites like ONTD (Oh No They Didn't). 5 January 2012.

[361] Kelly, Laura. "'I've Been the Next Big Thing for about 10 Years." *The Big Issue* (Scotland edition). 16-22 May 2011, p. 19.

[362] "Checking out the Competition? Benedict Cumberbatch Celebrates His Golden Globe Nomination with a Night Out at the Cinema." *Daily Mail.* 14 December 2012.

[363] Walker, Tim. "Sherlock Star Benedict Cumberbatch is Cyberstalked." *The Telegraph.* 13 March 2013.

[364] Webb, Claire. "Father Brown's Mark Williams on Following in Benedict Cumberbatch's Footsteps." *Radio Times.* 13 January 2013.

[365] Rutter, Claire. "Sherlock Star Who Stripped Nude for Benedict Cumberbatch to Play 'Bond Girl.'" Entertainmentwise. 25 January 2013.

[366] Harris, Mark. "What Stars Are For." *Entertainment Weekly.* 2 January 2009.

[367] Gabler, Neal. "Toward a New Definition of Celebrity." The Norman Lear Center. PDF, p. 5.

[368] "Benedict Cumberbatch: Jonny Lee Miller Took 'Elementary' Role for the Paycheck." *Hollywood Reporter.* Updated. 30 August 2012.

[369] John, Emma. "Benedict Cumberbatch Interview: On the Couch with Mr. Cumberbatch." *The Guardian.* 4 September 2011.

[370] Britten, Nick. "'Posh Baiting' May Drive Benedict Cumberbatch to US." *The Telegraph.* 14 Aug. 2013.

[371] Glosswitch. "Posh-baiting: It's Enough to Make You Want to Leave the Bullingdon Club." *New Statesman.* 15 August 2012.

[372] "Is Benedict Cumberbatch Right That Posh-bashing Has Gone Too Far?" *The Guardian.* 14 August 2012.

[373] Aitkenhead, Decca. "Benedict Cumberbatch on Parade's End, Sherlock, Being a Sex Symbol, and Living the LA Dream." *Radio Times.* 24 August 2012.

[374] Spero, Josh. "Josh Spero Talking about Benedict Cumberbatch on BBC Radio Wales Aug. 2012." YouTube. 15

August 2012. See also "Josh Spero Talking about Benedict Cumberbatch on BBC Radio Wales." Spear's. 15 August 2012.

[375] McElvoy, Anne. "Lose the Chip, Benedict—All Actors Have a Class Range." *London Evening Standard.* 15 August 2012.

[376] "Benedict Cumberbatch Fears for Fans." *Belfast Telegraph.* 27 September 2012.

[377] Wilson, Benji. Cover Story: "A Classic on Parade." *The Sunday Times, Culture* magazine. 12 August 2012, p. 4.

[378] Wilson, Benji. "Benedict Cumberbatch." *Reader's Digest.* August 2012.

[379] Lazarus, Susanna. "Is Benedict Cumberbatch Headed to Downton Abbey? *Radio Times.* 17 August 2012.

[380] Ferguson, Euan. "Benedict Cumberbatch: Naturally He's a Class Act." *The Guardian.* 18 August 2012.

[381] Ausiello, Michael. "Eye on Emmy, Benedict Cumberbatch on Playing Sherlock at 50, His Mad Men Envy, and That 'Mortifying' Downton Abbey 'PR Disaster.'" TVLine.com. 14 June 2012.

[382] WENN.com. "Benedict Cumberbatch Upset Over Jonny Lee Miller Misquote." 31 August 2012.

[383] Ventre, Michael. "Tax Breaks Created TV Party." *Variety.* 15 August 2012.

[384] "Benedict Cumberbatch—The One Show 24 August 2012." YouTube.

[385] "Fresh Faces to Watch." E! Promo shown during 2013 Golden Globes red carpet coverage. 14 January 2013. Broadcast.

[386] "Live From the Red Carpet." E! 14 January 2013. Broadcast.

[387] Live Blog. 7:17 p.m. *The Guardian.* 14 January 2013.

[388] "Benedict Cumberbatch—BBC Interview at BAFTA Tea Party 2013 & Other Snippets." YouTube. 14 January 2013.

[389] Sullivan, Kevin P. "Benedict Cumberbatch Unleashes 'Star Trek' Villain." MTV. 14 January 2013.

[390] Cumberbuddy. 14 January 2013. Cumberbatchweb.

[391] RAS. "Golden Globes 2013: Live Blogging the Show." *The Wall Street Journal.* 14 January 2013.

[392] Snierson, Dan. "'The Simpsons': Watch Benedict Cumberbatch Play the British Prime Minister AND Snape— Exclusive Video." *Entertainment Weekly.* 8 February 2013.

[393] Kelly, Laura. "'I've Been the Next Big Thing for about 10 Years." *The Big Issue* (Scotland ed.). 16-22 May 2011, p. 19.

[394] Brew, Simon. "Benedict Cumberbatch on Why He Chose Star Trek." Den of Geek. 21 March 2013.

[395] Blay, Zeba. "Benedict Cumberbatch: 'I Worry for My Obsessive Fans." Digital Spy. 18 August 2012.

[396] The fan's original Tumbler post has been removed, but articles "republishing" the announcement are still available online, such as http://www.celebitchy.com/241770/benedict_cumberbatch_was_incredibly_sweet_to_a_cumberbitch_in_nola/.

[397] Pavia, Lucy. "Hollywood's Most Wanted." *InStyle* (UK). August 2012, p. 110.

[398] Twitter posts. 25 March 2013.

[399] BBC Fangirl. "Sherlock: #Setlock: Portland Square, Monday 26th [incorrect date] 2013." Blog.

[400] EchoMichael. "Sherlock Star Benedict Cumberbatch Makes Teen Girl's Day in Cheltenham." *This is Gloucestershire.* 3 April 2013.

[401] "The 2012 Time 100 Poll." *Time.* 18 April 2012.

[402] Rutter, Claire. "Sherlock's Benedict Cumberbatch Beats David Beckham & Harry Styles to 'Sexiest Man.'" Entertainmentwise.com. 7 May 2012.

[403] Lazarus, Susanna. "Is Clare Balding More Fascinating Than Benedict Cumberbatch?" *Radio Times.* 29 January 2013.

[404] Sherlockology. "Sponsor Benedict Cumberbatch for the Palace to Palace London Bike Ride in Aid of the Prince's Trust." October 2012. and Cumberbatchweb. Same title.

[405] "Cumberbatch Today: Participated in Charity Bike Ride." OhNoTheyDidn't. 14 October 2012. Oh No They Didn't. Livejournal.

Chapter 8

[406] Jeffery, Morgan. "Benedict Cumberbatch on 'Parade's End': 'My Look Suits a Period Drama.'" Digital Spy. 21 August 2012.

[407] Seale, Jack. "Benedict Cumberbatch on Fame, Science and His New Radio 3 Play, Copenhagen." *Radio Times.* 11 January 2013.

[408] Dessau, Bruce. "Nominally a Star." *The Times.* 3 November 2007, p. 17.

[409] Brown, David. "Sherlock-Steven Moffat: We Hope We Can Hang on to Benedict Cumberbatch and Martin Freeman." *Radio Times.* 30 January 2013.

[410] Fleming, Mike, Jr. "Benedict Cumberbatch in Talks to Play Alan Turing in 'The Imitation Game.'" Deadline.com. 1 February 2013.

[411] Day, Elizabeth. "Una Stubbs: I Just Think 'Oh I Hope I Can Be Good Enough." *The Guardian.* 30 June 2012.

[412] The Naked Scientists. Special Editions. "Benedict Cumberbatch, Naked." 6 March 2013. Transcript and podcast.

Bibliography

"The 2012 Time 100 Poll." *Time.* 18 April 2012. http://www. time.com/time/specials/packages/article/0,28804,2107952_ 2107959_2107960,00.html

After the Dance, by Terence Rattigan, National Theatre. Programme. 2010.

After the Dance. Recording. Accessed at the National Theatre Archives, London, 5 December 2010.

After the Dance bible. Niks Cue Sheet. Act One Notes. Note 6. April 2010. All of the following were accessed at the National Theatre Archives, London, 5 December 2011.

___. Rehearsal Notes, 23 April 2010.

___. Rehearsal Notes, Number 13, 14 May 2010.

___. Rehearsal Notes, Number 8, 6 May 2010.

___. Rehearsal Notes, Number 2, 27 April 2010.

___. Rehearsal Notes, Number 16, 20 May 2010.

___. Rehearsal Notes, Number 2, 27 April 2010.

Aitkenhead, Decca. "Welcome to the Pleasure Zone." *Radio Times,* 18-24 August 2012, 11-13.

Alan Carr: Chatty Man. 24 January 2011 (original broadcast). http://www.youtube.com/watch?v=XzDG4xKioBA

"The Allure of Benedict." *Jaguar Magazine* #5. iPad. Or http://microsites.jaguar.com/UK/

"Almeida Brand Video." YouTube. 6 March 2011. http://www. youtube.com/watch?v=Hx-vWoHJHwQ

Anderson, Kyle. "Neil Gaiman's 'Neverwhere' Radio Play's All-Star Cast." Nerdist. 5 December 2012. http://www. nerdist.com/2012/12/neil-gaimans-neverwhere-radio-plays-all-star-cast/

Annand, Simon. "The Half." http://www.simonannand.com/ the-half/

___. *The Half: Photographs of Actors Preparing for the Stage.* London: Faber & Fabre, 2008.

301

"*The Arsonists* Post-Show Talk." Royal Court Theatre. Recording. 13 November 2007. Accessed at the British Library, London, 25 June 2012.

Ausiello, Michael. "Eye on Emmy, Benedict Cumberbatch on Playing Sherlock at 50, His Mad Men Envy, and That 'Mortifying' Downton Abbey 'PR Disaster.'" TVLine.com. 14 June 2012. http://tvline.com/2012/06/14/sherlock-season3-benedict-cumberbatch/

BAFTA. Press Release. "Benedict Cumberbatch Announced as Juror for the 2013 EE Rising Star Award." December 2012. http://www.bafta.org/press/beneditct-cumberbatch-ee-rising-star-jurer,233,SNS.html

Barnes, Henry. "Benedict Cumberbatch Landed Star Trek Role with Pitch Filmed on iPhone." *The Guardian.* 27 April 2012.http://www.guardian.co.uk/film/2012/apr/27/benedict-cumberbatch-star-trek-iphone

BBC Fangirl. "Sherlock: #Setlock: Portland Square, Monday 26th [incorrect date] 2013." http://bbcfangirl.blogspot.co.uk/2013/03/sherlock-setlock-portland-square-monday.html

BBC Media Centre. "Interview with Benedict Cumberbatch." 1 August 2012. http://www.bbc.co.uk/mediacentre/media packs/paradesend/benedict-cumberbatch.html

___. "Interview with Sir Tom Stoppard." 1 August 2012. http://www.bbc.co.uk/mediacentre/mediapacks/paradesend/tom-stoppard.html

BBC Press Office. "William Golding's *To the Ends of the Earth.*" 5 May 2005. http://www.bbc.co.uk/pressoffice/pressreleases/stories/2005/05_may/19/earth5.shtml

___. "William Golding's 'To the Ends of the Earth.'" 19 May 2005. _http://www.bbc.co.uk/pressoffice/pressreleases/stories/2005/05_may/19/earth5.shtml

___. *Hawking.* Press release. 2 April 2004. http://www.bbc.co.uk/pressoffice/pressreleases/stories/2004/04_april/02/hawking_cumberbatch.shtml

BBC Science and Nature. *Hawking.* August 2006. http://www.bbc.co.uk/sn/ tvradio/programmes/hawking/

"Behind the Scenes of Copenhagen." BBC Radio. 2013. http://www.bbc.co.uk/programmes/ galleries/p013mqmf

"Behind the Scenes on *The Turning Point.*" *Sky Arts Live!* 14 September 2010. http://www.youtube.com/watch?v=mD2 Kw-NJaMU

Bell, Jack. "The Solid Gold Girl Comes Back." *Daily Mirror,* 29 October 1977, 15.

"Benedict Cumberbatch." *Short List.* August 2012. http://www. shortlist.com/entertainment/tv/benedict-cumberbatch

"Benedict Cumberbatch: Dream Come True to Work with Steven Spielberg on War Horse." *The Telegraph.* ITV video. 9 January 2012. http://www.telegraph.co.uk/news/ newsvideo/celebrity-news-video/9001185/Benedict-Cumberbatch-Dream-come-true-to-work-with-Steven-Spielberg-on-War-Horse.html

"Benedict Cumberbatch: 'I Think Like Holmes.'" What's On TV. 9 December 2012. http://www.whatsontv.co.uk/article/ tv-news/benedict-cumberbatch-i-think-like-holmes

"Benedict Cumberbatch: Jonny Lee Miller Took 'Elementary' Role for the Paycheck." Hollywood Reporter. Updated. 30 August 2012. http://www.hollywoodreporter.com/news/ benedict-cumberbatch-jonny-lee-miller-elementary-sherlock-366932

"Benedict Cumberbatch: 'Sherlock,' Smaug, and Spying." *Morning Edition.* NPR. 3 May 2012. http://www.npr.org/ 2012/05/04/151956011/sherlock-leads-cumberbatch-to-acclaimed-films

"Benedict Cumberbatch—BBC Interview at BAFTA Tea Party 2013 & Other Snippets." 14 January 2013. http://www. youtube.com/watch?v+KhEgkKB4PAU&feature=youtu.be &a

"Benedict Cumberbatch—*The City* (Royal Court Theatre) Cast and Creatives Podcast April 2008." 14 January 2012. Accessed 22 September 2012. http://www.youtube.com/watch?v=wqSNjOpni7E This video is no longer available.

"Benedict Cumberbatch—The One Show 24 August 2012." http://www.youtube.com/watch?v+BH4VFNbPXmE

"Benedict Cumberbatch—Rhinoceros Stage Play—Casting the Lead." 15 August 2010. http://www.youtube.com/watch?v=OJVCv1dbnPk. Accessed 22 September 2012. This video is no longer available.

"Benedict Cumberbatch 'Desperate' for U.S. Success." NME. 27 April 2012. http://www.nme.com/filmandtv/news/benedict-cumberbatch-desperate-for-sherlock-us/266929

"Benedict Cumberbatch Fears for Fans." *Belfast Telegraph.* 27 September 2012. http://www.belfasttelegraph.co.uk/entertainment/news/benedict-cumberbatch-fears-for-fans-28867763.html

"Benedict Cumberbatch Talks about Sherlock and War Horse." *Mirror.* 31 December 2011. http://www.mirror.co.uk/tv/tv-news/benedict-cumberbatch-talks-about-sherlock-and-war-99003

"Benedict Cumberbatch Used Sherlock Skills to Survive Armed Kidnapping Ordeal." *The Mirror.* 12 January 2012. http://www.mirror.co.uk/3am/celebrity-news/benedict-cumberbatch-used-sherlock-skills-171955

Benedict, David. "*The Arsonists.*" *Variety.* 14 November 2007. http://www.variety.com/review/VE1117935431?refcatid=33

Billington, Michael. "After the Dance." *The Guardian.* 8 June 2010. http://www.guardian.co.uk/stage/2010/jun/09/after-the-dance-theatre-review

___. "Rhinoceros, Royal Court, London." *The Guardian.* 27 September 2007. http://www.guardian.co.uk/stage/2007/sep/28/theatre2

Blay, Zeba. "Benedict Cumberbatch: 'I worry for My Obsessive Fans." Digital Spy. 18 August 2012. http://www. digitalspy.co.uk/showbiz/news/a400328/benedict-cumberbatch-i-worry-for-my-obsessive-fans.html

Boucher, Geoff. "'Sherlock' and 'Star Trek': Benedict Cumberbatch Lights It Up." *Los Angeles Times.* 9 May 2012. http://herocomplex.latimes.com/2012/05/09/sherlock-and-star-trek-benedict-cumberbatch-lights-it-up/#/0

Brealey, Louise. "Sherlock: Meet Lara Pulver, Louise Brealey and Una Stubbs—the Baker St Babes." *Radio Times.* 16 January 2012. http://www.radiotimes.com/news/2012-01-15/sherlock-meet-lara-pulver-louise-brealey-and-una-stubbs---the-baker-st-babes

Brew, Simon. "Benedict Cumberbatch on Star Trek: Into Darkness." Den of Geek. 5 December 2012. http://www. denofgeek.com/movies/star-trek/23717/benedict-cumberbatch-on-star-trek-into-darkness

___. "Benedict Cumberbatch on Why He Chose Star Trek." Den of Geek. 21 March 2013. http://www.denofgeek.com/movies/star-trek/24903/benedict-cumberbatch-on-why-he-chose-star-trek

Britten, Nick. "'Posh Baiting' May Drive Benedict Cumberbatch to US." *The Telegraph.* 14 August 2013. http://www.telegraph.co.uk/culture/tvandradio/9473337/Post-baiting-may-drive-Benedict-Cumberbatch-to-the-US.html

Brown, David. "Sherlock-Steven Moffat: We Hope We Can Hang on to Benedict Cumberbatch and Martin Freeman." *Radio Times.* 30 January 2013. http://www.radiotimes.com/news/2013-01-30/sherlock---steven-moffat-we-hope-we-can-hang-on-to-benedict-cumberbatch-and-martin-freeman

Cabin Pressure. "Cremona." BBC Radio. 16 July 2008 (original broadcast).

___. "Wokingham." Dir. David Tyler. BBC Radio 4. 6 February 2013 (original broadcast).

Cambridge Spies. Episode 2. Dir. Tim Fywell. BBC. 16 May 2003 (original broadcast).

Carnicke, Sharon Marie. "Screen Performance and Directors' Visions." In Cynthia Baron, Diane Carson, and Frank P. Tomasulo (Eds.), *More than a Method: Trends in Contemporary Film Performance* (pp. 42-67). Detroit: Wayne State University, 2004.

Chater, Eos. "How I Taught Sherlock Holmes to Play the Violin." *The Guardian.* 4 January 2012. http://www. guardian.co.uk/tv-and-radio/shortcuts/2012/jan/04/how-taught-sherlock-holmes-violin

"Checking out the Competition? Benedict Cumberbatch Celebrates His Golden Globe Nomination with a Night Out at the Cinema." http://www.dailymail.co.uk/tvshowbiz/ article-2247990/Benedict-Cumberbatch-Celebrates-Golden-Globe-nomination-date-night-inema.html#ixzz2F3qAQX2h

Cheltenham Music Festival. "Benedict Cumberbatch— Cheltenham Music Festival." 13 July 2012. YouTube. http://www.youtube.com/watch?v=JZbce9oMmVc

Child, Ben. "Benedict Cumberbatch and Gemma Arterton Up For Absolutely Anything Monty Python Film." *The Guardian.* 7 November 2012. http://www.guardian.co.uk/ film/2012/nov/07/cumberbatch-arterton-python-absolutely-anything

___. "Benedict Cumberbatch as Julian Assange in the WikiLeaks Movie—First Picture." *The Guardian.* 23 January 2013. http://www.guardian.co.uk/film/2013/jan/ 23/benedict-cumberbatch-julian-assange-first-picture

Christie, Nicola. "Bright Star." *The Times,* 10 April 2004, 29.

"City Post-show Talk." Royal Court Theatre. Recording. 8 May 2008. Accessed at the British Library, London, 25 June 2012.

Clifton, Jane. "Van Gogh Seen in Letters to His Brother." *The Dominion Post*, 12 December 2012, A13.

"Co-Creator Live Chat: Mark Gatiss." PBS. 14 May 2012. Video. http://www.pbs.org/wgbh/masterpiece/ sherlock/season2_chat_gatiss.html

Cole, Tom. "Benedict Cumberbatch 'Force-Fed' Himself Doughnuts for Parade's End Role." *Radio Times*. 24 August 2012. http://www.radiotimes.com/news/2012-08-24/benedict-cumberbatch-force-fed-himself-doughnuts-for-parades-end-role

___. "Benedict Cumberbatch Joins Stephen Hawking at the Premiere of His New Documentary Series." *Radio Times*. 6 September 2012. http://www.radiotimes.com/news/2012-09-06/benedict-cumberbatch-joins-stephen-hawking-at-the-premiere-of-his-new-documentary-series

Comey, Jeremiah. *The Art of Film Acting: A Guide for Actors and Directors*. Oxford: Focal Press, 2002.

Conlan, Tara. "Sherlock is Cheeky Entertainment, Insists BBC after Nudity Complaints." *The Guardian*. 11 January 2012. http://www.guardian.co.uk/media/2012/jan/11/sherlock-bbc-nude-scenes

Cook, Mark. Review of *Oh! What a Lovely War*. *Time Out*. 31 July 2002. Rep. *Theatre Record*, 22(15), 980.

Copenhagen. Frayne, Michael. Harding, Emma, dir. BBC Radio 3. 13 January 2013 (original broadcast).

Costa, Maddy. "Frankenstein: Man or Monster?" *The Guardian*, 17 January 2011, http://www.guardian.co.uk/culture/2011/jan/17/a-monster-role-frankenstein-danny-boyle.

Coveney, Michael. Review of *The Lady from the Sea*. *Daily Mail*. 16 May 2003. Rep. *Theatre Record*, 23(10), 650.

___. Review of *Love's Labour's Lost*. *Daily Mail*. 22 June 2001. Rep. *Theatre Record*, 21(12), 757.

Crimp, Martin. *The City*. London: Faber and Faber, 2008.

"Cumberbatch Late for Spielberg Meet." *Belfast Telegraph*. 11 January 2012. http://www.belfasttelegraph.co.uk/entertain

ment/film-tv/news/cumberbatch-late-for-spielberg-meet-28701732.html

"Cumberbatch Today: Participated in Charity Bike Ride." Oh No They Didn't. 14 October 2012. http://ohnotheydidnt. livejournal.com/72744580.html

Cumberbatch, Benedict. "Holiday Holmes: Benedict Cumberbatch in the Seychelles." *London Evening Standard.* 25 November 2011. http://www.standard.co.uk/lifestyle/ esmagazine/ holiday-holmes-benedict-cumberbatch-in-the-seychelles-6372248.html

___. *Inspired by Music: Personal Reflections of How Music Changed Our Lives.* London: Shoehorn Publishing, 2009.

___. *Star Trek: Into Darkness* teaser. December 2012. Paramount.

"Cumberbatched in Berlin." 1 February 2013. http://dude ufugly.tumblr.com/post/42026670797/cumberbatched-in-berlin

Cumberbatchweb. "Cheltenham Literary Festival." http://www. benedictcumberbatch.co.uk/benedict-cumberbatch-and-louise-brealey-discuss-sherlock-at-cheltenham-literary-festival/

___. "Review of The Children's Monologues." 2010. http://www.benedictcumberbatch.co.uk/theatre/cumberbatc hweb-review-of-the-childrens-monologues/

___. September 2012. http://www.benedictcumberbatch.co.uk/ 2012/10/13/team-bc-raise-over-23000-for-the-princes-trust/

___. "The Times—New Benedict Cumberbatch Interview Promoting Third Star." 14 May 2011. http://cumberbatch web.tumblr.com/day/2011/05/14

___. Transcript of *Frankenstein* Q&A. http://www.benedict cumberbatch.co.uk/frankenstein-qa-transcript.html

Cumberbuddy. 14 January 2013. Cuberbatchweb. http:// cumberbatchweb.tumblr.com/

Curtis, Nick. "Benedict Cumberbatch—Stepping into the Lead." *London Evening Standard.* 1 June 2010. http://www.standard.co.uk/showbiz/starinterviews/benedict-cumberbatch--stepping-into-the-lead-6475519.html

Dalglish, Darren. "Benedict Cumberbatch." LondonTheatre.co. uk. 19 July 2010. http://www.londontheatre.co.uk/lon dontheatre/questionsandanswers/benedictcumberbatch.htm

Day, Elizabeth. "Benedict Cumberbatch: 'I Felt Like I Had Rabies or Was a King.'" *The Guardian.* 6 November 2010. http://www.guardian.co.uk/tv-and-radio/2010/nov/07/ benedict-cumberbatch-sherlock-childrens-monologues

___. "Una Stubbs: I Just Think 'Oh I Hope I Can Be Good Enough." *The Guardian.* 30 June 2012. http://www. guardian.co.uk/stage/2012/jul/01/una-stubbs-curious-incident-interview

de Moraes, Lisa. "*Sherlock* Premiere Scores High Ratings." *The Washington Post.* 9 May 2012. http://www. washingtonpost.com/blogs/tv-column/post/sherlock-pre miere-scores-high-ratings-still-no-match-for-downton-abbey/2012/05/07/gIQAZofw8T_blog.html

Deacon, Michael, Horsford, Simon, O'Donovan, Gerard. and Reynolds, Gillian. "The Daily Telegraph's TV Desk's Pick of 5 April's Television and Radio Available on the BBC's Catch-up Service, the iPlayer." *The Telegraph.* 5 April 2010. http://www.telegraph.co.uk/ culture/tvandradio/tv-on-demand/7560909/BBC-iPlayer-choices-Monday-5-April.html

Dessau, Bruce. "Benedict Cumberbatch's Rising Star." *The Times.* 3 November 2007. http://entertainment.timesonline .co.uk/tol/arts_and_entertainment/stage/theatre/article27729 03.ece

___. "Nominally a Star." *The Times,* 3 November 2007, 17.

Dibdin, Emma. "Benedict Cumberbatch 'Emailed Regularly by Julian Assange.'" Digital Spy. 25 March 2013.

http://www.digitalspy.com/movies/news/a468369/benedict-cumberbatch-emailed-regularly-by-julian-assange.html

Dowell, Ben. "Parade's End Marches Away with Four Broadcasting Press Guild Awards." *The Guardian.* 14 March 2013. http://www.guardian.co.uk/media/2013/mar/14/parades-end-broadcasting-guild-awards

Drake, Philip. "Reconceptualizing Screen Performance." *Journal of Film and Video,* 58(1-2), 85. Cited in Shingler, Martin. *Star Studies: A Critical Guide.* London: Palgrave Macmillan/BFI, 2012, 45.

Earth Observing System. "Sherlock on the Fiddle." 2 January 2012. http://earthobservingsystem.tumblr.com/post/151885 32235/sherlock-on-the-fiddle

EchoMichael. "Sherlock Star Benedict Cumberbatch Makes Teen Girl's Day in Cheltenham." *This is Gloucestershire.* 3 April 2013. http://www.thisisgloucestershire.co.uk/Sherlock-star-Benedict-Cumberbatch-makes-teen/story-18596969-detail/story.html#axzz2PO1DXViz

Edwards, Jane. Review of *Hedda Gabler. Time Out.* 23 March 2005. Rep. *Theatre Record,* 25(6), 348.

"Eee! It's Wanda's Little Wonder." *Daily Mirror.* 24 July 1976, 5.

Elbert, Lynn. "Benedict Cumberbatch Defends 'Sherlock' Nude Scene." *The Huffington Post.* 6 January 2012. http://www.huffingtonpost.com/2012/01/06/benedict-cumberbatch-sherlock-nude-scene_n_1189147.html

Elmhirst, Sophie. "The Man with the Child in His Eyes." *New Statesman.* 17 November 2011. http://www.newstatesman.com/fiction/2011/11/war-horse-morpurgo-children

Evans, Lloyd. Review of *Period of Adjustment. Spectator.* 25 March 2006. Rep. *Theatre Record,* 26(6), 306.

"Extracts from the Introduction to Songs." *The Harrovian.* 1 December 2012. CXXVI(11), 114.

Ferguson, Euan. "Benedict Cumberbatch: Naturally He's a Class Act." *The Guardian*. 18 August 2012. http://www.guardian.co.uk/theobserver/2012/aug/19/profile -benedict-cumberbatch-sherlock?newsfeed=true

Ferguson, Liz. "Cumberbabes: Listen to Benedict Cumberbatch Talk in a Brainy Way about Nuclear Physics, in the Play Copenhagen, on BBC Radio." *Montreal Gazette*. 17 January 2013. http://blogs.montrealgazette.com/2013/ 01/17/cumberbabes-listen-to-benedict-cumberbatch-talk-in- a-brainy-way-about-nuclear-physics-in-the-play- copenhagen-on-bbc-radio/

___. "Jimmy Kimmel Makes Fun of Actor Benedict Cumberbatch's Name—Not Polite, Not That Funny and Not Very Original, Either." *The Montreal Gazette*. 18 September 2012. http://blogs.montrealgazette.com/2012/ 09/18/jimmy-kimmel-makes-fun-of-actor-benedict- cumberbatchs-name-not-polite-not-that-funny-and-not- very-original-either/

Finnemore, John. "Cabin Pressure IV—Prepare for Boarding." 14 November 2012. http://johnfinnemore.blogspot.co.uk/ 2012/11/cabin-pressure-iv-prepare-for-boarding.html

___. "I Wish I Could Find the Setting for 'Jelly Babies to Automatic.'" 11 July 2011. http://johnfinnemore.blogspot .co.uk/2011/07/imagine-trying-to-play-it-in-new-york.html

___. "Newcastle." 19 July 2011. http://johnfinnemore.blogspot .co.uk/2011/07/newcastle.html

___. "'Ours Blanc.' Or 'Ours Polaire.'" 1 July 2011. http://johnfinnemore.blogspot.co.uk/ 2011/07/ours-blanc- or-ours-polaire.html

___. "Stage Direction: [DING] Ding! [DING] Ding! [DING] Ding!" 9 July 2011. http://johnfinnemore.blogspot.co.uk/ 2011/07/stage-direction-ding-ding-ding-ding.html

___. "Two Things You Might Be Interested In." 2 May 2008. http://johnfinnemore.blogspot.co.uk/2008/05/two-things-you-might-be-interested-in.html

___. "Yverdon-Les-Bains." 15 February 2013. http://john finnemore.blogspot.com/2013_02_01_archive.html

First Look: The Making of Tinker Tailor Soldier Spy. Focus Features, 2011. HBO.

Fisher, Philip. "Rhinoceros." British Theatre Guide. 2007. http://www.britishtheatreguide.info/ reviews/rhinocerosRC-rev

Fleming, Mike, Jr. "Benedict Cumberbatch in Talks to Play Alan Turing in 'The Imitation Game.'" Deadline.com. 1 February 2013. http://www.deadline.com/2013/02/benedict-cumberbatch-in-talks-to-play-alan-turing-in-the-imitation-game/

___. "DreamWorks Julian Assange Pic Talk Focusing on Benedict Cumberbatch and Joel Kinnaman?" Deadline New York. 2 October 2012. http://www.deadline.com/2012/10/dreamworks-julian-assange-pic-talk-focusing-on-benedict-cumberbatch-and-joel-kinnaman/

Fortysomething. ITV. Dir. Hugh Laurie. 2003. Episode 1.2. 6 July 2003 (original broadcast).

Fox, Hilary. "From 'Sherlock' to 'Star Trek' for Cumberbatch." 14 December 2011. http://omg.yahoo.com/news/sherlock-star-trek-cumberbatch-133455288.html

Frankenstein, alternate casting. Dir. Danny Boyle. Technical rehearsal recording. All recordings accessed at the National Theatre Archives, London, 3 June 2011.

Frankenstein, alternate casting. Dir. Danny Boyle.

Frankenstein, original casting. Dir. Danny Boyle.

Frankenstein, Olivier Theatre 2011. Costume Bible. Sections Benedict Cumberbatch, Jonny Lee Miller, and Misc. Accessed at the National Theatre Archives, London, 8 March 2013.

Frankenstein, Olivier Theatre 2011, Stage Management Bible. Section 26—Rehearsal Notes, Wednesday, 8th December 2010 Frankenstein Issue 3. All of the following accessed at the National Theatre Archives, London, 6 December 2011.

___. Section 26—Rehearsal Notes, Thursday, 9th December 2010 Frankenstein Issue 4..

___. Section 26—Rehearsal Notes, Thursday 16th December 2010 Issue 9.

___. Section 26—Rehearsal Notes, Thursday 23rd December 2010 Issue 14.

___. Section 26—Rehearsal Notes, Wednesday 19th January 2011 Issue 28.

___. Section 26—Rehearsal Notes, Tuesday 11th January 2011 Issue 21.

___. Section 26—Rehearsal Notes, Friday 14th January 2011 Issue 24.

___. Section 26—Rehearsal Notes, Saturday 15th January 2011 Issue 25.

___. Section 26—Rehearsal Notes, Friday 21st January 2011 Issue 30.

___. Section 26—Rehearsal Notes, Saturday 22nd January 2011 Issue 31.

___. Section 20, Pre-show rehearsal schedule, Frankenstein Production Schedule 09-issued (p. 4), Saturday 5th February.

___. Section 10, Frankenstein—Tash's Notes, Version A-Benedict –'Creature', Jonny-'Victor'.

Frankenstein: A Modern Myth. Dir. Adam Low. Lone Star Productions and National Theatre, 2012.

Frankenstein Q&A. National Theatre. 21 April 2011. London. Excerpts were once available at the National Theatre website.

"Fresh Faces to Watch." E! 14 January 2013 (original broadcast).

Frisch, Max. *The Arsonists*. London: Methuen Drama, 2007.

Frost, Caroline. "Sherlock Star Benedict Cumberbatch's Curious Incident In The Night-Time, During 'Parade's End' Filming." 12 September 2012. http://www.huffingtonpost .co.uk/2012/09/12/sherlock-benedict-cumberbatch-parades-end_n_1877725.html?ir=UK+Entertainment

Gabler, Neal. "Toward a New Definition of Celebrity." The Norman Lear Center. PDF, 5. http://www.learcenter.org/ pdf/Gabler.pdf

Gilbert, Gerard. "Parade's End: A Series to Challenge Downton." *The Independent*. 11 August 2012. http://www.independent.co.uk/arts-entertainment/tv/ features/parades-end-a-series-to-challenge-downton-8026636.html

___. "A Series to Challenge *Downton*." *The Independent, Radar* magazine, 11 August 2012, 7, 9.

Glanfield, Tim. "Benedict Cumberbatch As You've Never Seen Him Before." *Radio Times*. 21 February 2012. http://www.radiotimes.com/news/2012-02-21/benedict-cumberbatch-as-youve-never-seen-him-before

Glosswitch. "Posh-baiting: It's Enough to Make You Want to Leave the Bullingdon Club." *New Statesman*. 15 August 2012.http://www.newstatesman.com/lifestyle/2012/08/posh - bashing-enough-make-you-want-leave-bullingdon-club

Grant-West, Charlotte. "Benedict Cumberbatch Not Too Big for Radio 4 Sitcom." 21 November 2012. http://www. entertainmentwise.com/news/95401/Benedict-Cumberbatch-Not-To-Big-For-Radio-4-Sitcom

Gross, John. Review of *As You Like It*. 16 June 2002.Rep. *Theatre Record*, 22(12), 768.

Harris, Mark. "What Stars Are For." *Entertainment Weekly*. 2 January 2009. http://www.ew.com/ew/article/0,,20250042, 00.html

Harris, Neil Patrick. "My Hollywood Survival Guide." *Entertainment Weekly.* 22 September 2011. Highlights at http://popwatch.ew.com/2011/09/22/neil-patrick-harris-this-weeks-cover/

Hawking. BBC. Dir. Philip Martin. 13 April 2004 (original broadcast).

HD Warrior (Philip Johnston). "Van Gogh 'Painted with Words' BBC Docu-drama . . . Filmed During December 2009." 5 April 2010. http://www.hdwarrior.co.uk/2010/04/05/van-gogh-painted-with-words-bbc-docu-drama-filmed-during-december-2009/

Heartbeat. "No Hard Feelings." Dir. Judith Dine. ITV. 11 April 2004 (original broadcast).

___. "The Good Doctor." Dir. Paul Walker. ITV. 30 January 2000 (original broadcast).

Hedda Gabler. Produced by Robert Fox at the Almeida Theatre. Recorded 13 July 2005 at a matinee performance for the National Video Archive of Performance. Accessed 22 March 2013 at the Victoria and Albert Museum's performance archives at Blythe House, London.

"Highlights from the PBS/Masterpiece Sherlock Series 2 Event in NYC." 2 May 2012. http://storify.com/PBS/pbs-masterpiece-sherlock-series-2-event-in-nyc

Hinckley, David. "Super Bowl XLVII Scores 3rd Highest Ratings in U.S. Television History." *New York Daily News.* 4 February 2013. http://www.nydailynews.com/entertainment/tv-movies/super-bowl-xvlii-scores-highest-audience-article-1.1254933

Hitchings, Henry. "After the Dance Shows the National Theatre At its Best." *The London Evening Standard.* 9 June 2010. http://www.standard.co.uk/arts/theatre/after-the-dance-shows-the-national-theatre-at-its-best-7420215.html

Hood, D R. Email. 17 November 2012.

Hopewell, John, and McNary, Dave. "Berlin Fest's Big Bang Theory." *Variety.* 11 February 2013. http://www.variety.com/article/VR1118066092/

Hutchison, Tom. "Sherlock Star's Gun Scare." 12 January 2012. http://www.dailystar.co.uk/news/view/229719/SHERLOCK-STAR-GUN-SCARE/

Inseparable. Dir. Nick White. Area 17, 2007. http://www.area17.com/drama.html

Ionesco, Eugene. *Rhinoceros.* Trans. Martin Crimp. London: Faber and Faber, 2007.

"Is Benedict Cumberbatch Right That Posh-bashing Has Gone Too Far?" *The Guardian.* 14 August 2012. http://www.guardian.co.uk/commentisfree/poll/2012/aug/14/posh-bashing-benedict-cumberbatch

Israel, Sara. National Theatre. Email. 25 July 2012.

Itzkoff, Dave. "Role to Role, from 'Sherlock' to Star Trek." *New York Times.* 26 April 2012. http://www.nytimes.com/2012/04/29/arts/television/benedict-cumberbatch-moves-from-role-to-role.html?_r=2

Jarvis, Alice-Azania. "Benedict Cumberbatch: Success? It's Elementary." *The Independent.* 29 January 2011. http://www.independent.co.uk/news/people/profiles/benedict-cumberbatch-success-its-elementary-2197808.html

Jeffery, Morgan. "Benedict Cumberbatch on 'Parade's End': 'My Look Suits a Period Drama.'" Digital Spy. 21 August 2012. . http://www.digitalspy.com/british-tv/interviews/a400530/benedict-cumberbatch-on-Parades-end-my-look-suits-a-period-drama.html

JimmyKimmelLive. "What is a Cumberbatch?" 18 September 2012. http://www.youtube.com/watch?v=qnWnUFf5hD8

John, Emma. "Benedict Cumberbatch Interview: On the Couch with Mr. Cumberbatch." *The Guardian.* 3 September 2011. http://www.guardian.co.uk/tv-and-radio/2011/sep/04/benedict-cumberbatch-ford-madox-ford

Johnson, Carrie, and Dockser, Ellen. "PBS' Masterpiece Mystery! 'Sherlock, Series 2' Uncovers Remarkable Ratings." PBS. 7 May 2012. http://www.pbs.org/about/news/archive/2012/sherlock2-premiere-ratings/

Kaufman, Anthony. "Atonement." *Variety.* 15 November 2007. http://www.variety.com/article/VR1117976091/

Kay, Jeremy. "FilmNation Acquires International Rights to 'The Imitation Game.'" *Screen Daily.* 7 February 2013. http://www.screendaily.com/festivals/berlin/european-film-market/filmnation-brings-the-imitation-game-to-efm/5051498.article

Kelly, Laura. "'I've Been the Next Big Thing for about 10 Years." *The Big Issue* (Scotland ed.), 16-22 May 2011, 16, 19.

Kennedy, Hannah. "20 Questions with Benedict Cumberbatch." What's On. 25 April 2005. http://www.whatsonstage.com/interviews/theatre/london/E8821113997955/20+Questions+With...Benedict+Cumberbatch.html

Key, Graeme. "Copenhagen—The Director's Blog." BBC Radio. 10 January 2013. http://www.bbc.co.uk/blogs/radio3/2013/01/copenhagen---the-directors-blo.shtml

Kingsley, Hilary. "Is Wanda Laughing All the Way to Bed?" *Daily Mirror,* 6 December 1980, 15.

Kinnear, Lucy. "The 5-minute Interview: Benedict Cumberbatch, Actor." *The Independent.* 7 February 2008. http://cumberbatchweb.tumblr.com/day/2011/05/14

Knowles, Stewart. "Timothy, Wanda . . . and the Rose That Changed Her Mind About Marriage." *ITV Playhouse/TV Times,* 28 July 1979, 9-10.

Koch, Emily. "Sherlock Filming Causes Stir in Bristol." *The Post.* 26 March 2013. http://www.thisisbristol.co.uk/Sherlock-filming-causes-stir-Bristol/story-18522504-detail/story.html#

Kroll, Justin. "Benedict Cumberbatch to Star in Del Toro's 'Crimson Peak' (Exclusive)." *Variety.* 4 April 2013. http://variety.com/2013/film/news/benedict-cumberbatch-joins-del-toros-crimson-peak-exclusive-1200333091/

LAMDA. The Acting Courses. http://www.lamda.org.uk/drama/courses/1acting.htm

LAMDA—The London Academy of Music and Dramatic Art. "Where Are They Now?" http://www.lamda.org.uk/alumni/wherearethey.htm

Lawson, Mark. "Under Their Skins." *The Guardian.* 28 April 2008. http://www.guardian.co.uk/stage/2008/apr/29/theatre

Lazarus, Susanna. "Is Benedict Cumberbatch Headed to Downton Abbey?" *Radio Times.* 17 August 2012. http://www.radiotimes.com/news/2012-08-17/is-benedict-cumberbatch-heading-for-downton-abbey

___. "Is Clare Balding More Fascinating Than Benedict Cumberbatch?" *Radio Times.* 29 January 2013. http://www.radiotimes.com/news/2013-01-29/is-clare-balding-more-fascinating-than-benedict-cumberbatch

___. "Sherlock Takes Home Two Prizes at the Royal Television Society Programme Awards." *Radio Times.* 19 March 2013. http://www.radiotimes.com/news/2013-03-19/sherlock-takes-home-two-prizes-at-the-royal-television-society-programme-awards

Legendary Pictures. http://www.legendary.com/about/

Live Blog. *The Guardian.* 7:17 p.m. 14 January 2013. http://www.guardian.co.uk/film/2013/jan/13/golden-globes/tina-fey-amy-poehler-live

"Live From the Red Carpet." E! 14 January 2013 (original broadcast).

Lobb, Adrian. "The Lonely Detective." *The Big Issue* (Scotland), 20-26 August 2012, 25.

Loveridge, Charlotte. *"The Arsonists." Curtain Up.* 13 November 2007. http://www.curtainup.com/arsonists lond.html

Lowry, Brian. "Parade's End." *Variety.* 19 February 2013. http://www.variety.com/VE1117949282/

Macauley, Alistair. Review of *Hedda Gabler. Financial Times.* 21 March 2005. Rep. *Theatre Record,* 25(6), 348.

___. Review of *Period of Adjustment. Financial Times.* 22 March 2006. Rep. *Theatre Record,* 26(6), 306.

Malkin, Marc. "Star Trek Sequel Trailer: Why Co-star Zoe Saldana Made Benedict Cumberbatch Blush Over It." E!online. 7 December 2012. http://au.eonline.com/news/369423/star-trek-sequel-trailer-why-zoe-saldana-made-costar-benedict-cumberbatch-blush-over-it

Marmion, Patrick. Review of *Oh! What a Lovely War. Mail on Sunday.* 28 July 2002. Rep. *Theatre Record,* 22(15), 980.

___. Review of *Period of Adjustment. Daily Mail.* 17 March 2006. Rep. *Theatre Record,* 26(6), 304.

"Martin Freeman: 'Sherlock' is Best Written Thing." What's On TV. 27 December 2012. http://www.whatsontv.co.uk/drama/tv-news/news/martin-freeman-sherlock-is-best-written-thing/18638

Masterpiece. The Last Enemy. PBS. http://www.pbs.org/wgbh/masterpiece/lastenemy/characters.html

Masterpiece. Sherlock Season 2. Co-Creator Live Chats: Mark Gatiss. PBS. 14 May 2012. http://www.pbs.org/wgbh/masterpiece/sherlock/season2_chat_gatiss.html

McDonald, Paul. "Why Study Film Acting? Some Opening Reflections." In Cynthia Baron, Diane Carson, and Frank P. Tomasulo (Eds.), *More Than a Method: Trends in Contemporary Film Performances* (pp. 23-41). Detroit: Wayne State University, 2004.

McElvoy, Anne. "Lose the Chip, Benedict—All Actors Have a Class Range." *London Evening Standard.* 15 August 2012.

http://www.standard.co.uk/comment/lose-the-chip-
benedict-all-actors-have-a-class-range-8049557.html

McNary, Dave. "'Twelve Years a Slave' Dated for Dec. 27 by
Fox Searchlight." *Variety.* 28 March 2013.
http://variety.com/2013/film/news/twelve-years-a-slave-
dated-for-dec-27-by-fox-searchlight-1200330527/

Mellow, Louisa. "Benedict Cumberbatch on the Future of
Sherlock." Den of Geek. 19 December 2012.
http://www.denofgeek.us/37229/benedict-cumberbatch-on-
the-future-of-sherlock

Millar, Paul. "Benedict Cumberbatch's Van Gogh Docudrama
Fetches 960k." Digital Spy. 6 April 2010.
http://www.digitalspy.com/british-tv/news/a329146/
benedict-cumberbatchs-van-gogh-docu-drama-fetches-
960k.html

Mitchison, Amanda. "Benedict Cumberbatch on Playing
Sherlock Holmes." *The Guardian.* 16 July 2010.
http://www.guardian.co.uk/tv-and-radio/2010/
jul/17/benedict-cumberbatch-sherlock-holmes

Moore, Ronnie. "Title Revealed for Benedict Cumberbatch-led
WikiLeaks Film." The Film Stage. 20 December 2012.
http://thefilmstage.com/news/title-revealed-for-benedict-
cumberbatch-led-wikileaks-film-downtown-abbey-star-
joins/

Muir, Kate. "Benedict Cumberbatch on Fame, Death, and a
New Film." *The Times.* 14 May 2011. http://www.
thetimes.co.uk/tto/arts/film/article3017186.ece

Mumford, Gwilym. "Sherlock Returns to the BBC: 'He's
Definitely Devilish.'" *The Guardian.* 16 December 2011.
http://www.guardian.co.uk/tv-and-radio/2011/dec/
17/sherlock-bbc-cumberbatch-freeman-interview

Myall, Steve. "Benedict Cumberbatch Talks about Sherlock
and War Horse." *Daily Mirror.* 31 December 2011.

http://www.mirror.co.uk/tv/tv-news/benedict-cumberbatch-talks-about-sherlock-and-war-99003

The Naked Scientists. Special Editions. "Benedict Cumberbatch, Naked." 6 March 2013. Transcript at http://www.thenakedscientists.com/HTML/podcasts/specials/show/20130306/nocache/1/?cHash=483872490db6e3af548252727500f7d6&tx_nakscishow_pi1[transcript]=1. Podcast at http://www.thenakedscientists.com/HTML/podcasts/specials/show/20130306/.

Nathan, Sara. "Sherlock Star Has Forged 'Very Special' Relationship with Blonde Daughter of Patty Hearst." *Mail Online.* 28 February 2012. http://www.dailymail.co.uk/news/article-2107978/Sherlock-star-forged-special-relationship-blonde-daughter-Patty-Hearst.html#axzz2JyAJTY3g

"Next Stop the Oscars for Star Trek's Benedict Cumberbatch?" Contactmusic.com. 7 December 2012. http://www.contactmusic.com/news/next-stop-the-oscars-for-star-trek-s-benedict-cumberbatch_3407659

"Nicholas Hoult and Benedict Cumberbatch are Stars to Watch in 2013." *Forbes.* 7 January 2012. http://www.forbes.com/sites/dorothypomerantz/2013/01/07/nicholas-hoult-and-benedict-cumberbatch-are-stars-to-watch-in-2013/

O'Hare, Kate. "'Star Trek 2': 'Sherlock' Star Benedict Cumberbatch Dyes Hair, Loves J.J. Abrams." Zap2It. 25 April 2012. http://blog.zap2it.com/pop2it/2012/04/star-trek-2-sherlock-star-benedict-cumberbatch-dyes-hair-loves-jj-abrams.html

Oldman, Gary. Commentary. *Tinker Tailor Soldier Spy.* Universal. DVD. 2012.

Pahle, Rebecca. "Benedict Cumberbatch to Depress Audience Members with Alan Turing Biopic?" The Mary Sue. 2 February 2013. http://www.themarysue.com/alan-turing-benedict-cumberbatch-imitation-game/

Palmer, Martyn. "'I've Always Wanted to Play a Spy . . . You Are Never What You Seem': Benedict Cumberbatch on Fulfilling His Acting Dream." *Mail Online*. 13 July 2011. http://www.dailymail.co.uk/home/moslive/article-2012212/Tinker-Tailor-Soldier-Spy-Benedict-Cumberbatch-fulfilling-acting-dream.html

Parade's End. Mammoth Screen Ltd., 2012. DVD. Produced by BBC, HBO, Lookout Point, and Mammoth Screen. Dir. Susanna White. Episode Two.

___. Mammoth Screen Ltd., 2012. DVD. Produced by BBC, HBO, Lookout Point, and Mammoth Screen. Dir. Susanna White. Disc 2. "Behind the Scenes." Interview with Susanna White.

PBS/WNET. Livestream of the *Sherlock* Series 2 event.

Pedigree 4 a Day Official Ad (UK).YouTube. September 2012. http://www.youtube.com/ watch?v=aPYAaY1vhlk

Porter, Lynnette. "Celebrity and the Celebration of Art: The Transformation of Benedict Cumberbatch." PopMatters. 27 April 2011. http://www.popmatters.com/pm/feature/139431-celebrity-and-the-celebration-of-art/P1

___. "DR Hood and the 'Dramatic Poetry' of Wreckers." PopMatters. Deep Focus. 6 January 2011. http://www. popmatters.com/pm/column/152743-director-d-r-hood-and-the-dramatic-poetry-of-wreckers/

___. "'Third Star,' Making the Festival Rounds, Pits Benedict Cumberbatch Against a Taboo Topic." PopMatters. 1 June 2011. http://www.popmatters.com/pm/feature/141879-three-cheers-for-third-star/

Preston, John. "The Rattigan Enigma, BBC Four, The Camera That Changed the World, The Code, BBC Two, Review." *The Telegraph*. 30 July 2011. http://www.telegraph.co.uk/culture/tvandradio/8670854/The-Rattigan-Enigma-BBC-Four-The-Camera-That-Changed-the-World-The-Code-BBC-Two-review.html

"Radio Plays." BBC 4 Radio Plays by Year. http://www.suttonelms.org.uk/miscellany.html

RAS. "Golden Globes 2013: Live Blogging the Show." *The Wall Street Journal.* 14 January 2013. http://blogs.wsj.com/speakeasy/2013/01/13/golden-globes/2013-live-blogging-the-show/:mod=goodle_news_blog

The Rattigan Enigma. BBC. Benedict Cumberbatch, writer. 28 July 2011 (original broadcast).

Ray, Amber M. "Benedict Cumberbatch: The Uncensored 'Sherlock' Interview." *Metro.* 6 May 2012. http://www.metro.us/newyork/entertainment/article/1142298--benedict-cumberbatch-the-uncensored-sherlock-interview

Reynolds, Gillian. "Neverwhere is a Reminder that Radio is Already Innovative." *The Telegraph.* 26 March 2013. http://www.telegraph.co.uk/culture/tvandradio/tv-and-radio-reviews/9954811/Neverwhere-is-a-reminder-that-radio-is-already-innovative.html

Rhinoceros. Videorecording made at the Royal Court Theatre, matinee performance, 6 December 2007. Accessed at the Victoria and Albert Museum, performance archives, Blythe House, London, 22 March 2013.

"Rhinoceros Post-Show Talk." 20 September 2007. Accessed at the British Library Performance Archives, London, 14 March 2013.

Roach, Vicky. "Benedict Cumberbatch, Movies' Man of 2012?" *The Herald.* 29 December 2011. http://www.heraldsun.com.au/entertainment/movies-man-of-2012/story-e6frf96f-1226232459475

Rochlin, Margy. "Holmes at Last." *New York Post.* 6 May 2012. http://www.nypost.com/p/entertainment/tv/holmes_at_last_aJHMwbpvgFcTCKzoF4SDAK

Rollings, Grant. "Ben Has Trouble with Girlfriends Because He's So Like Sherlock." *The Sun.* 14 January 2012. http://www.thesun.co.uk/sol/homepage/showbiz/tv/4060874

/Benedict-Cumberbatch-Why-Sherlock-Holmes-actor-cant-get-a-girl.html#ixzz272NYN1KA

Rosenberg, Alyssa. "Steven Moffat on 'Sherlock's Return, the Holmes-Watson Love Story, and Updating the First Supervillain." ThinkProgress. 7 May 2012. http://think progress.org/alyssa/2012/05/07/479306/steven-moffat-on-sherlocks-return-the-holmes-watson-love-story-and-updating-the-first-supervillain/?mobile=nc

Rutter, Claire. "Sherlock Star Who Stripped Nude for Benedict Cumberbatch to Play 'Bond Girl.'" Entertainmentwise. 25 January 2013. http://www.entertainmentwise.com/news/102685/Woman-Who-Stripped-Nude-For-Benedict-Cumberbatch-To-Play-Bond-Girl

___. "Sherlock's Benedict Cumberbatch Announced as Guest Director of Cambridge Science Festival." 22 January 2013. http://www.entertainmentwise.com/news/102212/Sherlocks-Benedict-Cumberbatch-Annouced-As-Guest-Director-Of-The-Cambridge-Science-Festival

___. "Sherlock's Benedict Cumberbatch Beats David Beckham & Harry Styles to 'Sexiest Man.'" Entertainmentwise.com. 7 May 2012. http://www.entertainmentwise.com/news/75230/Sherlocks-Benedict-Cumberbatch-Beats-David-Beckham-Harry-Styles-To-Sexiest-Man

Sands, Sarah. "Many of Us are 'Fruitcakes' Now, Mr. Cameron." *London Evening Standard.* 22 November 2011. http://www.standard.co.uk/news/many-of-us-are-fruitcakes-now-mr-cameron-6370736.html

Seale, Jack. "Benedict Cumberbatch on Fame, Science and His New Radio 3 Play, Copenhagen." *Radio Times.* 11 January 2013. http://www.radiotimes.com/news/2013-01-11/bene dict-cumberbatch-on-fame-science-and-his-new-radio-3-play-copenhagen

___. "Danny Boyle: Benedict Cumberbatch is 'One of the Leading Actors in the World.'" *Radio Times.* 9 April 2012.

http://www.radiotimes.com/news/2012-04-09/danny-boyle-benedict-cumberbatch-is-one-of-the-leading-actors-in-the-world

Secher, Benjamin, "Plummy Depths," *The Telegraph*, 11 August 2012, 39.

Shakespeare, William. *Romeo and Juliet.* Act II, Scene II, Lines 45-49.

Shelley, Mary. *Frankenstein.* New York: Norton, 2012.

Sherlock. "The Hounds of Baskerville." BBC. Dir. Paul McGuigan. 8 January 2012 (original broadcast).

___. "A Scandal in Belgravia." BBC. Dir. Paul McGuigan. 1 January 2012 (original broadcast).

___. "A Study in Pink." BBC. Dir. Paul McGuigan. 25 July 2010 (original broadcast).

Sherlock: Season Two. DVD set. Commentary, Part 1. BBC Worldwide. 2012.

Sherlock 2 Fan Q&A in New York. PBS. 2 May 2012. http://video.pbs.org/video/2232626419

Sherlock Master Class. Edinburgh International Television Festival. 24 August 2012.

Sherlock screening. "A Scandal in Belgravia." British Film Institute. 7 December 2011. London.

Sherlock screening. "A Scandal in Belgravia." PBS. 2 May 2012. New York. Streaming video.

"Sherlock Speaks German: The Making of the German Version." *The Baker Street Chronicle.* Summer 2012, p. 15.

Sherlockology. "*Inseparable* review." 2011. http://sherlockology.tumblr.com/post/13160610719/inseparablereview

___. "The Playwright's Playwrights: Look Back in Anger." 7 July 2012. http://www.sherlockology.com/news/2012/7/7/look-back-in-anger-07072012

___. "Sponsor Benedict Cumberbatch for the Palace to Palace London Bike Ride in Aid of the Prince's Trust." October

2012. http://sherlockology.tumblr.com/post/32221610891/
sponsor-benedict-cumberbatch-for-the-palace-to-palace-lo

Shingler, Martin. *Star Studies: A Critical Guide*. London:
Palgrave Macmillan/British Film Institute, 2012.

Silent Witness. "Tell No Tales: Part 1." Dir. John Duthie. BBC.
19 October 2002 (original broadcast).

___. "Tell No Tales: Part 2." Dir. John Duthie. BBC. 20
October 2002 (original broadcast).

Singh, Anita. "Parade's End—'Who is This Benedict
Cumberbatch?'" *The Telegraph*. 27 July 2012.
http://www.telegraph.co.uk/culture/tvandradio/9432700/Par
ades-End-Who-is-this-Benedict-Cumberbatch.html

Sivell, Vaughan. "On Benedict Cumberbatch." *Mug7*. 9
September 2011. http://mug7.com/2011/09/09/on-benedict-
cumberbatch/

Snierson, Dan. "'The Simpson': Watch Benedict Cumberbatch
Play the British Prime Minister AND Snape—Exclusive
Video." *Entertainment Weekly*. 8 February 2013.
http://insidetv.ew.com/2013/02/08/the-simpsons-benedict-
cumberbatch-snape/

Spencer, Charles. "The Arsonists: A Blast, and Then a Damp
Squib." *The Telegraph*. 7 November 2007. http://www.
telegraph.co.uk/culture/theatre/drama/3669087/The-
Arsonists-A-blast-then-a-damp-squib.html

___. Review of *Period of Adjustment*. *Daily Telegraph*. March
18 2006. Rep. *Theatre Record*, 26(6), 305.

Spencer, Kathryn (Ed.). "When Veteran Elaine Knew a Star
Was Born." *The Express*. 14 September 2007. British
Library Newspaper Index. Record No. 58644804.

Spero, Josh. "Josh Spero Talking about Benedict Cumberbatch
on BBC Radio Wales Aug 2012." YouTube. 15 August
2012. http://www.youtube.com/watch?v=9duNquWFLak.
Also, on Spears.com. http://www.spearswms.com/press/

35707/josh-spero-talks-about-benedict-cumberbatch-on-bbc-radio-wales.thtml

Spielberg, Steven. *War Horse: The Making of the Motion Picture*. New York: It Books/HarperCollins, 2011.

Stanford, Peter. "It's No Good, Benedict Cumberbatch Can't Stop Us Liking Him." *The Telegraph*. 18 August 2012. http://www.telegraph.co.uk/comment/9485074/Its-no-good-Benedict-Cumberbatch-cant-stop-us-liking-him.html

Sullivan, Kevin P. "Benedict Cumberbatch Unleashes 'Star Trek' Villain." MTV. 14 January 2013. http://www.mtv.com/news/articles/1700140/star-trek/villain-benedict-cumberbatch.jhtml

Swashbuckled. "No Shit Sherlock." Blog. 16 May 2011. http://swashbuckled.wordpress.com/2011/05/16/no-shit-sherlock/

Sweeting, Adam. "The Rattigan Enigma, BBC Four." The Arts Desk. 29 July 2011. http://www.theartsdesk.com/theatre/rattigan-enigma-bbc-four

Taylor, Paul. "First Night: Rhinoceros, Royal Court Theatre." *The Independent*. 28 September 2007. http://www.independent.co.uk/arts-entertainment/theatre-dance/reviews/first-night-rhinoceros-royal-court-london-464772.html

___. Review of *As You Like It*. *The Independent*. 17 June 2002. Rep. *Theatre Record*, 22(12), 768.

Thomas, Simon. "*The Arsonists.*" *Music OMG*. 15 December 2007. http://www.musicomh.com/theatre/arsonists_1107.htm

Tipping the Velvet. Dir. Geoffrey Sax. BBC. 2 October 2002 (original broadcast).

"Tips for Nervous Santas." *Daily Express,* 17 December 1979, 17.

Torin, Douglas. "Benedict Cumberbatch and Rebecca Hall Take Acting Honours as Parade's End Wins 4 Prizes."

Broadcasting Press Guild. 14 March 2013. http://www. broadcastingpressguild.org/2013/03/14/benedict-cumberbatch-and-rebecca-hall-take-acting-honours-as-parades-end-wins-4-prizes/

Ventre, Michael. "Tax Breaks Created TV Party." *Variety.* 15 August 2012. http://www.variety.com/article/VR111 8057556/

Walker, Tim. "Sherlock Star Benedict Cumberbatch is Cyberstalked." *The Telegraph.* 13 March 2013. http://www.telegraph.co.uk/news/9925578/Sherlock-star-Benedict-Cumberbatch-is-cyberstalked.html

___. "Sherlock Actor Benedict Cumberbatch Plans to Play Hamlet." *The Telegraph.* 20 June 2012. http://www. telegraph.co.uk/news/celebritynews/9342061/Sherlock-actor-Benedict-Cumberbatch-plans-to-play-Hamlet.html

War Horse. Dir. Steven Spielberg. Dreamworks. 2011.

Webb, Claire. "Father Brown's Mark Williams on Following in Benedict Cumberbatch's Footsteps." *Radio Times.* 13 January 2013. http://www.radiotimes.com/news/2013-01-13/father-browns-mark-williams-on-following-in-benedict-cumberbatchs-footsteps

WENN.com. "Benedict Cumberbatch Snags The Simpsons Role." Hollywood.com. 5 July 2012. http://www.holly wood.com/news/Benedict_Cumberbatch_snags_The_Simps ons_role/32942469

___. "Benedict Cumberbatch Upset Over Jonny Lee Miller Misquote." 31 August 2012. http://www.hollywood.com/ news/Benedict_Cumberbatch_upset_over_Jonny_Lee_Mill er_misquote/38423677

"What's New: Arts Channel Open Week." *SkyWatch,* December 2012, 7.

White, Lesley. "The Fabulous Baker Street Boy." *The Sunday Times.* 15 August 2010. http://www.thesundaytimes.co.uk/ sto/Magazine/Interviews/article364344.ece

White, Nick. Email. 23 October 2012.

___. Email. 9 April 2013.

Willocks, Sarah. Review of *As You Like It*. *Time Out*. 19 June 2002. Rep. *Theatre Record*, 22(12), 68.

Wilson, Ben, and Elston, Charlotte. "Record Profits Driven by Rising International Creative Exports." BBC Worldwide. 12 July 2011. http://www.bbc.co.uk/pressoffice/bbcworld wide/worldwidestories/pressreleases/2011/07_july/annual_r eview.shtml

Wilson, Benji. "Benedict Cumberbatch." *Reader's Digest*. September 2012. http://www.readersdigest.co.uk/magazine/ readers-digest-main/benedict-cumberbatch

___. "Cover Story: A Classic on Parade." *The Sunday Times, Culture* magazine, 12 August 2012, 4.

Wilson, MacKenzie. "Benedict Cumberbatch and His Mom Chat with 'Saunders and French.'" BBC America. 3 January 2011. http://www.bbcamerica.com/anglophenia/ 2011/01/benedict-cumberbatch-and-his-mom-chat-with-french-and-saunders/

"Wreckers Q&A with Director D.R. Hood, Benedict Cumberbatch, and Shaun Evans." Curzon Cinemas Ltd. 22 December 2011. http://www.youtube.com/watch?v= WV85tpdlWiY

Young, Bill. "Sherlock Master Class Highlights." 25 August 2012. http://tellyspotting.org/2012/08/25/sherlock-master-class-highlights/

Zucker, Joseph. "Super Bowl Commercials 2013: Ranking Top Movie Trailers from Big Game." The Bleacher Report. 3 February 2013. http://bleacherreport.com/articles/1514567-super-bowl-commercials-2013-ranking-top-movie-trailers-from-big-game

Index

214, 215, 217, 218, 219, 220, 221, 228, 236, 238, 246, 264, 266; *see also* individual awards (e.g., Golden Nymph)

Ayrshire 191

backlash 225, 239, 240-43

BAFTA 1, 2, 3, 62, 96, 103, 105, 141, 185, 219, 266

BAFTA Cymru 2

BAFTA tea party 126, 247

Balding, Clare 258

Bana, Eric 102

Banff Rockie Awards 3

Barafundle Bay 111, 225

Barbados 16

Basner, Glen 221

BBC 1, 2, 8, 9, 10, 23, 70, 71, 78, 79, 80, 81, 91, 92, 96, 98, 99, 105, 117, 120, 136, 147, 149, 189, 193, 212, 232, 239, 243, 244, 247, 264

BBC Media Centre 231

BBC radio 2, 116, 117, 120, 126

BBC Wales 240

BBC Worldwide 6

Beale, Simon Russell 127, 130

Beaton, Alistair 47, 48

Beckham, David 9, 258

Berenger 41-46

Berlin 221, 225, 226

Bernard 84

Best, Eve 38, 42, 58

Bettany, Paul 103

The Biggest Secret 117

Birkin, Andrew 162

birth 15, 18

body language 67, 74, 100, 206, 233, 248; *see also* mannerisms

Bond, James 61, 159, 189, 235

Boyle, Danny 2, 160-61, 163, 164, 177, 179

331

343

Scott, Andrew 142

Scott-Fowler, David 40, 60, 62, 63, 64-70

The Sergeant's Mate 62

Serkis, Andy 219

Seven Women and the 12-Pound Look 118

Seychelles 71

Shakespeare 25, 36, 37, 62

Shappey, Arthur 119, 121, 223

Shappey, Carolyn Knapp 223

Sheen, Martin 33

Shepherd's Bush 35

Sherlock 2, 3, 4, 5, 6, 7, 8, 9, 19, 21, 28, 31, 40, 60, 61, 62. 63, 64, 75, 76, 85, 87, 89, 91, 92, 93, 96, 98, 99, 104, 107, 113, 119, 120, 121, 126, 127, 135, 138-61, 163, 172, 185, 190, 191, 198, 200, 202, 204, 209, 212, 215, 216, 217, 218, 220, 222, 223, 224-25, 227, 228, 229, 235, 239, 242, 243, 246, 249, 250, 251, 252, 254, 255, 257, 259, 261, 264, 265, 266, 270; "The Great Game" 155; "The Hounds of Baskerville" 140, 151; "The Reichenbach Fall" 140, 147, 155, 224; "A Scandal in Belgravia" 31, 139, 140, 141, 143, 147-52, 154, 155, 157, 160, 161; "A Study in Pink" 139

Sherlockology 105, 202, 250, 261

Shingler, Martin 217, 222

Silent Witness 62, 78

The Simpsons 7, 250-52

sister 5, 17

Sivell, Vaughan 112, 113, 225

SkyArts Theatre Live! 72

Slippery, Rory 80, 84

Small Island 62, 81, 84, 91, 96

Smaug 1, 11, 86, 219

Snape, Severus 7, 250, 251

social media 103, 238; *see also* individual media (e.g., Twitter)

Sodwana Bay 94

South Africa 24, 74, 93, 94, 95
Spellbound 118
Spero, Josh 86-87
Spielberg, Steven 115, 135, 190, 204, 206, 207, 248
Spock 212
Spooks 57, 62, 63
Star Trek: Into Darkness 1, 8, 11, 27, 28, 29, 30, 49, 86, 89,
109, 126, 135, 156, 190, 200, 201, 202, 208-11, 212, 214, 215,
216, 218, 219, 222, 230, 233, 246, 248, 249, 250, 253, 260, 261
stardom 13, 40, 77, 92, 95, 99, 126, 134, 161, 185, 201, 204,
217, 218, 222, 223, 224, 235, 236, 269
Starter for Ten 62, 81, 85, 102, 124, 202
Stephen Hawking's Grand Design 130
Stewart, Major Jamie 84, 87, 88, 89, 205
Stoppard, Tom 115, 189, 190, 193
Stritch, Elaine 20
Strong, Mark 189
Stuart: A Life Backwards 42, 57, 62, 80, 81, 85, 91, 92, 93, 97
Styles, Harry 258
Super Bowl 201-02
tabloids 12, 49, 93, 217, 224, 230, 234, 258
Talbot, Edmund 17, 83, 87, 93
television 2, 3, 4, 7, 9, 10, 11, 13, 15, 18, 24, 26, 29, 39, 40,
57, 60, 62, 63, 70, 71, 73, 76, 78-102, 117, 119, 134, 135, 141,
146, 155, 161, 172, 185, 189, 191, 197, 198, 201, 202, 207,
217, 218, 223, 228, 229, 235, 250, 252, 263, 266, 267; *see also*
individual titles (e.g., *Sherlock*)
Television and Radio Industries Club 3
Television Critics Association 3, 150
Tesman, George 37, 38, 58-60
theatre 2, 7, 8, 10, 11, 13, 18, 22, 24, 33-77, 79, 82, 91, 96,
117, 129, 154, 161-89, 198, 217, 218, 223, 227, 240, 261, 263;
see also individual productions (e.g., *Frankenstein*)
Theatre Record 38

Save Undershaw

The author and publisher support the campaign to save
and restore Sir Arthur Conan Doyle's former home.
Undershaw is where he brought Sherlock Holmes back to
life, and should be preserved for future generations of
Holmes fans.

Save Undershaw   www.saveundershaw.com

Facebook www.facebook.com/saveundershaw

You can read more about Sir Arthur Conan Doyle and
Undershaw in Alistair Duncan's book (share of royalties
to the Undershaw Preservation Trust) – An Entirely New
Country and in the amazing compilation Sherlock's
Home – The Empty House (all royalties to the Trust).

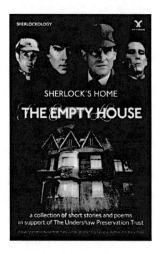 

Also from MX Publishing

From one of the world's largest Sherlock Holmes publishers, dozens of new books novels from top Holmes authors.

Visit the Sherlock Holmes Books page on Facebook for the latest releases:

www.facebook.com/BooksSherlockHolmes

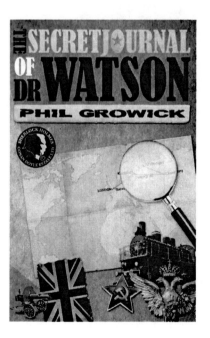

CPSIA information can be obtained at www.ICGtesting.com
Printed in the USA
LVOW06s0844141113

361136LV00009B/30/P